# MOONLIGHTING
## An Episode Guide

# MOONLIGHTING
## An Episode Guide

Written By
Grace Chivell
and Shawna Saari
***Moonlighting the Podcast***

TUCKER
DS

P R E S S

# **FOREWORD**

Several years ago, I became aware of a podcast devoted to a show I created and ran back in the 1980s called *Moonlighting*. I was surprised to discover that such a podcast existed; the show itself had been unavailable for viewing (except for bad copies on YouTube) for almost two decades. I listened to the podcast and discovered Grace Chivell and Shawna Saari. These two women created and hosted the podcast and were (and are) unashamedly passionate in their love for *Moonlighting*. Their mission? They set about to watch each and every episode and then devote a single podcast to it. Best laid plans. Sometimes the podcasts actually lasted longer than the episodes. Sometimes it required more than one podcast to adequately contain the thoughts and feelings these two women had about that episode. Sometimes (it seemed to me), Shawna and Grace put more thought into the episodes than me or any of the other writers on the show did. Clearly, there was something wrong with these two women. So I did what any responsible person would do in such a situation. I called the authorities. I am happy to report that both Grace and Shawna have served their time and are now productive members of the community. I'm further pleased to report that while incarcerated, they wrote a book. I have not read it. I started to. But honestly, the whole damn thing felt like déjà vu. Others tell me it's pretty great and a lot of fun. My feeling is, anything we can do to help these two women lead normal and productive lives, I'm for it. So buy the book. Give it to people you have to buy Xmas gifts for but don't really care about. That's what I'm going to do. And know, you're making the world a better place.

**Glenn Gordon Caron - November 3, 2023**

**Contact Information:**
**Email:** fans@moonlightingthepodcast.com

**Social Media:**
**Website:** moonlightingthepodcast.com
**Instagram:** @moonlightingthepodcast
**Facebook Page:** Fans of the Moonlighting Podcast
**X (Twitter):** @moon_podcast85

ISBN: 9781959748045

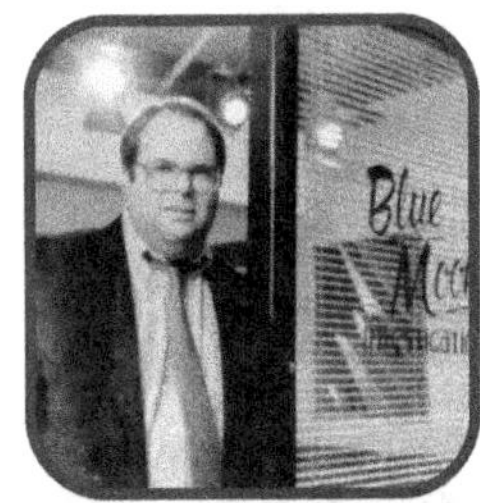

# THE CREATOR

## Glenn Gordon Caron

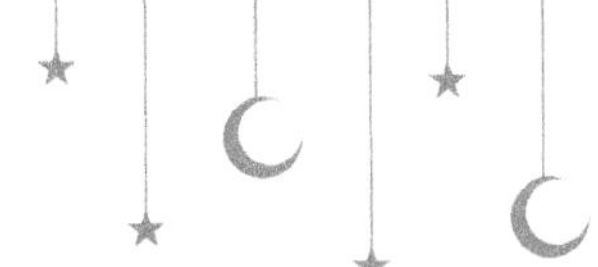

Glenn Gordon Caron has had an exemplary career in the entertainment industry. Glenn's career began as a copywriter. While working at an ad agency, Glenn was asked to write a pilot for NBC. The pilot didn't go anywhere, but James L. Brooks took notice of Glenn's work and invited him to write for *Taxi* (TV Series, 1978-1983), though he worked on only one episode. From there, Glenn went on to write an episode of *Good Time Harry* (TV Series, 1980), three episodes of *Breaking Away* (TV Series, 1980-1981), and an episode of *Fame* (TV Series, 1982 1987). Subsequently, Glenn was co-producer on the first twelve episodes of *Remington Steele* (TV Series, 1982-1987). ABC approached Glenn to write a TV movie pilot. The first two that he wrote were not picked up as series; however, before his third attempt at a pilot, the network told Glenn it wanted a TV series about a detective agency with a male and a female as leads . . . and that is how *Moonlighting* was born.

*Moonlighting* aired for five seasons and for a total of sixty-six episodes. Glenn was the executive producer of the show for four seasons. As the main writer, Glenn often opted to shine the light on other writers who put forth their story ideas by giving them the writing credit on an episode. However, every script went through Glenn's typewriter for final approval. Glenn's writing on *Moonlighting* harkened back to the days of screwball comedy, including double entendres, sharp repartee between the two leads, and fast-paced, overlapping dialogue for Bruce and Cybill, which they became very good at!

Glenn directed his first feature film between the third and fourth seasons of *Moonlighting*, called *Clean and Sober* (Movie, 1988), which starred Michael Keaton. He received four Emmy nominations, two for Outstanding Drama Series and two for Outstanding Writing in a Drama Series. Over its run, *Moonlighting* received six Emmy Awards, for editing, costume design, hairstyling, art direction, and Lead Actor in a Drama Series for Bruce Willis. Glenn also directed *Wilder Napalm* (Movie, 1993), *Love Affair* (Movie, 1994), and *Picture Perfect* (Movie, 1997) which starred Jennifer Aniston. He created the show *Medium* (TV Series, 2005-2011), and served as executive producer and wrote the series pilot and several other episodes of the series. Most recently, Glenn was a consulting producer on *Bull* (TV Series, 2016-2022) before becoming the series show-runner at the start of season two. Glenn has gone on to produce and write many other projects and is still very active in the industry.

## AWARDS

Glenn received an award from the Writers Guild of America for the pilot script of *Moonlighting* (1985) and won the award for Outstanding Television Writer at the Austin Film Festival (2007).

# THE CAST

## Cybill Shepherd

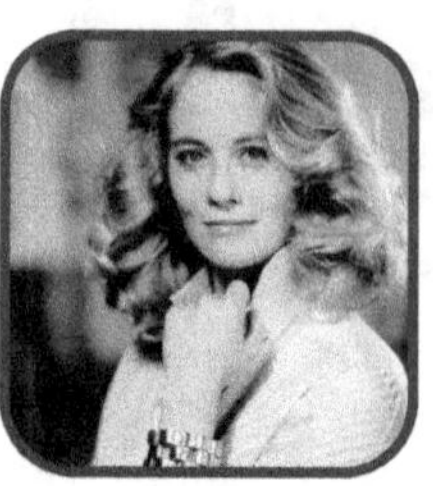

Cybill Lynne Shepherd, born in Memphis, Tennessee, was named after her grandfather Cy, and her father, Bill. In her early career, Cybill was a model appearing in many fashion magazines such as *Teen* and *Glamour*. At the age of sixteen, while still in high school, Cybill won the Miss Teenage Memphis title, and she went on to compete in the 1966 Miss Teenage America and Model of the Year pageants.

Soon she was being cast in various modeling campaigns and became the "it" girl on the cover of just about every magazine. In 1970, film director Peter Bogdanovich saw Cybill on the cover of *Glamour* magazine, and he knew he'd found just the girl to play Jacy Farrow in his upcoming movie, *The Last Picture Show* (Movie, 1971). The film was a huge success; it was nominated for eight Academy Awards, won two, and transformed Cybill into a movie star. Her subsequent films include *The Heartbreak Kid* (Movie, 1972) with Charles Grodin; *Daisy Miller* (Movie, 1974) and *At Long Last Love* (Movie, 1975), both directed by Bogdanovich, with whom she was then romantically involved; and Martin Scorsese's *Taxi Driver* (Movie, 1976) with Robert De Niro. Cybill then launched a music career by releasing an album named *Cybill Does It . . . To Cole Porter* (Studio album, 1974).

Cybill and Bogdanovich were good friends with the acclaimed actor, director, and writer Orson Welles, who lived with them off and on and whom Cybill says gave her sage advice about her acting career and encouraged her to get experience on stage in front of a live audience. His disclaimer was that it should not be in theaters in major cities such as New York or Los Angeles. So Cybill packed her bags and went back to Memphis to work in regional theater and toured around the country honing her craft.

**Continued...**

# Cybill Shepherd

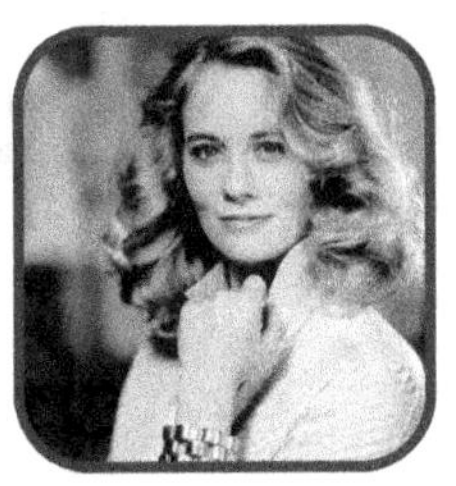

In 1983, Cybill returned to L.A. and was cast in the NBC television drama *The Yellow Rose* (TV Series, 1983-1984), which lasted only one season. But not to worry: the following year she was cast as Madolyn "Maddie" Hayes in *Moonlighting* (TV Series, 1985-1989). As the story goes, while Glenn Gordon Caron was writing the Pilot for *Moonlighting*, he realized he was writing the character of Maddie for Cybill Shepherd, so Glenn approached her to discuss the script. She loved the fast-talking "Hawksian"-style comedy and agreed to take the role: a role that defined her career and earned her the highest level of success she'd experienced up to that time.

In her personal life, Cybill has a daughter, Clementine (who has since made her a grandmother of two), and also a set of boy-girl twins, whom she gave birth to during season three of *Moonlighting*. Following *Moonlighting*, Cybill appeared in such films as *Chances Are* (Movie, 1989) and, reprising her role as Jacy Farrow from *The Last Picture Show*, *Texasville* (Movie, 1990). In 1997, she won her third Golden Globe, for her own television sitcom, *Cybill* (TV Series, 1995-1998).

In 2000, Cybill released her autobiography, *Cybill Disobedience: How I Survived Beauty Pageants, Elvis, Sex, Bruce Willis, Lies, Marriage, Motherhood, Hollywood, and the Irrepressible Urge to Say What I Think* (Book, 2000), which became a best seller. She appeared in *The L Word* (TV Series, 2004-2009) as Phyllis Kroll alongside her daughter Clementine, who portrayed Molly Kroll for nine episodes. Cybill made her Broadway debut in *The Best Man* (Play, 2012). Most recently, she starred in *Being Rose* (Movie, 2017) and in Lifetime's *How to Murder Your Husband: The Nancy Brophy Story* (TV Movie, 2023) opposite Steve Guttenberg. Cybill's career continues to thrive, but to *Moonlighting* fans, she will always be our beautiful Maddie Hayes.

# THE CAST

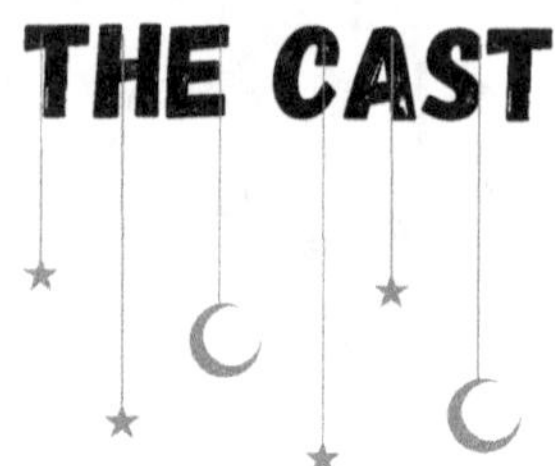

**Bruce Willis**

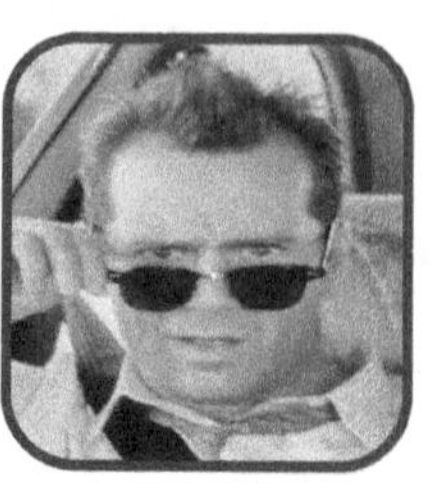

Walter Bruce Willis was born in Idar-Oberstein, Germany. His mother is German, and his father was an American soldier. After his father was discharged from the military, the family relocated to New Jersey. where Bruce eventually attended Penns Grove High School. As a kid, Bruce spoke with a stutter, but he found that when acting on stage, his stutter receded dramatically, so he decided to join the drama club. After high school, Bruce worked as a security guard and a private investigator (great preparation for his role on *Moonlighting*), but he decided acting was really his passion, so he enrolled in the drama program at Montclair State University.

Eventually, Bruce made his way to New York, where he was a popular bartender at various bars, including the Kamikaze Club and Chelsea Central. Meanwhile, he took on various uncredited roles such as "courtroom observer" in the Paul Newman's *The Verdict* (Movie, 1982) (when later working with Newman on *Nobody's Fool* (Movie, 1994), Bruce told him about this, and of course, Newman had no idea!). Bruce also appeared in an episode of *Miami Vice* (TV Series, 1984-1989) called "No Exit" and an episode of *The Twilight Zone* (TV Series, 1985-1989) titled "Shatterday" just before being cast in *Moonlighting* (TV Series, 1985-1989).

As we know now, his next role, as David Addison Jr., would be the turning point in his career. Every actor in Hollywood and beyond read for the role of David Addison, but as soon as Glenn Gordon Caron and the casting team saw Bruce's audition, they knew instantly he was the guy. It took some convincing to get ABC to see what Caron and the others saw in Bruce, but after a wardrobe change and a few screen tests, the network got on board, and the rest is TV history. Casting Bruce opposite Cybill Shepherd helped establish him as a leading man and showcased his talents in both comedic and dramatic acting. During *Moonlighting's* run, Bruce won an Emmy Award for 'Outstanding Lead Actor in a Drama Series' and a Golden Globe Award for 'Best Actor in Television Series Musical or Comedy.'

**Continued...**

## Bruce Willis

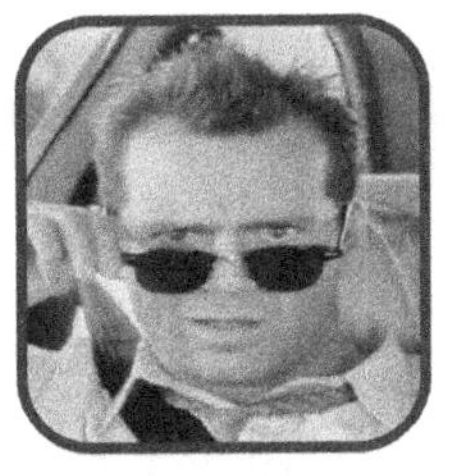

Many opportunities came Bruce's way with the success of *Moonlighting.* He recorded, "The Return of Bruno," (Studio album, 1987), which was accompanied by a mockumentary of the same name (TV Movie, 1987). He became the spokesperson for Seagram's Wine Coolers and made a couple of movies along the way. His first films were *Blind Date* (Movie, 1987), in which he starred opposite Kim Basinger, and *Sunset* (Movie, 1988), with James Garner. However, his big break came when Cybill announced she was pregnant during the third season of *Moonlighting,* which allowed Bruce time to take the role of John McClane in the highly successful action movie *Die Hard* (Movie, 1988).

This role catapulted Bruce from television actor to movie star and action hero. Bruce went on to take on many varied roles after *Moonlighting,* from the voice of Baby Mikey in *Look Who's Talking* (Movie, 1990) to boxer Butch Coolidge in Quentin Tarantino's acclaimed film *Pulp Fiction* (Movie, 1990). Due to disruptions while filming *Broadway Brawler* (Movie, 1997), Bruce signed a three-picture deal with Disney, going on to star in *Armageddon* (Movie, 1998), *The Sixth Sense* (Movie, 1999), and *Unbreakable* (Movie, 2000), all box office successes. Plus he reprised his role as McClane in the *Die Hard* franchise every few years.

In 2000, Bruce won another Emmy, for Outstanding Guest Actor in a Comedy Series for his role as Paul Stevens on *Friends* (TV Series, 1994-2004). Bruce made his Broadway debut in Stephen King's *Misery* (Play, 2015-2016), opposite Laurie Metcalf. Bruce is the father of five girls, and his oldest daughter, Rumer, recently made him a grandfather . . . another girl! Throughout his four decades in Hollywood, Bruce made over one hundred films in various genres before retiring from acting in 2022, but he will remain forever in our hearts as the loose and lovable David Addison.

# THE CAST

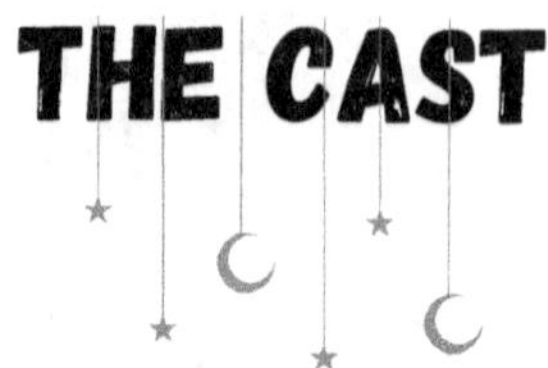

**Allyce Beasley**

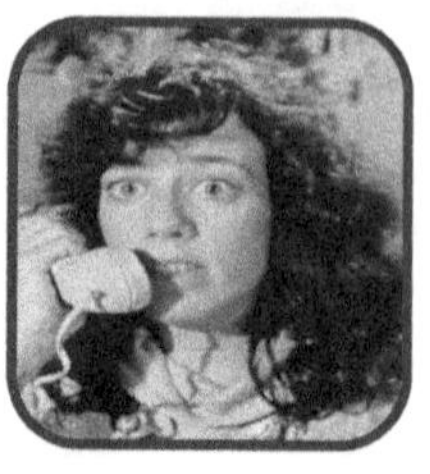

Allyce Beasley was born Alice Tannenberg, in Brooklyn, New York, and eventually developed her professional name by changing the spelling of her first name and choosing the surname Beasley after the football player Beasley Reece. Allyce was introduced to the theater through a guy she dated in college and decided to focus on acting from then on. After college, she acted for a time in local theater productions in Santa Fe, New Mexico, but eventually returned to New York and attended acting classes under Lee Strasberg during the day while working as a waitress at night. Allyce and Vincent Schiavelli, who would later become her husband, both appeared in the same episode of *Taxi* (TV Series 1978-1983). Allyce moved to LA in the early eighties and was cast as Coach Ernie Pantusso's daughter in the first season of *Cheers* (TV Series, 1982-1993) and also made an appearance in *Remington Steele* (TV Series, 1982-1983).

Allyce played Agnes Dipesto in all sixty-six episodes of *Moonlighting* (TV Series, 1985-1989) and became a much-loved character in the show. Whatever was going on between Maddie and David, Agnes was there to hold it all together. Dipesto wasn't just a receptionist; she gave her bosses advice without them even knowing it and spoke her mind when it was required. But what made Miss Dipesto so memorable was the way she answered the phones at the Blue Moon Detective Agency, in rhyme. Agnes would answer each call with a rhyme stating the types of cases Blue Moon could solve or sometimes mention specials they were running, and the person on the line just had to wait until the end to state their business. These rhymes certainly became a cute and comical feature of the show!

Allyce's other work includes *The Tommyknockers* (Mini Series, 1993), *Loaded Weapon 1* (Movie, 1993), *Stuart Little* (Movie, 1999), *Legally Blonde* (Movie, 2001), *Medium* (TV Series, 2005-2011), and *New Amsterdam* (TV Series, 2018-2023), and she is still a working actress today, but we *Moonlighting* fans will always love her portrayal of Miss Agnes Dipesto.

# THE CAST

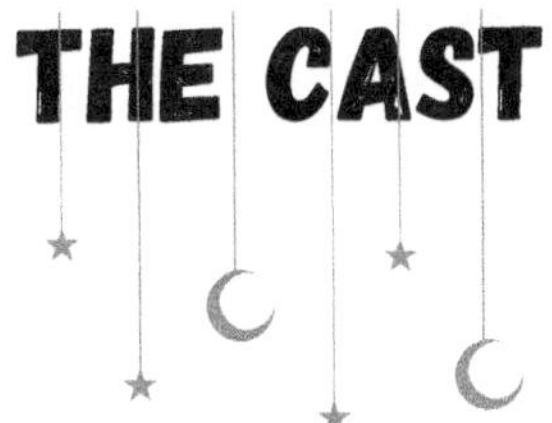

**Curtis Armstrong**

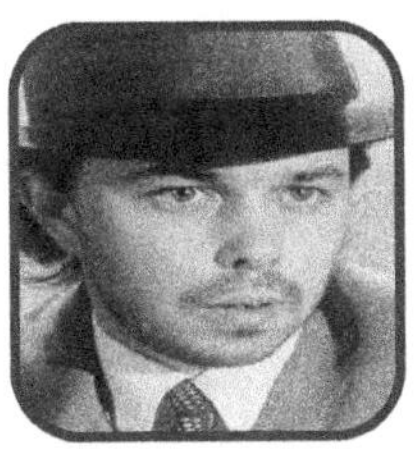

Curtis Armstrong was born in Detroit. He attended Western Michigan University and later transferred to the Academy of Dramatic Art at Oakland University in Rochester, Michigan, graduating in 1975. His first film role was Miles Dalby in *Risky Business* (Movie, 1983), but the role he will always be best known for came the next year when he played Dudley "Booger" Dawson in *Revenge of the Nerds* (Movie, 1984); all you have to say is "Booger" and people know who you're talking about. He also had roles in *Better Off Dead* (Movie, 1985) and *Bad Medicine* (Movie, 1985) before being cast as Herbert Quentin Viola in *Moonlighting* (TV Series, 1985-1989) as a love interest for Agnes Dipesto.

His first episode on *Moonlighting* was in season three's "Yours, Very Deadly," and Curtis went on to star in thirty-seven episodes. Due to the long hours required of Cybill and Bruce from episode to episode, Allyce's and Curtis's characters begin to get more airtime to give the two leads a break from filming. In the episode "Here's Living with You Kid," Allyce and Curtis do a parody of the *Casablanca* (Movie, 1942), an episode in which neither of the series's two leads appear at all. Curtis was a wonderful addition to *Moonlighting*, as he was the antithesis of David Addison, and their characters combined were a great comedic force. Meanwhile, he reprised his role as Booger in *Revenge of the Nerds II: Nerds in Paradise* (Movie, 1987).

Curtis is also a voice actor, having provided his voice as Mr. Moleguaco on *The Emperor's New School* (TV Series, 2006-2008), and Bugspit on *The Buzz on Maggie* (TV Series, 2005-2006). In *Ray* (Movie, 2004), he played music executive Ahmet Ertegun. Over the years, Curtis has accumulated a vast résumé of television and film credits, not only as an actor but also as a producer and writer. In 2013, he received a Daytime Emmy Award for Outstanding Performer in an Animated Program for his voice-over role as Dan in *Dan Vs.* (TV Series, 2011-2013), We know many will also remember Curtis for his film roles, but *Moonlighting* fans will always remember Curtis as Herbert Viola, and for loving Agnes and protecting her in so many ways.

# INTRODUCTION

### GRACE CHIVELL

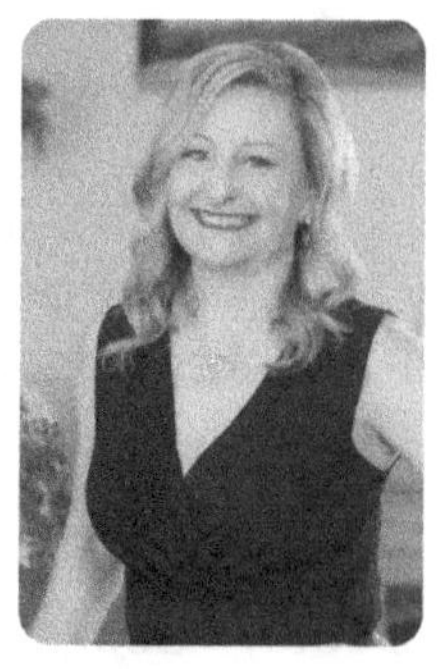

Grace is a best-selling author, and life coach, living in Melbourne, Australia. She is a mother of three girls and a grandmother to five grandsons. She is a longtime Bruce Willis fan, ever since she first laid eyes on him back in 1985 on *Moonlighting*, and has followed his career ever since. She has always enjoyed scrutinizing (and fantasizing etc, etc.) every episode of her favorite TV shows, especially *Moonlighting*. She has always enjoyed the details, such as the writing and the references in each episode. As you can imagine, she has watched the series over and over and over again, as a true fan should! She never missed an episode when it aired and was mesmerized by these two characters who radiated so much chemistry on screen. Listening to their double entendres and overlapping dialogue, Grace was hooked! She loves to travel the world and enjoys learning about other cultures, especially the food! Whatever is going on in her life, she often gets back into her comfort zone by watching *Moonlighting*.

### SHAWNA SAARI

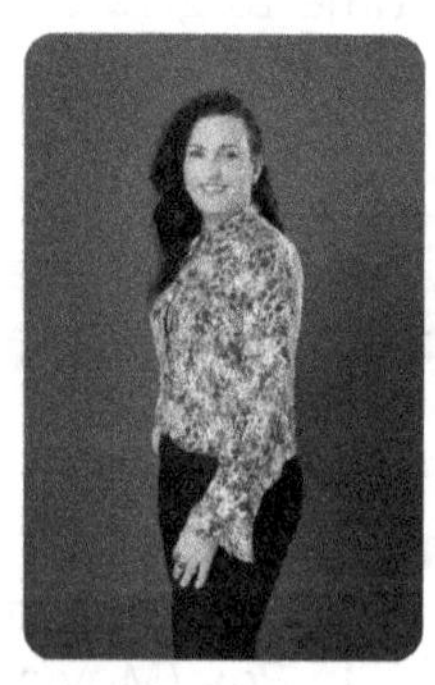

Shawna, a native Californian, currently resides in Shanghai, China. She has been an avid fan of *Moonlighting* since 1985 and has followed the careers of Bruce Willis and Cybill Shepherd closely ever since. Throughout the years, *Moonlighting* has been something she comes back to for the fun, the nostalgia, the banter! But it has been more than just a TV show to watch for her. *Moonlighting* has inspired her creativity over the years through fan fiction writing and editing videos featuring clips of the show set to music. Now, through hosting *Moonlighting the Podcast*, new people, experiences, and opportunities have come into her life. Who'd a thunk that a show she watched as a teen could lead to all this; it truly reaffirms the belief that you should follow your passion, no matter how silly it seems, because you never know where it might lead! Aside from analyzing the sixty-six episodes, Shawna "moonlights" as a teacher and often runs off to a foreign country (not necessarily to hide under a bed) where she can be found in a classroom, on a tennis court, cycling, or enjoying some food and drink in an exotic local.

# MOONLIGHTING THE PODCAST

## *How it all began . . .*

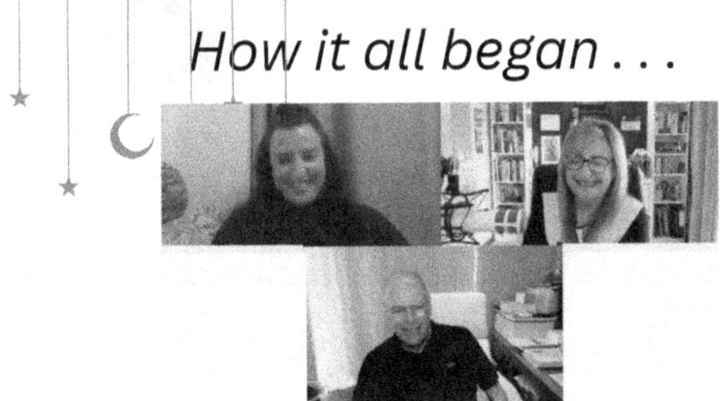

In 2018, Shawna Saari listened to a podcast that had a one-off episode about *Moonlighting* and enjoyed it so much she went looking for more. Surprised to find that no one had yet done a podcast about *Moonlighting*, she figured why not do it herself? After a few failed attempts to get a fellow *Moonlighting* fan to host with her, she was forced to put the project on hold.

Around the same time, on the other side of the world in Melbourne, Australia, Grace Chivell, with two podcasts already under her belt, *Your Road to Success* and *Conversations with Grace*, thought, "*Ba-bing!* I need to do a podcast about *Moonlighting*." The show needs a podcast. But who to cohost? She began to reach out to the masses to find a cohost.

After Grace posted on various sites looking for a cohost, the universe worked its "moonlight magic" as the planets aligned for Shawna and Grace to join forces. The rest, as David Addison would say, "is kismet," and *Moonlighting the Podcast* was born.

# S01 E01
## *Moonlighting* Pilot

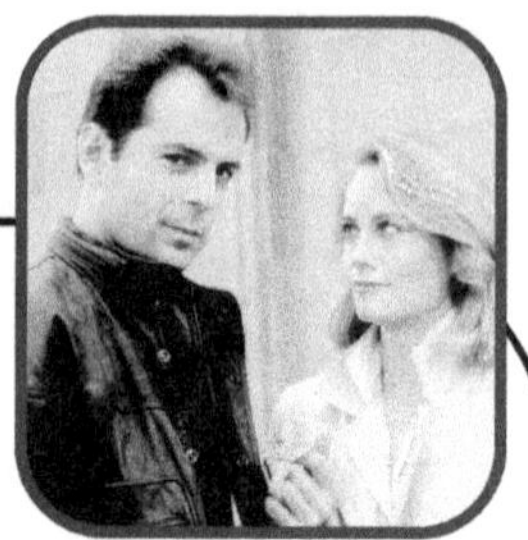

**Plot:**

Well-known model Madolyn "Maddie" Hayes is abruptly awoken one morning to find that her housekeeper and chef have not been paid. She makes a visit to her accountant, only to find that the building is empty and he has fled. She soon realizes that she has been stripped of most of her financial assets by her accountant. Her lawyer informs her that she still owns a number of floundering businesses, which were maintained as tax write-offs. She begins to visit them one by one to fire the staff, shut the businesses down, and liquidate the cash. One of the businesses is a detective agency called City of Angels Investigations.

During her visit to the agency, she breaks the bad news to David Addison, a wisecracking investigator who has been running the agency, that he is out of work, but David has no intention of letting Maddie close the business down. He begins to find ways to persuade her to keep the agency open and convince her they have a future together working as detectives.

During a madcap series of events, Maddie accidentally comes into the possession of a wristwatch that holds the key to the location of smuggled Nazi diamonds. After deciphering several clues, the pair retrieve the diamonds only to find that the mastermind behind the whole scheme has been following their every move including following them the Eastern Building. What follows is one of the most anxiety-provoking scenes in the history of *Moonlighting* when the man attempts to retrieve the diamonds from Maddie and David on the roof-top of the building.

**Air Date:** March 3, 1985

**Written by:** Glenn Gordon Caron

**Director:** Robert Butler

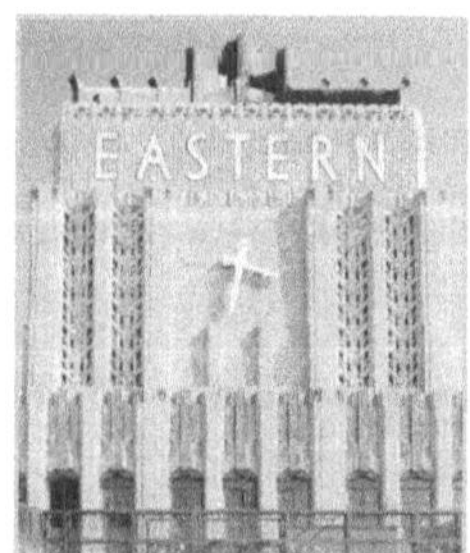

**#1 -** City of Angels Investigations, lost or stolen property our speciality, you dropped it, we'll spot it, he cheats, we'll peek, little one gone, we'll find him before dawn, no job is too big, no job is too small, we're here to please one and all.

**#2** - Blue Moon Detective Agency, we'll help you solve your case, we'll help you find your mate, if it's answers you need, we're eager to please, from stuff that's been took to people who rook, we're always on the case with a smile on our face, we're an agency with class, we really move our . . .

## STATS:

*Door Slams: 0*
*Feet out of Elevator: 2*
*Maddie's Outfit Changes: 7*
*Agnes Rhymes: 2*

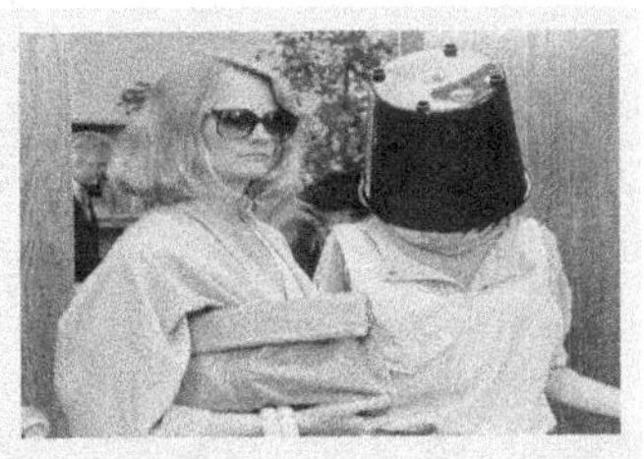

## REVEALING MISTAKE:
In the first shot, a semi-automatic pistol is being loaded from a box labeled "revolver" ammunition.

## FUN FACT:
Robert Ellenstein played Licht in Alfred Hitchcock's *North by Northwest* (Movie, 1959), which also starred Eva Marie Saint, who plays Maddie's mother.

## LOOK FOR:
The stuntman was injured during the end scene in which Heinz swings from the ladder and hits the wall.

## CONTINUITY:
When the guy with the blonde mohawk is running through the park, he's barefoot, but when he runs away, after the accident, he's wearing shoes.

## GREAT LINES:

All right! You're looking great, kid! I'm right behind ya. Now, don't look back and try and see me, just know that I'm right in back of you, and—yes, I am looking up your dress.

*~David Addison*

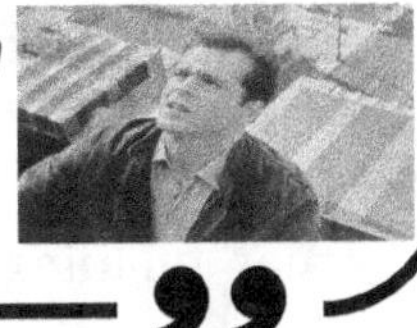

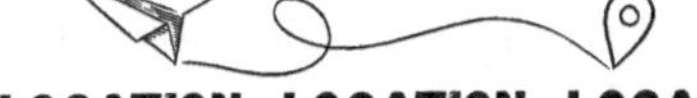

## LOCATION...LOCATION...LOCATION...

~ **Eastern Columbia Building** - 849 South. Broadway, Los Angeles, California, USA
~ **Century Plaza Towers, ABC Entertainment Center (Blue Moon exterior)** - 2040 Avenue of the Stars, Century City, Los Angeles, California, USA
~ **The Westin Bonaventure Hotel & Starline Room** - (**elevator chase**) - 404 South Figueroa Street, Los Angeles, California, USA

## WHERE IT ALL BEGAN:

*Moonlighting* started as an *ABC Sunday Night Movie* and first aired on ABC in America on March 3, 1985. The show then moved to its permanent time slot, Tuesdays at 9pm, with s01e02, "Gunfight at the So-So Corral," which first aired two days later, on March 5, 1985.

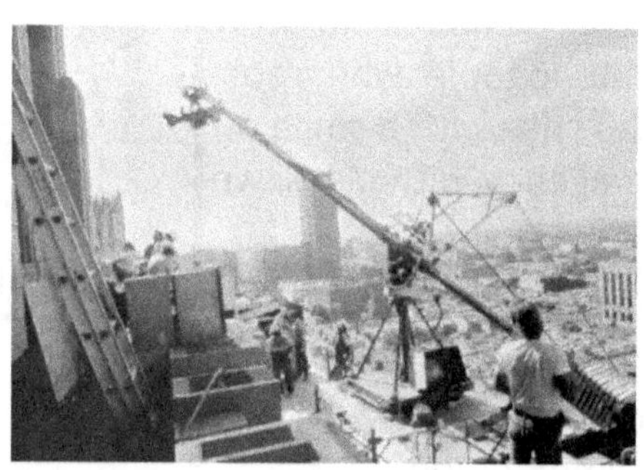

## FINDING SHOOTING LOCATIONS

When *Moonlighting*'s executive producer Jay Daniel joined Grace and Shawna on *Moonlighting the Podcast,* he spoke about finding the Eastern Building used in the Pilot episode. Jay said, "The show very often would present itself a problem where you'd go, 'Well, now what?' Look at the Pilot, look at that building in the Pilot where they're hanging off of the clock. Just finding that set, Glenn wasn't sure where to shoot that. So I thought of the Capitol Records building; it would be interesting. We went up there, and of course, there's not enough room and they couldn't play the scene up there — otherwise, it was great. But finding the [Eastern Building] was a blessing in that there's probably only one building in Los Angeles that you could shoot that scene the way that we shot it. The key to that was that there's not just one clock up there, there are four clocks, one on each side of the building."

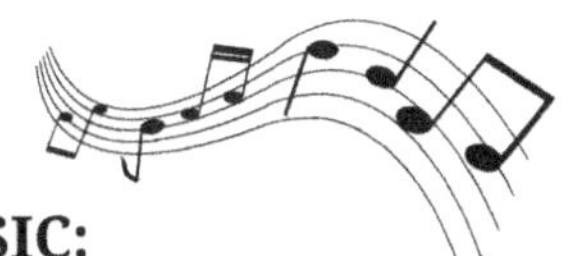


**"Moonlighting"**
By Al Jarreau and Lee Holdridge
Performed by Al Jarreau

**"Blue Moon"**
Written by Richard Rodgers and Lorenz Hart
Performed by Bruce Willis on harmonica

**"Crazy"**
Written by Willie Nelson
Performed by Patsy Cline

**"Since I Fell for You"**
Written by Buddy Johnson
Performed by Lenny Welch

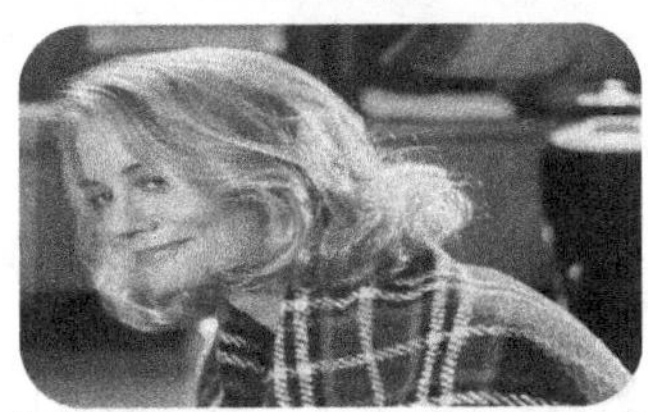

*Maddie listening to David play "Blue Moon" (Song, 1934) on his harmonica. She's starting to like this guy.*

**The meeting [with ABC] had clearly gone well, and I was walking away, and a door opened and I heard a voice . . . 'Glenn, what's it called?' and I said, *'Moonlighting.'***

*~Glenn Gordon Caron*
*Moonlighting the Podcast*

## CAST CREDITS

**Dennis Lipscomb** ... Simon
**Jim McKrell** ... Dr. Spellner
**Mary Hart** ... Herself
**Liz Sheridan** ... Selma
**Dennis Stewart** ... Klaus Gunter
(a.k.a. Blonde Mohawk)
**Sam Hennings** ... Jonathan Kaplan
**Rebecca Stanley** ... Susan Kaplan
**Robert Ellenstein** ... Heinz
**Fredrick Coffin** ... Pawnbroker
**James Karen** ... Alan Webb
**Joan McMurty** ... Mother
**Brian Thompson** ... Thug
**Joe Whipp** ... Investigator

# S01 E02
# Gunfight at
# the So-So Corral

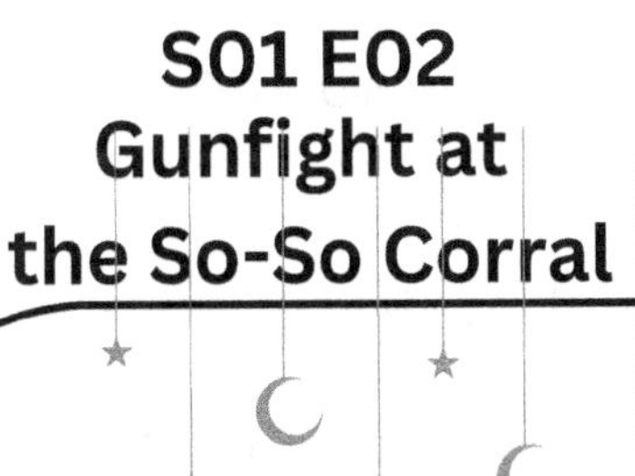



**Plot:**

Maddie shows up to her first day at the office excited and ready to work. The company name has now been changed from City of Angels to Blue Moon Investigations, after the shampoo ads Maddie is so well-known for. Everything is in place . . . the office, the secretary, the support staff. There's just one problem: there are no cases to solve.

Maddie confronts David over why the phones aren't ringing and there are no clients walking though the door. She questions whether she made the right decision in keeping this agency open. So in desperation, David runs across the road to a rival detective agency, steals a client, and brings him back to Blue Moon. The man, Farley Wrye, wants them to find his estranged son, but the plot thickens when Maddie and David realize that everything is not what it seems, and they find out that Wrye is not who he says he is.

**Air Date:** March 5, 1985

**Written by:** Michael Petryni

**Director:** Peter Werner

### CAST CREDITS

**Pat Corley** ... Franklin Tate/Farley Wrye
**Gary Graham** ... Michael Wrye
**Tim Robbins** ... Brummer
**Kim North** ... Secretary
**Tony Burton** ... Bartender

### Agnes Rhyme:

> Blue Moon Detective Agency, we're detectives with a heart, we're here to do our part, in your moment of need, we'll be there indeed, so please don't be shy, just give us a try, we're cooperative and discreet, we really can't be beat, and now, if I may be so bold, I'd like to put you on hold.

### POSSIBLE INSIDE JOKE:

Maddie says she is going to tell "Mr. Bruce" that David made her shake out her "do." Evidently, "Mr. Bruce" refers to Bruce Willis, who used to tease Cybill about having a "hair-do from another century." In s05e04, "Plastic Fantastic Lovers," David mentions that when they first met, he thought Maddie had a "hair-do from another century," so this is most likely an inside joke.

### PLACES AND FACES IN OPENING CREDITS:
- ~ The Nuart Theater
- ~ Hong Kong Low Restaurant
- ~ Angelyne
- ~ Century Plaza Towers
- ~ Los Angeles Skyline
- ~ Wilshire Boulevard

### STATS:

*Door Slams: 0*
*Feet out of Elevator: 0*
*Maddie's Outfit Changes: 5*
*Agnes Rhymes: 1*

### — 66 — GREAT LINES:

*Soon we'll be handling it all, robbery, grand larceny, felonious assault . . . felonious with no salt.*

**~David**
— 99 —

### FUN FACT:
This episode is the first time David says:
**Do bears bare?**
**Do bees be?**

### *MOONLIGHTING* MENTION:
**Muppet Babies** - "Bug-Busting Babies"
(TV Episode, 1988)

**Gonzo says, "Do bees be? Do bears bare?"**

### OUTFIT ROLE CALL:
- Maddie wears the pink dress again at the beginning of s02e04, "The Dream Sequence Always Rings Twice."

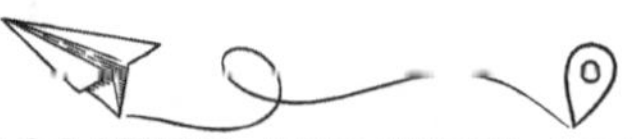

## LOCATION...LOCATION...LOCATION...

~ **Century Plaza Towers (Blue Moon)** - 2029 and 2049 Century Park East, Los Angeles, California, USA

~ **Fox Studio Lot** - 10201 Pico Boulevard, Eastern Columbia Building, 849 South Broadway, Los Angeles, California, USA; Stage 10, Stage 11, and Stage 20 at Fox Studios, Century City, California, USA)

~ **Rocco's Auto & Truck Wrecking** - 555 North Mission Rd., Los Angeles, California, USA

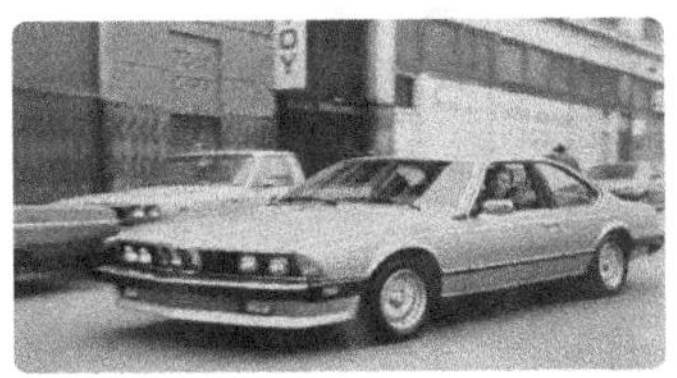

*Maddie's car was a BMW 635CSi in bronzit beige.*

## CULTURAL REFERENCES:

~ David is watching *Family Feud* (TV Game Show, 1975-1985)

**David mentions:**

~ **McLean Stevenson,** who played Lieutenant Colonel Henry Blake in *M*A*S*H* (TV Series, 1972-1983).

~ **Wyatt Earp**, which is a reference to *Gunfight at the O.K. Corral,* (Movie, 1957).

~ **Tony Orlando** - Sang "Tie a Yellow Ribbon Round the Old Oak Tree." (Musical Act Tony Orlando and Dawn, 1973)

~ **Charo** - Spanish-American, actress, singer, and comedian.

~ *My Fair Lady* (Movie, 1964), starring Rex Harrison & Audrey Hepburn.

~ **Brave the Wild Wind,** by Johanna Lindsey (Novel, 1980) - the book Agnes is reading.

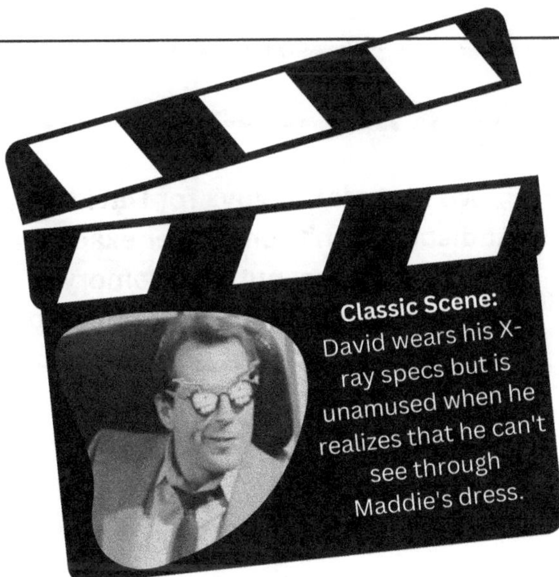

**Classic Scene:** David wears his X-ray specs but is unamused when he realizes that he can't see through Maddie's dress.

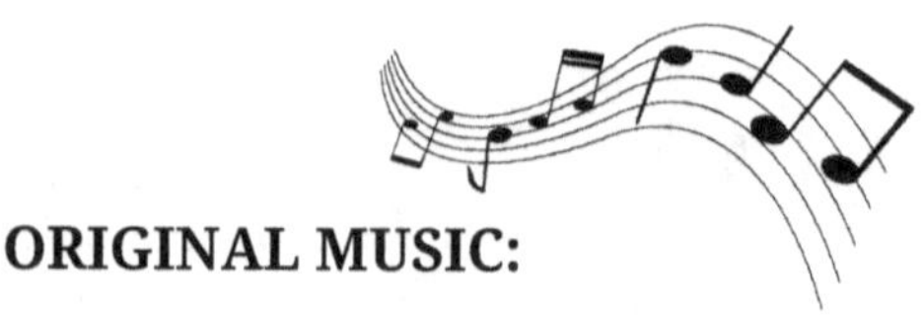

## ORIGINAL MUSIC:

**"Moonlighting"**
By Al Jarreau and Lee Holdridge
Performed by Al Jarreau

**"Tutti Frutti"**
Lyrics by Little Richard  and Dorothy LaBostrie
Performed by Little Richard

**"Do Wah Diddy Diddy"**
Written by Manfred Mann
Performed by Bruce Willis

**"Knock on Wood"**
Lyrics by Eddie Floyd  and Steve Cropper
Performed by Eddie Floyd
*(Replaced with new music on Hulu streaming)*

**"She Advertises"**
Composed and performed by John Hunter
*(Replaced with new music on Hulu streaming)*

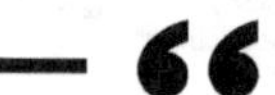

**We saw a lot of guys for David Addison. I don't remember exactly how many it was, but the memory of when Bruce [Willis] finally appeared Is something you just don't forget.**

*~Executive Producer Jay Daniel*
*Moonlighting the Podcast*

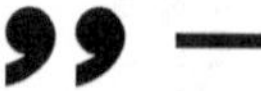

# S01 E03
# Read the Mind...
# See the Movie



**Plot:**

In an attempt to make money other ways while waiting for detective work to pick up, Blue Moon is hired by SRT Industries to provide security. The company is a family-owned business run in part by one of Maddie's closest friends, Vivian Baker. SRT has been plagued by information leaks and sabotage. The company's main competitor, Preston Holt, claims that he has been receiving inside information from a psychic named Omar Gauss.

 David and Maddie soon discover that Vivian Baker's father also visits Gauss and conclude that he is selling company secrets. However, the case turns out not to be that clear-cut when they discover the leaks might be a little closer to home.

**Air Date:** March 12, 1985

**Written by:** Joe Gannon

**Director:** Burt Brinckerhoff

**The Working Title**
**"An Inkling of Murder"**

**CAST CREDITS**

**Cotter Smith** ... Brian Baker

**Lenore Kasdorf** ... Vivian Baker

**Bill Morey** ... Carl Baker

**Joe Lambie** ... Preston Holt

**John Harkins** ... Omar Gauss

**Paul Reid Roman** ... Randolph

**Garnett Smith** ... Maître d

**Agnes Rhyme:**

> Blue Moon Detective Agency, we're here to unravel, events that might baffle, we'll figure it out, and leave you no doubt, so tell us what's wrong, it won't take us long, we do our work well . . . there's no need to yell.

## FUN FACT #1:

The scene in which Maddie and David are on the roof is similar to Alfred Hitchcock's *To Catch a Thief* (Movie, 1955).

## FUN FACT #2:

This is the one and only time Maddie chews gum in the series.

## REVEALING MISTAKE #1:

A mannequin, and not a human, is clearly present just before Vivian is crushed by the concrete.

## REVEALING MISTAKE #2:

When Maddie is in the limousine with Preston Holt, she is looking in the wrong direction while talking to him. Cybill preferred to be filmed camera left, so this might be one reason she seems to be looking in the wrong place.

## REVEALING MISTAKE #3:

When Maddie and David run from Gauss's home, they leave in a red Corvette and not a red Porsche (which is said to be the company car).

## STATS:

*Door Slams: 0*
*Feet out of Elevator: 0*
*Maddie's Outfit Changes: 9*
*Agnes Rhymes: 1*

## GREAT LINES:

> **David**: *I'll stake my professional reputation, such as it is, on it.*

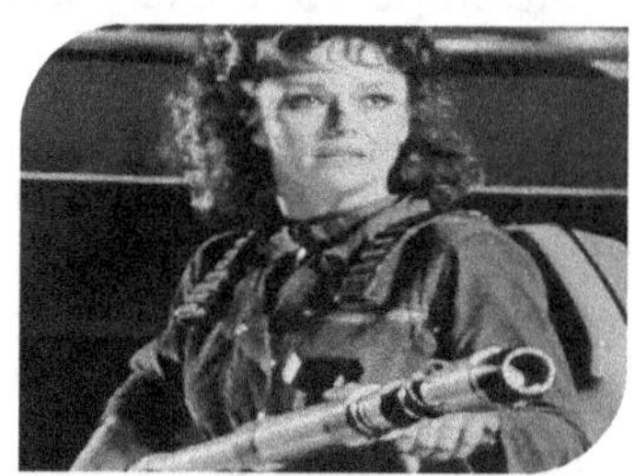

*Vivian Baker, played by Lenore Kasdorf, dressed up to the nines with her laser gun.*

## OUTFIT ROLE CALL:

- Maddie wears the brown skirt/top outfit again in s02e01, "Brother, Can You Spare a Blonde," (with a pink blouse) and s02e13, "In God We Strongly Suspect."

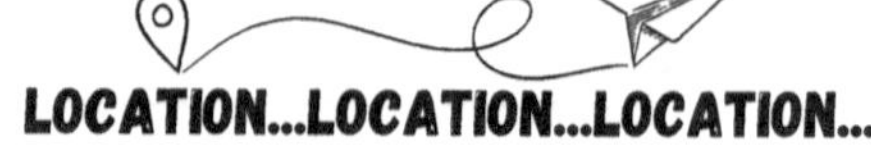

## LOCATION...LOCATION...LOCATION...

~ **Gauss Mansion** - Located in the city of Monrovia, California, USA

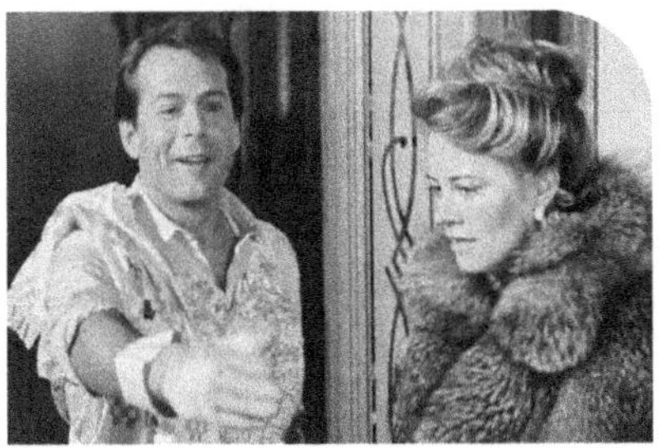

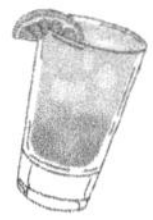



## CULTURAL REFERENCES:

~ **Winchester** - The Winchester rifle developed by Henry Rifle in the 1800s.

~ **Colt** - Samuel Colt, firearms manufacturer.

~ **Nobel** - Alfred Bernhard Nobel was a Swedish chemist, engineer, and inventor. He invented dynamite, which he patented in 1867. He acquired 355 patents in his lifetime. He bequeathed his fortune to establish the Nobel Prize.

### David mentions:

~ **Tang** - Tang is a drink mix from General Foods Corporation food scientist William A. Mitchell.

~ **The Amazing Kreskin** - The Amazing Kreskin (born George Joseph Kresge) was a mentalist in American in the seventies who became popular on television.

~ ***The Twilight Zone*** (TV Series, 1959-1964) - David hums the theme and parodies the intro. Earlier that year,  just before being cast in *Moonlighting,* Bruce starred in an episode of *The Twilight Zone* called "Shatterday."

~ **Yabba Dabba Doo** - "Yabba-Dabba-Doo!" is the catchphrase of Fred Flintstone in the *The Flintstones* (Cartoon Series, 1960-1966)

~ **Herman and Katnip** - *Herman and Katnip* (Cartoon Series, 1944–1959), are two cartoon characters, Herman is a mouse and Katnip is a cat.

# S01 E04
# The Next
# Murder You Hear



**Plot:**

Popular late-night KRKD radio DJ Paul McCain works 2:00 to 6:00 a.m. hosting a show called "Heartbreak Hotline." During a live broadcast one night, those working the graveyard shift listen as McCain is gunned down live in the studio. The event is recounted on the front page of the newspaper the next morning, and David gets an idea.

 David understands that it would be great publicity for Blue Moon if they solve the crime . . . but Maddie prefers a paying client with a contract. Of course, in true *Moonlighting* fashion, David convinces Maddie to take on the case, so they begin to investigate the on-air shooting of McCain.

 Maddie is against taking the case once she finds out that McCain was having an affair with a married woman, but after listening to the man on tape, she becomes intrigued and decides Blue Moon should investigate after all. The DJ soon turns up alive, having faked his own death to keep the affair from his boss, but is then accused of the murder of his lover's husband, who was also his boss, (are you following?). Both the host and his mistress hire Blue Moon to prove their innocence, and Maddie and David disagree over who they believe actually did it.

**Air Date:** March 19, 1985

**Written by:** Peter Silverman

**Director:** Peter Werner

**CAST CREDITS**

**Gregg Henry** ... Paul McCain

**Barbara Stock** ... Laura Boyd

**James Sloyan** ... Sonny Brezner

**Ross Evans** ... Bartender

**Richard Epcar** ... Blue Moon Employee

**Frantz Turner** ... Blue Moon Employee

**Joan Ryan** ... Blue Moon Employee

**Nora Gaye** ... Caller

**Chino (Fats) Williams** ... Cook

## LOOK FOR: 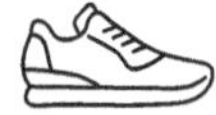

Cybill Shepherd, who famously hates wearing heels, is wearing sneakers the first time Maddie and David visit the KRKD radio station.

## FUN FACT #1:

*The Killing Fields* (Movie, 1984) is playing at the movie theater that Maddie drives past.

## FUN FACT #2:

The line used by Paul McCain "Go to a foreign country and hide under a bed" is used again by Maddie in s04e01, "A Trip to the Moon."

## FUN FACT #3:

Chino (Fats) Williams is also in s03e04, "Yours, Very Deadly."

## FUN FACT #4:

Maddie's periodontist, Dr. Fishbine, gets another mention in s02e05, "My Fair David."

**On Location:**
**from our personal photo album**

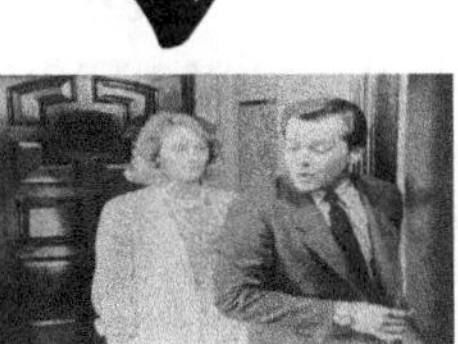

*Mr. Stickpin Door*

## STATS:

*Door Slams: 0*
*Feet out of Elevator: 0*
*Maddie's Outfit Changes: 8*
*Agnes Rhymes: 0*

## GREAT LINES:

# BOINK

*~ David Addison*

## REVEALING MISTAKE #1:

When Maddie inserts the "Heartbreak Hotline" cassette into her car stereo, it starts playing before the cassette fully descends into the tape deck.

## REVEALING MISTAKE #2:

When Maddie kicks David out of the car there are people standing on the street watching filming.

## CONTINUNITY:

Maddie and David's offices magically have "back doors" in this episode!

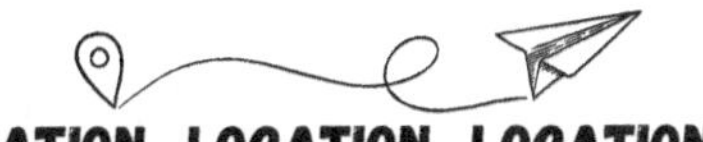

## LOCATION...LOCATION...LOCATION...

**~ KRKD Radio Station** - 541 South Spring St., Los Angeles, California, USA

**REVEALING MISTAKE #3:**
When they arrive at the radio station to tell Laura and Paul who killed Laura's husband, the twenty-four-hour clock says 2:00 a.m. not 8:00 p.m., which was their meeting time.

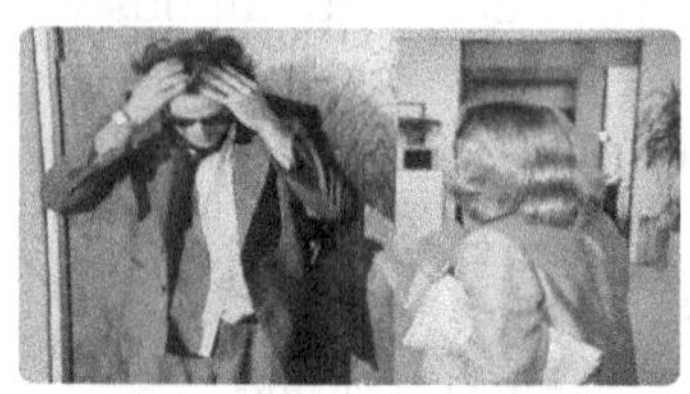

*"Oh my God, they dropped the bomb."*

**REVEALING MISTAKE #4:**
The scene In which Sonny starts shooting at KRKD, he shoots seven times, but David says he has shot only six times, thinking he has run out of bullets. Sonny then takes another shot.

**REVEALING MISTAKE #6:**
When Sonny is electrocuted, initially he is falling backward, but in the next shot, he's facing forward as he summersaults off the platform to the his death.

**REVEALING MISTAKE #5:**
There is a cut of a bullet going through glass that is used twice, once at beginning and once at the end of the episode.

**OUTFIT ROLE CALL:**
- Maddie wears the purple suit again in s02e09, "Atlas Belched."

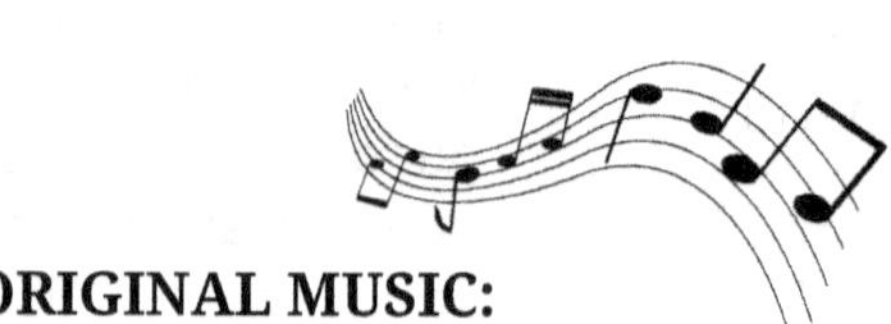

## ORIGINAL MUSIC:

**"Ooh Ooh Baby"**
Written by Smokey Robinson and Warren Moore
Performed by Linda Ronstadt
*(Replaced with new music on Hulu streaming)*
**"Respect"**
Written by Otis Redding
Performed by Aretha Franklin and Bruce Willis
**"The Hokey Pokey"**
**"The Hokey Pokey" Hokey Cokey"**
Written by Taft Baker,
Roland Lawrence LaPrise and Charles Macak
Performed by Bruce Willis

# S01 E05
# Next Stop Murder

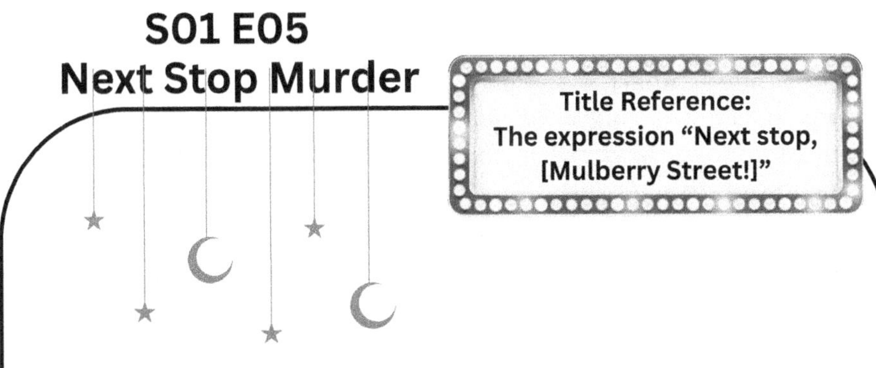


**Plot:**

When Ms. Dipesto wins the J. B Harland murder magazine essay contest, she is invited to spend twenty-four hours on his yearly "murder train," to solve a crime that happens during the trip. Maddie and David agree to drop Dipesto at the train station because she doesn't want to leave her car there overnight.

Due to David's antics on the train, Maddie and David miss exiting before it leaves the station and now have to stay on as it won't stop at all for the next twenty-four hours. While the train is in motion, J. B. Harland is murdered for real. Everyone on the train becomes suspicious of everyone else, so Maddie and David are left to solve the mystery. The episode concludes with an epic showdown atop the moving train with the killer trying to escape.

**Air Date:** March 26, 1985

**Written by:** Ali Marie Matheson and Kerry Ehrin

**Director:** Kevin Conner

### CAST CREDITS

**Vincent Schiavelli** ... Rodney Dillon

**Leonard Frey** ... Skyler Cantrell

**Lisa Blake Richards** ... Janet McCall

**Rick Jason** ... J. B.Harland

**Ben Slack** ... Sebastian Rhodes

## MISSING SCENE?
When Maddie and David are in the train car alone, in one scene they sit apart, Maddie seemingly not talking to David, but when they cut back, David sits across from Maddie speaking intimately.

## REVEALING MISTAKE:
In the scene where J. B. Harland is found dead, Skyler Cantrell incorrectly calls Janet "Jennifer."

## STATS:

*Door Slams: 0*
*Feet out of Elevator: 0*
*Maddie's Outfit Changes: 3*
*Agnes Rhymes: 2*

## GREAT LINES:
— " —

*The mind reels.*
**~David Addison**
——— " —

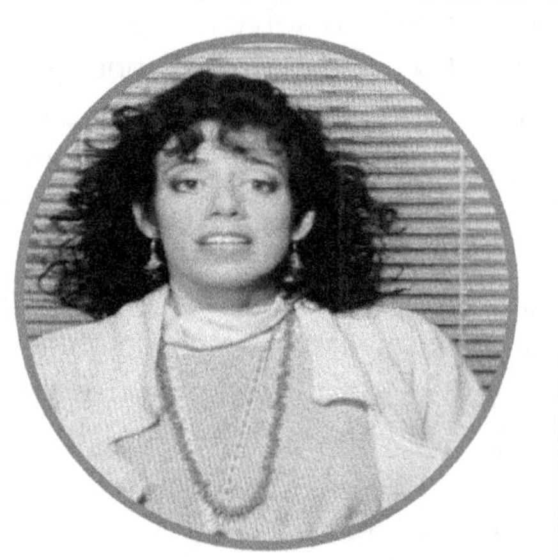

## FUN FACT
Agnes delivers this oft-quoted (by *Moonlighting* fans) phrase:

*"You guys are great; in fact, you're better than great. . . .*
**"You're great, great!"**

## CONTINUITY:
When Maddie and David get out of the folding bed, Maddie is wearing her left shoe. She gets up to open the curtains, and she is now wearing her right shoe. Then she goes down the hallway with one shoe off and one shoe on and is now wearing her left shoe again.

## OUTFIT ROLE CALL:
- Maddie wears the gray blouse with the pink flowers again in s03e06, "Big Man on Mulberry Street."

## LOCATION...LOCATION...LOCATION...
~ **Union Station** - 800 North Alameda St., Downtown, Los Angeles, California, USA

## Agnes Rhymes:

Agnes's rhymes were a staple of the show. She would answer the phone with a rhyme offering great bonuses with Blue Moon's services to entice the client to hire Maddie and David to take their case. It was a wonderful and entertaining addition to the show. The rhymes were not in every episode, but in this particular episode there were two.

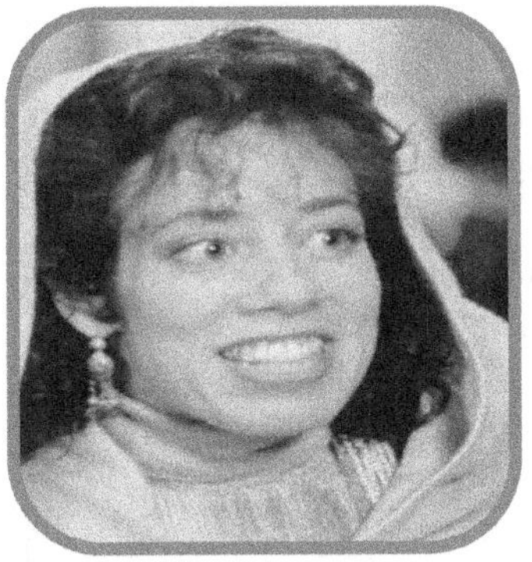

*Agnes is very excited as she is about to board the "J. B. Harland Murder Train."*

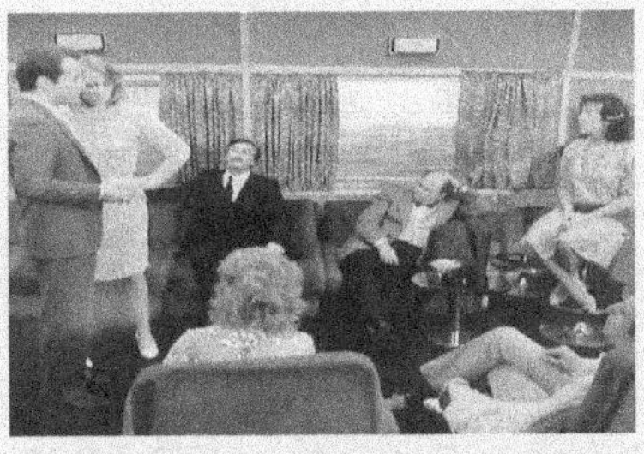

*David rounds up the suspects to announce who the murderer is.*

## Agnes Rhyme #1:

*My luck is on the rise,*
*I listen as fate cries,*
*the time is here,*
*so give a cheer,*
*Dipesto won a prize.*

## Agnes Rhyme #2:

*My goose is really cooked,*
*my nerves are really shook,*
*J.B. is dead, it's on my head,*
*life is such a rook,*
*my prints are on the knife,*
*it's going to cost my life,*
*I'm going to fry,*
*I'm going to cry,*
*Oh why, oh why, oh why!*

**ART IMITATES LIFE:**
Ms. Dipesto (Allyce Beasley) falls in love with Rodney Dillon (Vincent Schiavelli), the technical assistant to the victim. In real life, Beasley and Schiavelli were married in 1985.

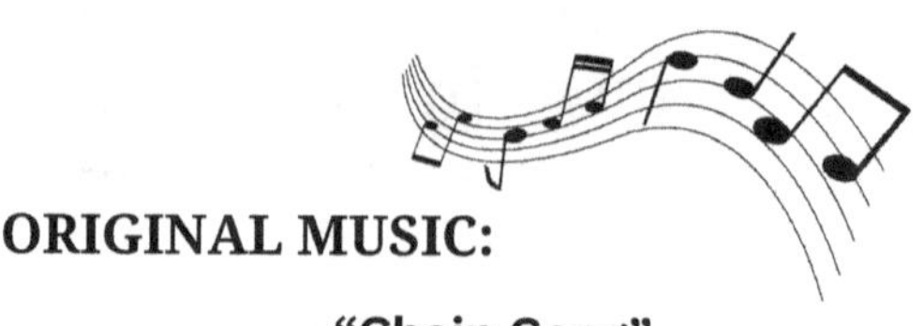

## ORIGINAL MUSIC:

**"Chain Gang"**
Written by Sam Cooke
Performed by Allyce Beasley

---

### CULTURAL REFERENCES:

~ Sebastian fawns better than ***Bambi*** (Movie, 1942).

~ Agnes mentions ***Cinderella*** (Movie, 1950).

~ Agnes says, "According to ***Donahue*** (TV Series, 1967–1995), I am at my physical and sexual peak . . . right now."

~ Everyone says goodnight to each other as they did on ***The Waltons*** (TV Series, 1972–1981), including "Good night, John-Boy."

~ ***Dynasty*** (TV Series, 1981–1989) - David mentions *Dynasty* Episode #88, which is "The Nightmare" (TV Episode, 1984).

---

### FIRST "DIPESTO EPISODE"

The "Dipesto Episodes," as they became known, were born out of necessity as Glenn Caron needed a way to give Cybill and Bruce, who were in every scene, a break. In the beginning, Maddie and David just had smaller parts in these episodes, then gradually appeared less and less. By s04e13, "Here's Living with You, Kid," neither Maddie or David plays a role in the episode - the only episode of the series in which neither Cybill or Bruce appears.

# S01 E06
# The Murder's in the Mail

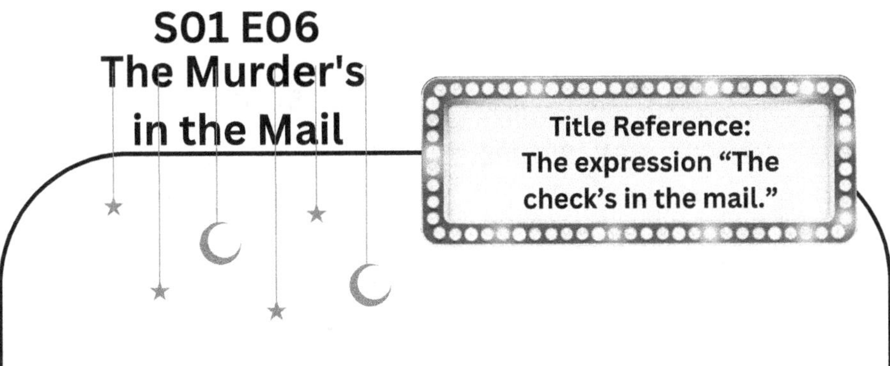



**Plot:**

Maddie has major concerns about Blue Moon's financial situation. So David convinces Maddie that they should become consultants for a debt collection agency to earn some extra cash. Upon visiting one of the debtors, they discover his dead body in his armchair. But when they return with the police, the body has disappeared and a completely different man answers the door of the apartment in which they found the dead body.

One thing leads to another, and the duo unknowingly becomes involved in an assassination plot in which Russians plan to kill a Chinese diplomat with a mole on his nose. However, a maître d' will not let them enter the formal dinner event at which several Chinese diplomats are enjoying their dinner.

So as usual, they have to get creative, and they enter the event as waiters and succeed in preventing the murder by apprehending the assassin, which then culminates in a huge food fight in the ballroom among all the event's attendees.

**Air Date:** April 2, 1985

**Written by:**
Maryanne Kasica &
Michael Scheff

**Director:** Peter Werner

**CAST CREDITS**

**Jon Cedar** ... Roy Hirsch
**Art Koustik** ... Taxi Driver
**James Walch** ... Priest
**Arthur Taxier** ... Nestavincenko
**Michael Halsey** ... The Blond Man
**Patricia Allison** ... Woman Outside Building
**Will Gill Jr.** ... Man in Airport
**Raymond O'Keefe** ... Maître d
**Lomax Study** ... Man in Elevator
**Nick Angotti** ... Detective
**Rio Fukuda** ... Guest
**Robert Moberly** ... Guest
**Bill Saito** ... Guest

### Agnes Rhyme:

Blue Moon Detective Agency, if persons are missing, if objects are lost, we'll find them for you at reasonable cost, your runaway husband, that nonpaying louse, we'll find them for you, bring them back to the house, lost a prize-winning dog, lost a prize-winning cat, we'll find them both for you in just no time flat. So tell us your problem, it'll all work out fine, just tell me your problem, it's why I'm on the line.

## CONTINUITY #1:

When David breaks the mirror, there is no envelope hidden behind the glass. The envelope appears later, after Maddie comes in to bandage David's injured hand.

## CONTINUITY #2:

Throughout the car chase, both Cybill's and Bruce's headrests are visible. However, when Cybill is driving in reverse, they have been removed!

## FUN FACT #1:

When Maddie and David get blocked in the alleyway, there is graffiti on the wall that says "Roy." They were trying to locate Roy Hirsch.



### GREAT LINES:

> **David**: *We're looking for a man with a mole on his nose.*
>
> **Security Officer**: *A mole on his nose?*
>
> **Maddie**: *A mole on his nose.*

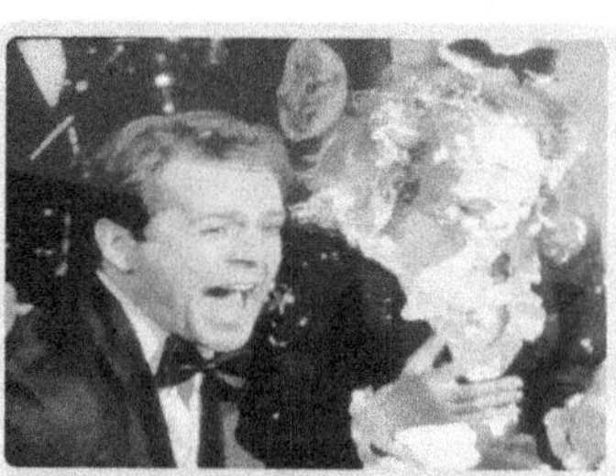

*Cybill and Bruce reported in an interview with "Good Morning America" in 1985 that a cream pie to the face is very satisfying!*

### LOCATION...LOCATION...LOCATION...

~ **Millennium Biltmore Hotel, Tiffin Room (food fight)** - 506 South Grand Ave., Los Angeles, California, USA

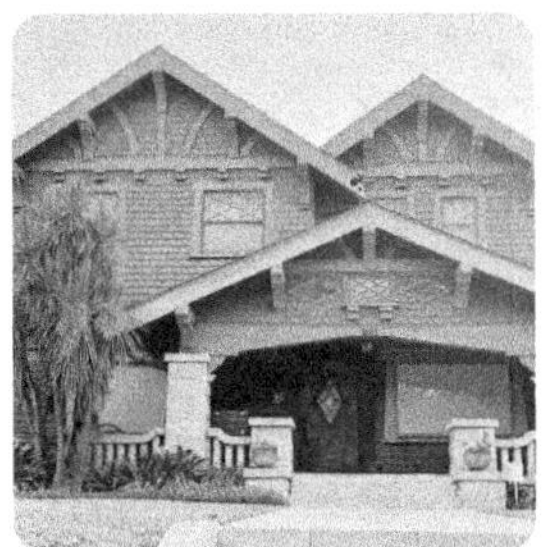

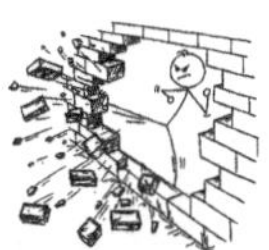

***The House on Pooh Corner***
*Where Maddie and David go to collect money from Larry (from our personal photo archive)*

**LOOK FOR:**
Maddie and David in their first car chase!

**FUN FACT #2:**
The policeman (Nick Angotti) was in *Die Hard 2* (Movie, 1990) as an engineer.

**BREAKING THE FOURTH WALL:**
David holds up a book he has been reading, "Being Second Stinks," written by J. D. Caron (inside joke in reference to Jay Daniel & Glenn Gordon Caron).

---

**CULTURAL REFERENCES:**

~ David mentions **Camp Kennybrook,** a New York summer camp.

~ The man in the elevator with Roy Hirsh looks like **Alfred Hitchcock** and is viewed from the side, similar to Alfred's famous silhouette.

~ David mentions "The House at Pooh Corner" when they arrive at Larry's house,  referring to **Winnie the Pooh** (Movie, 1961).

~ Maddie compares Larry to **Paul Bunyan,** referring to to *Paul Bunyan,* who was a giant lumberjack and folk hero in American and Canadian folklore.

~ David mentions the **Santini Bros.,** a New York moving company that was opened in 1905 by six brothers.

~ David: We've replaced this banquet hall's coffee with frozen crystals (referring to an ad for **Folger's** frozen crystals coffee)

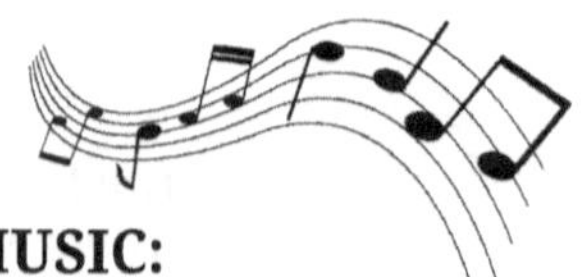

**ORIGINAL MUSIC:**

**"My Girl"**
Written by Smokey Robinson
and Ronald White
Performed by Bruce Willis while playing the harmonica

## The Man With the Mole on His Nose

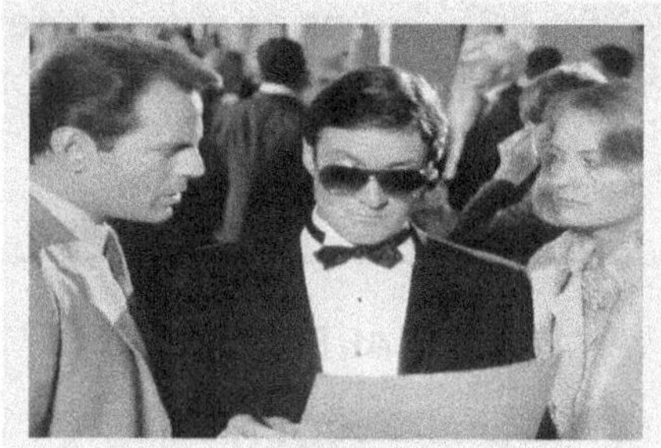

This episode contains the infamous "man with the mole on his nose" scene at the entrance to the ballroom with Maddie, David, and the Maître d' (Raymond O'Keefe). The scene is written as an homage to Dr. Seuss. Watch the bloopers at the end of s03e09, "The Straight Poop," to see how much trouble O'Keefe had with the rhyming dialogue.

# S02 E01
# Brother, Can You Spare a Blonde?



**Plot:**

When down-on-his-luck Richard Addison finds $100,000 under the hood of his car, instead of going to the police he takes the money and heads to LA to throw his "wealth" in his brother David's face. Richie also flirts with Maddie, making David very jealous. Meanwhile, Maddie finds out that she owes the IRS $35,000.

David asks his Richie for a loan to help Maddie but tells him not to say a word to her about it. David explains the extra cash to Maddie by saying that he found an agency bank account with money in it that no one knew about.

David gets angry when he is attacked in the men's room at Blue Moon. The thug wants his money back and has mistaken David for Richie. David now realizes that all this money that Richie has been flaunting does not belong to him.

The money belongs to a drug dealer, Mr. Navarone, who eventually confronts the Addison brothers and Maddie at a shopping mall. However, before Navarone can take the cash back, the team scatters the money over a third-floor mall balcony, to the excitement of all the shoppers below and to the dismay of Mr. Navarone.

**Air Date:** September 24, 1985

**Written by:**
Glenn Gordon Caron

**Director:** Peter Werner

## CAST CREDITS

**Charles Rocket** ... Richard "Richie" Addison (Recurring Role)
**Ed O'Ross** ... Navarone
**Jonathan Stark** ... Undercover Cop
**Patrick Alan** ... Rapper
**Russell Hines** ... Rapper
**Terry Wills** ... Store Owner
**Beau Billingslea** ... Announcer
**Adriano Rebora** ... Undercover Cop

### CONTINUITY #1:
When Navarone attacks David in the stall, he pulls David's head from the  toilet bowl and his hair and shirt are dry but were wet just a moment earlier.

### CONTINUITY #2:
When Maddie is running in the mall, her shoes are on, then off, then on again; she couldn't have taken her shoes off and put them on that quickly.

### CONTINUITY #3:
Maddie needs 35k, David tells Richie he needs 37k. David gives Maddie 37k . . . but later in the episode she reminds them of the 35k they gave her.

### CONTINUITY #4:
When Navarone pulls Maddie through the coatrack, her dress is pulled open and her bra is visible.

### FUN FACT:
At Maddie's house, Ritchie is reading a Trivial Pursuit card, but the game board on her coffee table is clearly not Trivial Pursuit.

### LOOK FOR:
A stunt double for Cybill sliding down the middle of the escalator behind Bruce.

## LOCATION...LOCATION...LOCATION...

**~ Bullocks Wilshire (Mall) -**
3050 Wilshire Boulevard,
Los Angeles, California, USA
**~ Adriano's Ristorante -**
2930 Beverly Glen Circle,
Los Angeles, California, USA

### STATS:

*Door Slams: 0*
*Feet out of Elevator: 1*
*Maddie's Outfit Changes: 6*
*Agnes Rhymes: 0*

### GREAT LINES:
— 66 —
**David** *(to Richie): You're a dead man!*
*(Richie checks his pulse)*
**Richie:** *Beg to differ with you, bro.*
— 99 —

### OUTFIT ROLE CALL:
- Maddie wore the brown skirt/top outfit in s01e03, "Read the Mind  . . .  See the Movie," and again in s02e13, "In God We Strongly Suspect."

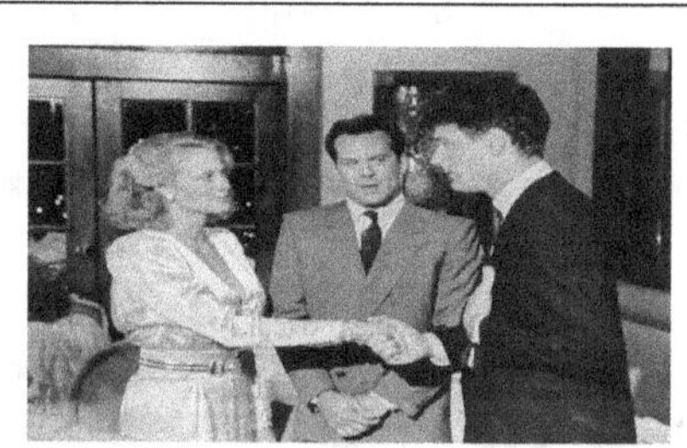

### FAMILY TIES:
This is the first time we meet David's younger brother, Richard (Richie) Addison, played by the late Charles Rocket. Glenn Caron originally wrote the role for David Lee Roth, the lead singer of Van Halen.

## CULTURAL REFERENCES:

~ *Gone with the Wind* (Movie, 1939) - David says, "Ooh, Scarlett, Tara ain't on the block yet."

~ *Leave It to Beaver* (TV Series, 1957–1963) - David and Richie greet each other with "Wally!" and "Beav!"—the names of the two brothers in the series.

~ *The Twilight Zone* (TV Series, 1959–1964) - Richie says it was "like the *The Twilight Zone*" when he found the money.

~ *The Guns of Navarone* (Movie, 1961) - Navarone wants David, Maddie, and Richie to join him in a theater where this movie is playing.

~ *The Waltons* (TV Series, 1972–1981) - The Trivial Pursuit question Richie asks Maddie is about this show.

~ David says, "Mr Iacocca," referring to **Lee Iacocca**, an automobile executive who was president of Chrysler (1978–1992.)

~ Maddie asks Agnes if they have any appointments. Agnes says, "John Gavin was made ambassador to Mexico again!" **John Gavin** was an actor who was the president of the Screen Actors Guild from 1971–1973 and then the US ambassador to Mexico from 1981–1986.

~ *The Titanic* - Maddie says "David, we're standing on the decks of the *Titanic* and you're suggesting songs to the band." The *RMS Titanic* was a British ship that sank in 1912.

~ Richie asks David, "How much ya got?" David replies: "Are we speaking strictly American currency or do **Krugerrands** count?" Krugerrands are South African coins.

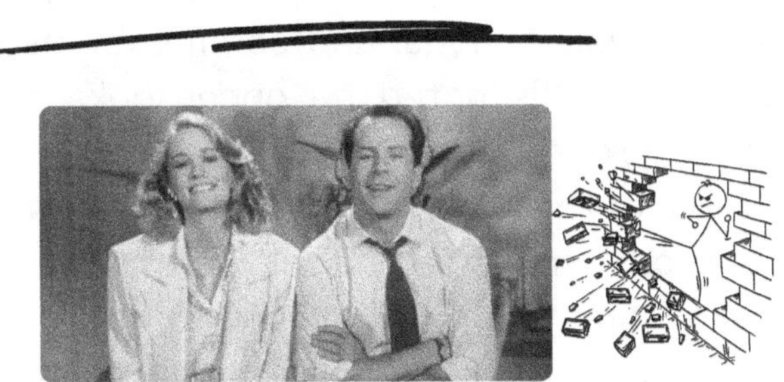

**BREAKING THE FOURTH WALL:**
David and Maddie speak directly to viewers,
welcoming them back to the second season.

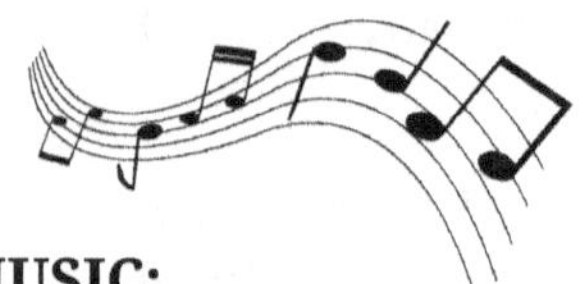

## ORIGINAL MUSIC:

**"Guido the Killer Pimp"**
Written by Edgar Froese,
Christopher Franke, and Johannes Schmölling
Performed by Tangerine Dream
*(Replaced with new music on Hulu streaming)*

**"Rappin' Duke"**
Written by Shawn Brown
Performed by Charles Rocket

**"For the Love of Money"**
Written by Kenny Gamble, Leon Huff, and Anthony Jackson
Performed by The O'Jays

**"If Only You Knew"**
Performed by Patti LaBelle
*(Replaced with new music on Hulu streaming)*

---

## BREAKING THE FOURTH WALL:

*Moonlighting* often broke the fourth wall of television with direct references to the plot, the writers, in-jokes about the show itself, or winks, nods, and comments made directly to viewers. Bruce Willis noted he once spoke directly to the camera as a joke, which got a big laugh, and it became a regular staple of the show from there. Due to the series's fast dialogue, producers often found themselves with a few minutes of airtime to fill, which led to cold opens in which Cybill and Bruce (in character as Maddie and David), would welcome the viewers back to another season, read fan mail, or get funky with famous Motown singers!

# S02 E02
# The Lady
# in the Iron Mask

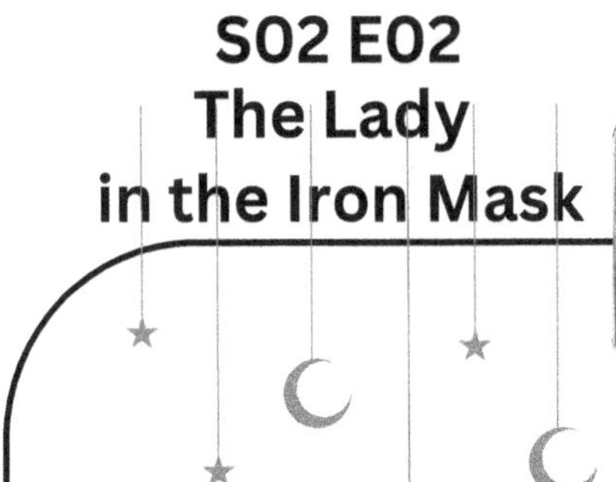

**Title Reference:**
*The Man in the Iron Mask*
(Novel, 1850)

**Plot:**

Maddie and David are hired by a veiled Barbara Wylie to track down her ex-boyfriend Frank Harbert, who has recently been paroled. Twelve years earlier, Harbert threw acid in Barbara's face in a fit of anger when he found out she was to marry another man. However, Barbara claims she wants to give Frank another chance. Maddie is reluctant to take the case, but David reasons that Blue Moon is hired to solve cases, not judge them. Maddie finally agrees, and they track down the man, though shortly after they find him, Maddie and David find out he has been murdered.

Later, they discover that the person who actually hired them was an impostor and not really Barbara Wylie, so now they must find the real killer. This leads to a chaotic and hilarious chase scene in which Maddie, David, Benjamin Wylie, and Barbara Wylie, all dressed alike, run through the halls of a hotel and end up sliding through soapsuds to end the chase in the hotel lobby.

**Air Date:** October 1, 1985

**Written by:** Roger Director

**Director:** Christopher Leitch

### CAST CREDITS

**Judith Hanson** ... Barbara Wylie
**Joel Polis** ... Frank Harbert
**Dennis Christopher** ... Benjamin Wylie
**Paul Willison** ... Desk Clerk No. 1
**Stan Barnett** ... Hotel Guest
**Howard Mann** ... Man in Elevator
**C. Thomas Howell** ... Waiter

**FUN FACT #1:**
This is the first real client to walk through the door and hire Blue Moon.

**FUN FACT #2:**
Plot based on the real-life "love story" of Linda and Burt Pugach.

**FUN FACT #3:**
Actor C. Thomas Howell's father, Chris Howell, was the stunt coordinator for nineteen episodes.

**FUN FACT #4:**
Actor C. Thomas Howell makes a cameo appearance in this episode as a waiter.

**CONTINUITY:**
Maddie and David walk out of Blue Moon and walk to the right, but the elevators are to the left.

**OUTFIT ROLE CALL:**
- Maddie wears the white striped suit again in s02e09, "Atlas Belched," and s02e17, "Funeral for a Door Nail."

**STATS:**

*Door Slams: 0*
*Feet Out of Elevator: 1*
*Maddie's Outfit Changes: 4*
*Agnes Rhymes: 0*

### — ❝ ——— GREAT LINES:

*I'm glad you're my partner . . . partner.*
*~**Maddie***

——— ❞ —

**REVEALING MISTAKE #1:**
The news story playing in the store window is on a loop.

**REVEALING MISTAKE #2:**
When David walks towards Harbert in the church, gaffers tape on the floor marks the spot for him to stand.

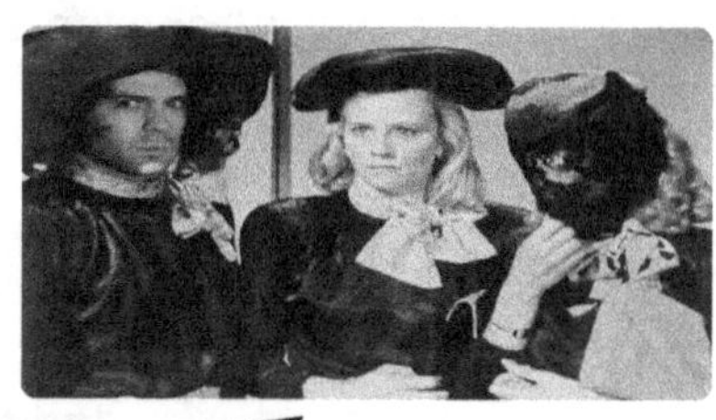

## LOCATION...LOCATION...LOCATION...
~ **Calvary Baptist Church** - Avenue G and 220th St., Hi Vista California, USA
~ **Hollenbeck Park** - 415 South Saint Louis St., Los Angeles, California, USA
~ **Ambassador Hotel** - 3400 Wilshire Boulevard, Los Angeles, California, USA (no longer there)
~ **The Sharper Image** - 611 Wilshire Boulevard, Los Angeles, California, USA

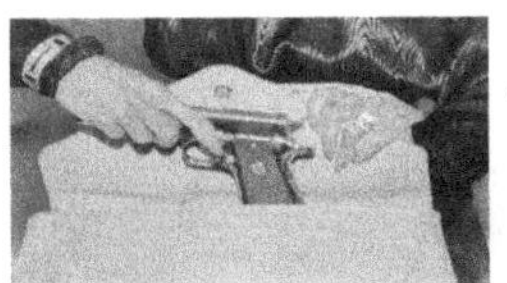

**On Location:**
**from our personal archive**

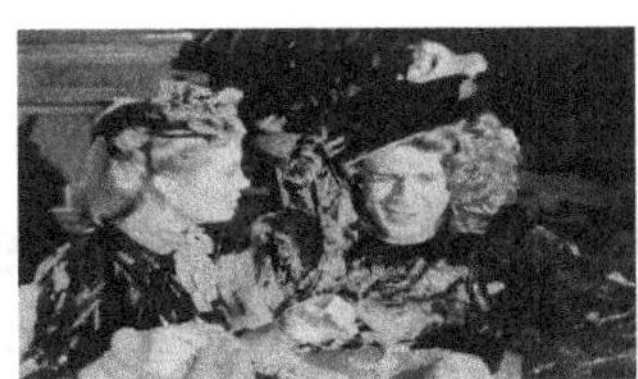

*"Anybody wanna play Twister?" ~David Addison*

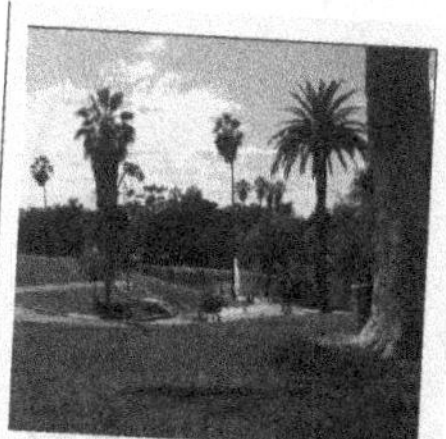

*Hollenbeck Park*

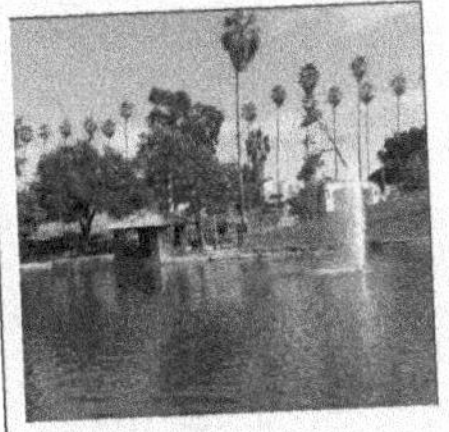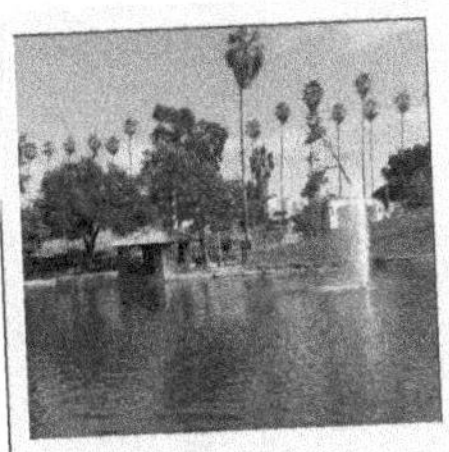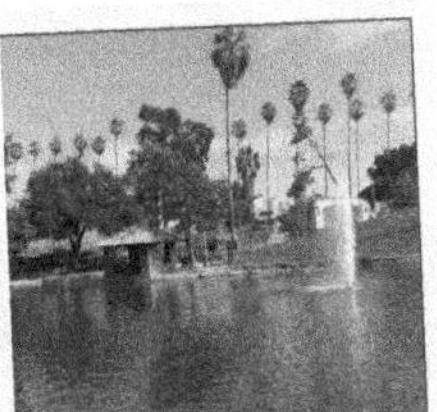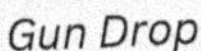

*Gun Drop*

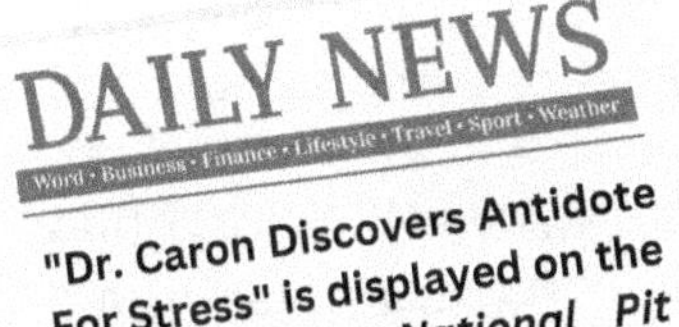


**"Dr. Caron Discovers Antidote For Stress"** is displayed on the cover of *The National Pit* newspaper David is holding.

## BREAKING THE FOURTH WALL:

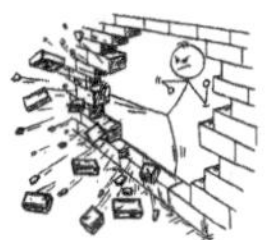

**Maddie**: You were framed.

**David**: For the murder of Frank Harbert.

**Maddie**: By your husband.

**David**: By your husband.

(Maddie annoyed with David)

**David**: Sorry, I lost my place.

## MUSIC CHANGE:

Originally, the chase was scored to the "William Tell Overture," but on DVD, that music was replaced by a more sedate orchestration before being restored on Hulu.

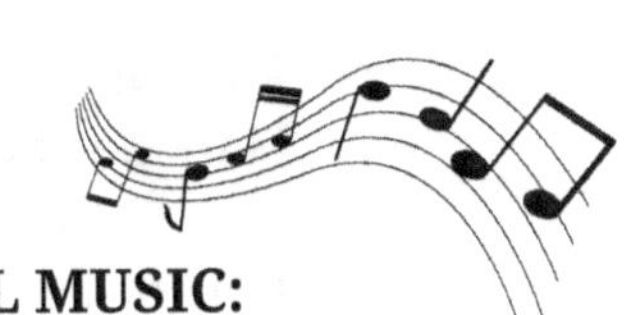

## ORIGINAL MUSIC:

**"The William Tell Overture"**
Composed by Gioachino Rossini.

**"Powerhouse"**
Composed by Raymond Scott
Whistled by Bruce Willis

# S02 E03
# Money Talks, Maddie Walks



**Plot:**

While talking an old friend, Charles, off the ledge after he finds out all his money has been taken, Maddie discovers he is a victim of the same accountant who stole her money, Ron Sawyer. She learns through Charles that Sawyer is in Argentina and has bought a casino with the millions of dollars that he's stolen from his clients. Maddie is determined to travel to Buenos Aires to confront him, against David's advice.

 In Buenos Aires, Maddie approaches Sawyer but soon finds out she won't be getting her money back. David arrives in a timely manner while she is drowning her sorrows in the casino restaurant on Sawyer's dime. David is determined to help Maddie win back some of her money in the casino, and the finale involves a poker game in which Sawyer loans her $100,000 to play. Maddie stakes everything she owns on the game, including the Blue Moon Detective Agency—but David stops the game short, afraid she'll lose everything.

 Later, Maddie finds out that she did in fact have the winning hand, and furious that David told her to fold, she leaves him stranded in Buenos Aires with no money.

**Air Date:** October 8, 1985

**Written by:** Ali Marie Matheson and Kerry Ehrin

**Director:** Christian I. Nyby II

## CAST CREDITS

**Alan Blumenfeld** ... Charles
**Mark Lonow** ... Ron Sawyer
**Rick Fitts** ... The Cop
**Anthony Alexander** ... The Croupier
**Anthony Gordon** ... Maître d'
**Robert Z'dar** ... Garcia
**Tony Giorgio** ... Tony
**Charles Seixas** ... Security Guard
**Paco Vela** ... Security Guard

## FUN FACT #1:
Ron Sawyer's dealer, Tony, is played by Tony Giorgio, who also played Bruno Tattaglia in the *The Godfather* (Movie, 1972).

## CULTURAL REFERENCES:
~ David imitates Ricky Ricardo from the *I Love Lucy* (TV Series, 1951–1957).
~ **Barbie and Ken Doll** - Mattel fashion dolls.
~ David references *Birdman of Alcatraz* (Movie, 1962).
~ Agnes says "Martin forgave Lewis" - referencing **Dean Martin and Jerry Lewis**, a comedy team that split in 1956 when Martin felt Lewis was hogging the spotlight.
~ **Tom Sawyer -** A book character created by Mark Twain.
~ Maddie and Charles used to eat **Cheetos,** a crunchy corn puff snack made by Frito-Lay.

## ART IMITATING LIFE:
David says he can pour the champagne because he's "in the union." Bruce used to work as a bartender in NYC, where he was in the hospitality union.

## FUN FACT #2:
We have our first door slam(s) of the series! Can you believe there were no door slams in season one!? As Grace would say, "Get outta town!"





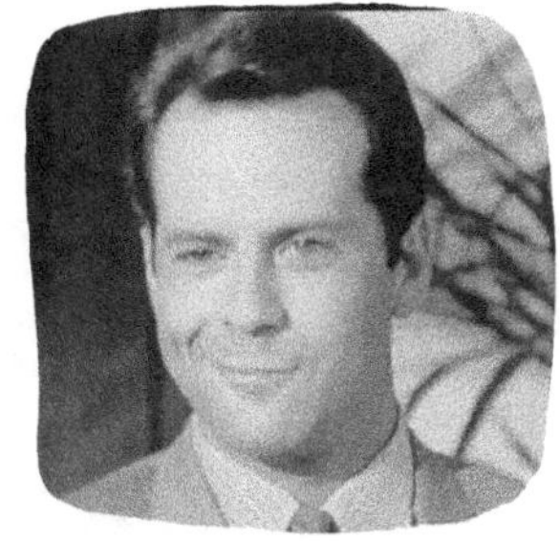

*That smirk....*

## OUTFIT ROLE CALL:
- Agnes wears the dress Maddie is wearing in the casino in s02e12, "North by North Dipesto."

## REVEALING MISTAKE (fixed!):
On the DVD release, there was no sound over Tony shuffling the cards before the poker game with Sawyer, but the card shuffling sound has now been added on Hulu streaming.

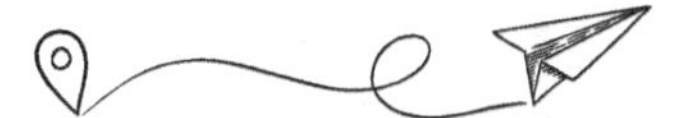

## LOCATION...LOCATION...LOCATION...
~ **Chicken Lickin' Office Building** - 510 South Spring Street, Los Angeles, California, USA

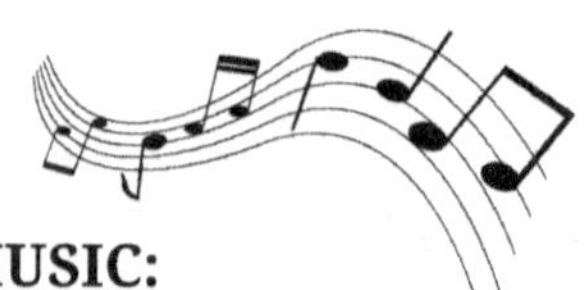

## ORIGINAL MUSIC:

**"You Wear It Well"**
Written by Chico DeBarge and El DeBarge
Performed by El DeBarge
*(Replaced with new music on Hulu streaming)*

**"The Nutcracker Suite: Dance of the Sugar Plum Fairy"**
Ballet by Pyotr Ilyich Tchaikovsky

**"Murphy's Law"**
Written by Steve Kipner and Paul Bliss
Performed by Al Jarreau

---

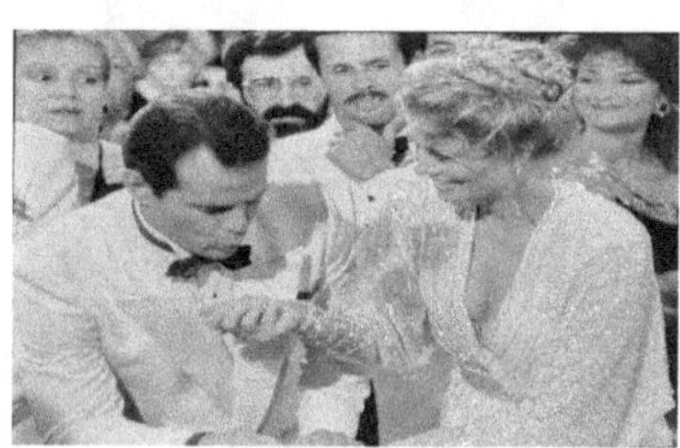

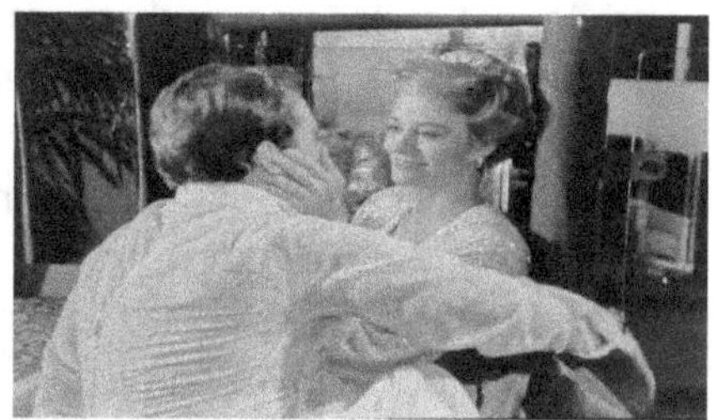

## *The Perfect Moonlighting Recipe*

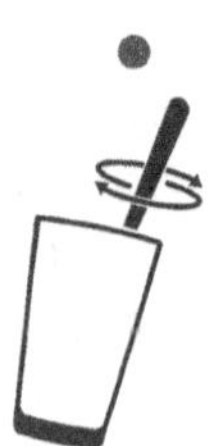

1 x car talk
1 x overlapping dialogue
2 x door slams
1 x upset Maddie
1 x Maddie in a gown
1 x David in a tux

*Stir well and serve.*

# S02 E04
# The Dream Sequence
# Always Rings Twice

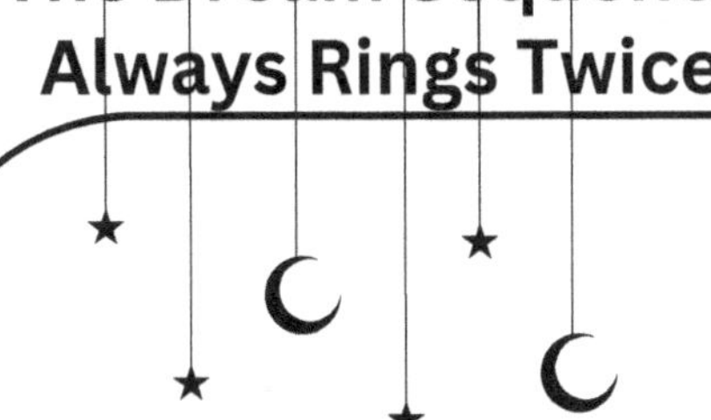



**Plot:**

This iconic episode is set in the 1940s and is a tribute to film noir. With extraordinary attention to detail, the episode is shot in two different styles of black and white starting at approximately twelve minutes into the episode, representing the different perspectives of Maddie's and David's individual dreams. While working a case, Maddie and David learn of a murder committed at a theater in the 1940s and have a disagreement about who may have committed the murder.

That night, both Maddie and David have dreams in which they take on the role of the convicted murderer and the circumstances leading to the crime, of course. Each perspective is influenced by the bias of the dreamer. Cybill Shepherd performs the songs "Blue Moon" and "I Told Ya I Love You, Now Get Out." Orson Welles introduces the episode, warning viewers about their color TVs turning to black and white twelve minutes into the episode. This was his last performance, filmed exactly one week before his death.

**Air Date:** October 15, 1985

**Written by**: Debra Frank and Carl Sautter

**Director:** Peter Werner

### CAST CREDITS

**Orson Welles** ... Himself
**Jack Bannon** ... Club Owner/Jerry Adams
**Phil Rubenstein** ... Mr. Bigelow/Sloane
**Frank McCarthy** ... Lieutenant Matthews
**Nick DeMauro** ... Priest
**Bill Handy** ... Jailor
**Raleigh Bond** ... Mr. Potter
**Freeman King** ... Bartender

**REVEALING MISTAKE:**
In the final scene, you can see the shadow of a boom mic drop in behind the door as David goes to close it.

**FUN FACT #1:**
08069 is written on Zach's prison uniform; that is the Penns Grove, NJ, zip code (Bruce Willis's hometown).

**FUN FACT #2:**
Raleigh Bond, who played Mr. Potter, played the insurance salesman in the remake of *The Postman Always Rings Twice* (Movie, 1981).

**FUN FACT #3:**
A split diopter lens was used to put both Bruce and Cybill in focus during the scene where they're both sitting on the bed in David's dream.

**OUTFIT ROLE CALL:**
- Maddie wore the pink dress she's wearing in the opening scene in s01e02, "Gunfight at the So-So Corral."

**Cultural References:**
- *The Wizard of Oz* (Movie, 1939) - David says, "Auntie Em? Uncle Henry?"
- *Dynasty* (TV Series, 1981–1989) - David says that without infidelity there wouldn't be this show.

**LOCATION...LOCATION...LOCATION...**
~ **Aquarius Theater** - 6230 Sunset Boulevard, Hollywood, Los Angeles, California, USA (no longer there)

**STATS:**

*Door Slams: 3*
*Feet out of Elevator: 3*
*Maddie's Outfit Changes: 15*
*Agnes Rhymes: 0*

**GREAT LINES:**

**Orson Welles** (*in cold open*): *Gather the kids, the dog, Grandma and lock them in another room. And sit back and enjoy this very special episode of* Moonlighting.

**LOOK FOR:**
Maddie has a picture of herself on her piano at home which is taken from promo shots for the pilot episode.

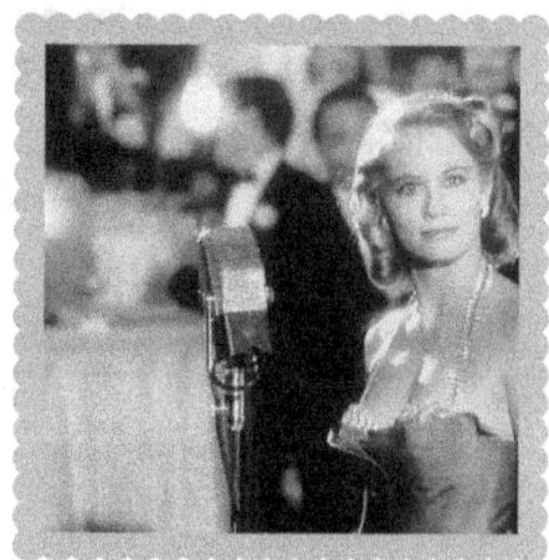

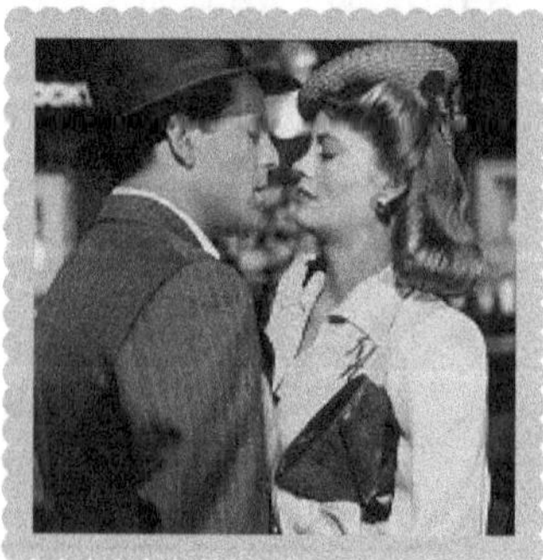

# Orson Welles

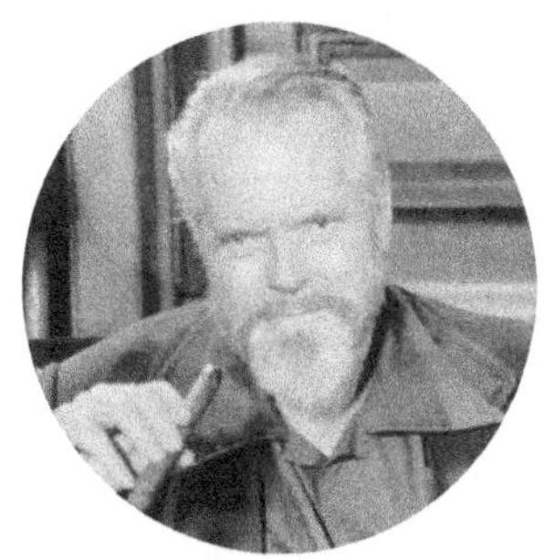

The late Orson Welles opens this episode with an introduction warning viewers that their television screens are about to go from color to black and white. Welles died five days before the episode was broadcast. A slide at the beginning of the episode reads, "This program is dedicated to the memory of Orson Welles 1915-1985."

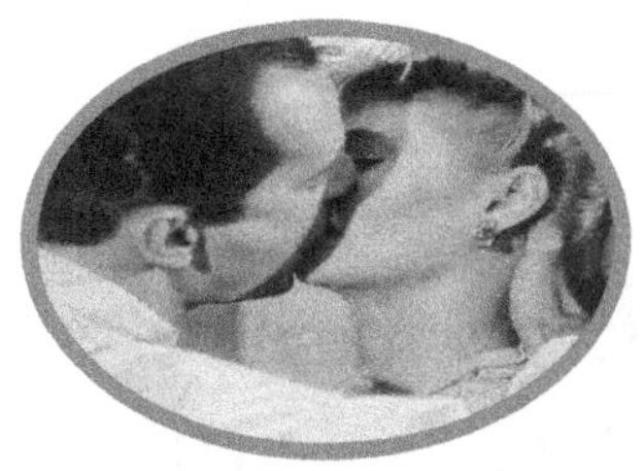

## COUPLEY THINGS

The chemistry between Maddie and David (Bruce and Cybill) was so white-hot during the original run of the show . . . fans were just dying to see them "get it on" and hoped to see them as a couple one day. For the real thing, we had to wait . . . and wait . . . and wait (*Moonlighting* fans know how to wait). But every once in a while, we'd get a taste of our favorite couple . . . as a couple . . . or, let's be honest, what we really wanted . . . to see them sleep together. Some of the ways Glenn satiated fans were through alternate universe romances - Zach and Rita; Kate and Petruchio! Fantasies and dream sequence - "Big Man," "The Man Who Cried Wife," and "Tracks!" Watching them work cases was another way we saw David and Maddie "play house" - Papa Bear and Sweetcakes, they'd have "the kids and the dog in the car," a "meatloaf in the oven at home," or they'd "promised the sitter they'd be home in an hour." In whatever way we got to see them "be together" while we waited for them to *be together*, we gladly accepted.

## ORIGINAL MUSIC:

**"Blue Moon"**
Written by Richard Rodgers and Lorenz Hart
Performed by Cybill Shepherd

**"I Told Ya I Love Ya, Now Get Out"**
Written by Herb Ellis, Johnny Frigo, and Lou Carter
Performed by Cybill Shepherd

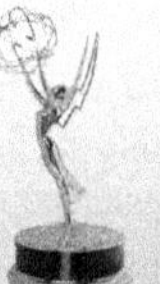

**"Powerhouse"**
Composed by Raymond Scott
Whistled by Bruce Willis

---

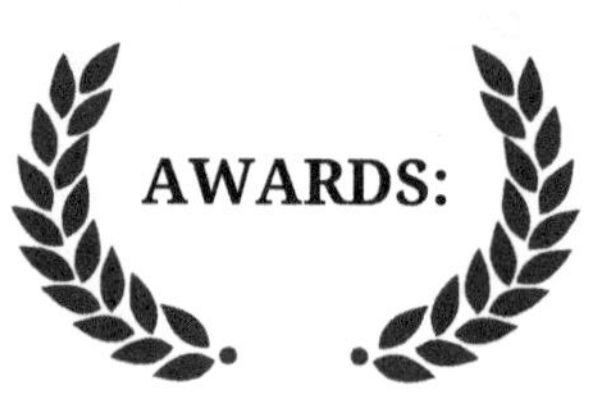

## AWARDS:

Neil Mandelberg received his first Emmy Award for Outstanding Editing for a Series - Single Camera Production for this episode.

*1986 Winner DGA Award (Comedy Series): Peter Werner*

*TV Guide's 100 Greatest Episodes of All-Time (TV Special, 1997)*

*"The Dream Sequence Always Rings Twice" (1985) is #34*

# S02 E05
# My Fair David



**Plot:**

Maddie arrives at work to find David and all the employees having a limbo contest. After a heated argument, Maddie and David bet that David can't behave like a mature adult for one week. If he loses, he must fire two employees; if she loses, she must limbo in front of the entire staff. Meanwhile, a wealthy client, Emily Greydon, whose stepson, Clark, a gifted concert pianist, has been kidnapped, and the kidnappers want $100,000 for the return of her son.

Mrs. Greydon has come to Blue Moon so that Maddie and David can negotiate for Clark's life with built-in incentives for them if they get him back cheaply. However, when Maddie and David go to drop off the money, they find out that Clark has faked his own kidnapping for the ransom.

Maddie and David agree not to tell Emily that they have reached an agreement with her son and that he is the kidnapper. However, they are shocked when they find out that he has been kidnapped for real the very next day. The effort to act so maturely takes its toll on David, which in turn changes the office atmosphere for the worse, as all the employees turn against Maddie. Maddie then has a change of heart and wants her old David back.

**Air Date:** October 29, 1985

**Written by:** Bruce Franklin Singer

**Director:** Will Mackenzie



### CAST CREDITS

**Robert Joy** ... Clark Greydon

**Barbara Bain** ... Emily Greydon

**Billy Drago** ... Gangster

**Will Nye** ... Simmons

**Irwin Keyes** ... Thug

## Agnes Rhyme:

> Blue Moon Detective Agency, domestic entanglement's our forte, if he plays around, we'll track him down, we'll catch him with his fling, take shots of the whole thing, black and white and color too, big ones, little ones . . .

## CONTINUITY #1:

When they park on the city street, Maddie's car window is down when she opens the door but is rolled up in the next shot.

## CONTINUITY #2:

Maddie's necklace strand alternates positions several times during one of the car talks.

## LOOK FOR:

Cybill is wearing white sneakers the first time  Maddie and David meet Mrs. Greydon in Maddie's office.

## FUN FACT #1:

Maddie's periodontist, Dr. Fishbine, was also mentioned in s01e04, "The Next Murder You Hear."

## CULTURAL REFERENCE:

Bruce asked if he could say **"In-a-Gadda-da-Vida"** in this episode, which is one of his "70s references," to the song by **Iron Butterfly** (American rock band, 1966-present); David mentions the song again in s5e03, "The Color of Maddie."

## STATS:

*Door Slams: 14*
*Feet out of Elevator: 0*
*Maddie's Outfit Changes: 3*
*Agnes Rhymes: .5*

## GREAT LINES:

**Maddie:** *. . . and what do I get?*
**David:** *What do you mean?*
**Maddie:** *When you lose, what do I get?*
**David:** *Moi.*
**Maddie:** *The whole thing, or just your head on a platter?*

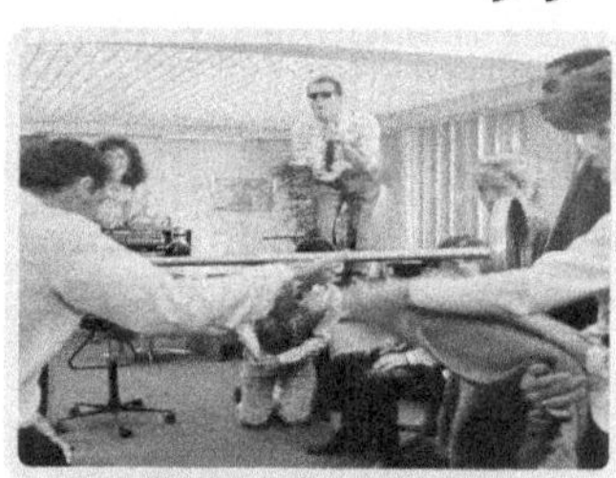

## Influences for *Moonlighting*

During his visit with Shawna and Grace on *Moonlighting the Podcast,* Glenn Gordon Caron discussed some of his influences for *Moonlighting*, which were Bugs Bunny cartoons, the Three Stooges, and Restoration comedy (thus the door slamming), and of course, Shakespeare's *Taming of The Shrew* (Play, 1594). He also mentioned that very little ad-libbing happened on set and, instead, Bruce and Cybill coped with receiving late scripts by being "dutiful to the writing on the pages."

## FUN FACT #2:

According to Cybill Shepherd, the office doors had to be replaced each season because they slammed them so hard! With fourteen door slams in this episode, it must have contributed to some faulty frames by the end of the season.

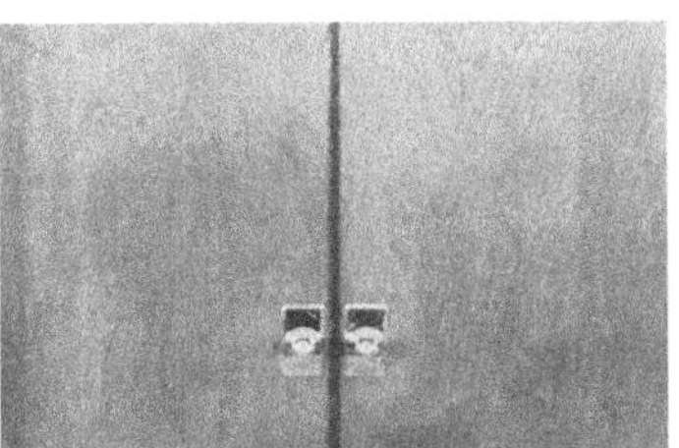

## HOW DID MADDIE AND DAVID EARN THE $50,000?

Emily Greydon was prepared to pay the $100,000 ransom with a $5,000 delivery fee to Blue Moon, although she preferred to pay a lower amount. Maddie and David make an agreement with Clark that he will receive $10,000 of the ransom. Because Maddie and David saved Emily $90,000, Blue Moon earned half that amount, which was the agreement with Emily. Therefore they were paid $45,000 plus the $5,000 delivery fee, making it $50,000! In summary, Clark received $10,000, Blue Moon received $50,000, and Emily paid out only $60,000 total (saving her $40,000).

**On location: from our personal photo archive**

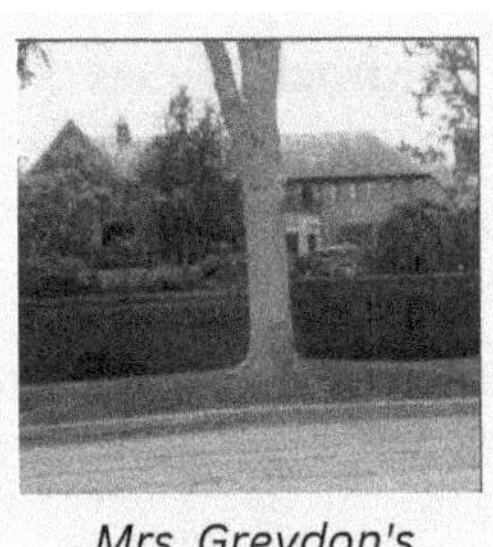

*Mrs. Greydon's Mansion*

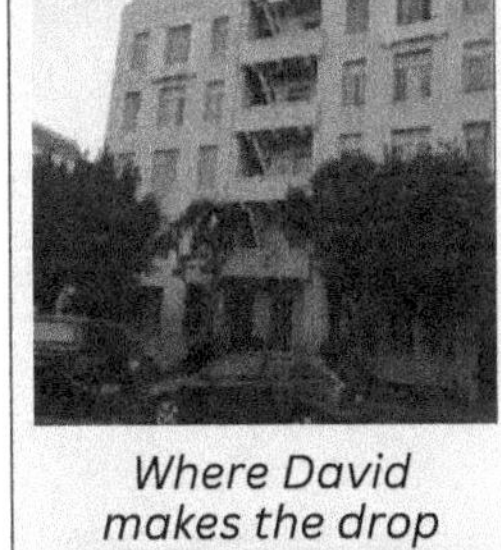

*Where David makes the drop*

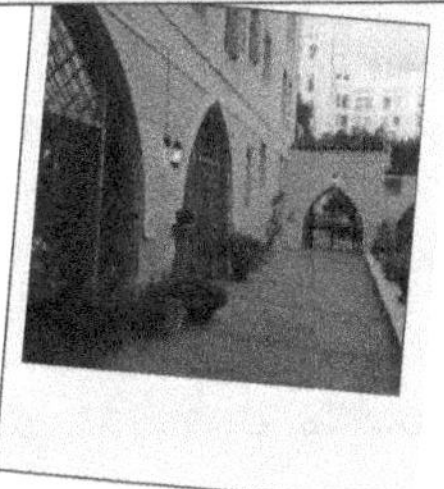

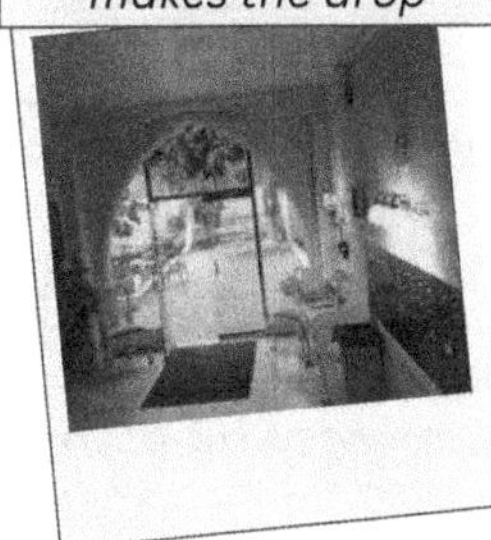

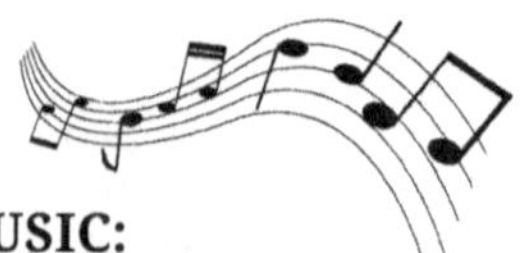



**"Limbo Rock"**
Written by Kal Mann and Billy Strange
Performed by Chubby Checker and Bruce Willis
**"Pop Goes the Weasel"**
Composed by Anthony Newley
**"The William Tell Overture"**
Composed by Gioachino Rossini
Performed by Robert Joy on the piano
**"Moonlight, Piano Sonata No. 14"**
Composed by Alfred Brendel
*Performed on the piano in the opening scene*
**"Money (That's What I Want)"**
Written by Janie Bradford and Berry Gordy
Performed by Bruce Willis
**"You Can't Always Get What You Want"**
Written by Mick Jagger and Keith Richards
Performed by The Rolling Stones
*(Replaced with new music on Hulu streaming)*

---

## ...OR WHAT?

There are many "Davidisms" but here are some examples of David's regular phrase, **"... *or what?*"**

**s03e03, "Symphony in Knocked Flat":**
*"Are we talkin' fun evening, or what?"*

**s01e04, "The Next Murder You Hear":**
*(About Dipesto) "Is she great, or what?"*

*"Women from all over the country will send me letters, make lewd suggestions . . . is this a wild country, or what?"*

*"Alright, is the kid a natural born salesman, or what?"*

**s03e012, "Sam and Dave":**
*"We show those guys what we're made of tonight, or what?"*

**s02e05, "My Fair David":**
*"... the smell of an armpit, the roar of a crowd, is this a great moment in sports, or what!?"*

# S02 E06
# Knowing Her

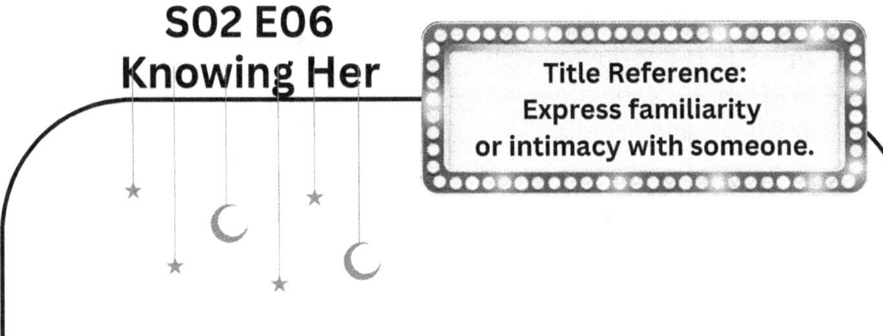



**Plot:**

Maddie has a bad morning trying to change a flat tire in the rain. After she arrives at the office, a wealthy client, Gillian Armstrong (Dana Delaney), walks into Blue Moon and wants to hire Maddie to find a locket that her grandmother gave her, which she says has been stolen from her hotel room.

David walks in and is stunned when he sees Gillian sitting in Maddie's office because he used to be in a relationship with her. Blinded by his emotions for Gillian, David begins to pursue her and then suspects that her estranged husband is trying to kill her when she is in a series of near-death "accidents."

One night, Gillian shoots her husband during a confrontation in his car. This is witnessed by David, who confirms with the police that it was a matter of self-defense. However, Maddie is not convinced.

**Air Date:** November 12, 1985

**Written by:** Jeff Reno and Ron Osborn

**Director:** Peter Werner

**Working Title**
**"Blast from the Past"**

**CAST CREDITS**

**Dana Delany** ... Gillian Armstrong
**Joel Colodner** ... Harlan Armstrong
**Richard McGonagle** ... Detective Barber
**Freddie Dawson** ... Blue Moon Employee
**Tyra Ferrell** ... Hooker
**Bill Marcus** ... Cop
**Dianne Turley Travis** ... Secretary
**James A. Williams** ... Man at Funeral

**CULTURAL REFERENCE:**
~ *Singin' in the Rain* (Musical, 1952) The title song plays over the opening scene.

**OUTFIT ROLE CALL:**
- Maddie wears the yellowish blouse/belt combo again in s02e13, "In God We Strongly Suspect."

## Past the Censors:

*Maddie:* "You're in my seat."

*David:* "Please, there are children watching!"

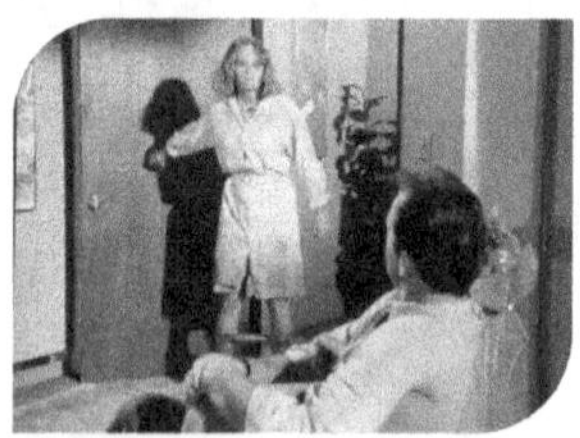

**FUN FACT #1:**
Glenn Caron wrote an episode of *Breaking Away* (TV Series 1980–1981) called "Knowing Her." On *Medium* (TV Series 2005–2011), which Glenn created, there is also an episode called "Knowing Her."

**REVEALING MISTAKE:**
In the end scene David kicks the light switch with his foot and the light turns off, but his foot is nowhere near the light switch.

**STATS:**

*Door Slams: 6*
*Feet out of Elevator: 1*
*Maddie's Outfit Changes: 5*
*Agnes Rhymes: 0*

**GREAT LINES:**

*David:* One bullet, alive.

*Maddie:* Two bullets, dead!

**LOOK FOR:**
In Gillian's hotel room, when she says, "Well, you'll be happy to know I only got half of what I wanted," Bruce's mouth is clearly moving delivering lines, but the sound has been removed.

**FUN FACT #2:**
Bruce Willis chose the original song "This Old Heart of Mine (Is Weak For You)"(Song, 1966) for the scene with Gillian in the park.

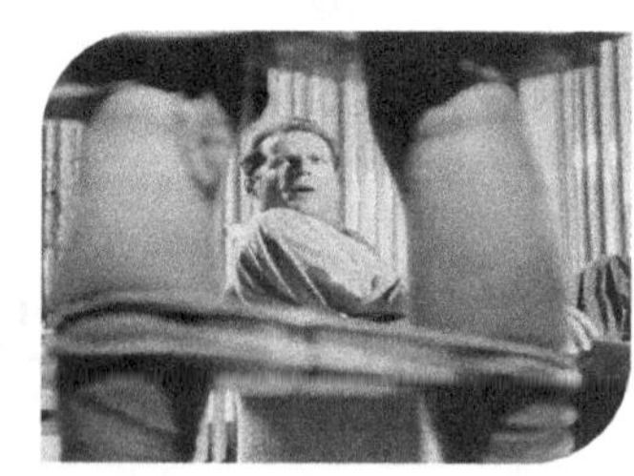

**LOCATION, LOCATION, LOCATION...**
~ **Inglewood Park Cemetery (Funeral)** - 720 East Florence Avenue, Inglewood, California, USA

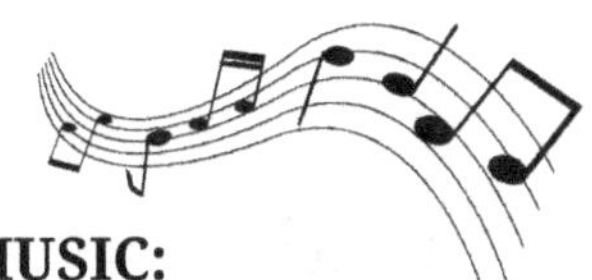

## ORIGINAL MUSIC:

**"Singin' in the Rain"**
Music by Nacio Herb Brown
Lyrics by Arthur Freed
Performed by Gene Kelly

**"This Old Heart of Mine" (Is Weak for You)"**
Written by Brian Holland, Lamont Dozier,
Eddie Holland, Sylvia Moy
Performed by the Isley Brothers
*(Replaced with new music on Hulu streaming)*

**"The Man on the Flying Trapeze"**
**"The Daring Young Man on the Flying Trapeze"**
**"The Flying Trapeze"**
Composed by Gaston Lyle, Alfred Lee
Lyrics by George Leybourne

**"No Escape from the Blues"**
Written by Charlie Williams & Muddy Waters
Performed by Bruce Willis

**"Itsy Bitsy Spider"**
By Anonymous

**"Take Me Out to the Ball Game"**
Written by Jack Norworth and Albert Von Tilzer
*(Replaced with new music on Hulu streaming)*

**"Piano Sonata No. 2 (Funeral March)"**
Composed by Frederic Chopin

*Glenn Gordon Caron:* Dana [Delany] came by way of Bruce. I was writing the part and he went, "Oh, I know somebody!" and he told me about Dana.

*Moonlighting the Podcast:* Because they knew each other from New York.

*Glenn Gordon Caron:* Yes, exactly!

# S02 E07
# Somewhere Under the Rainbow

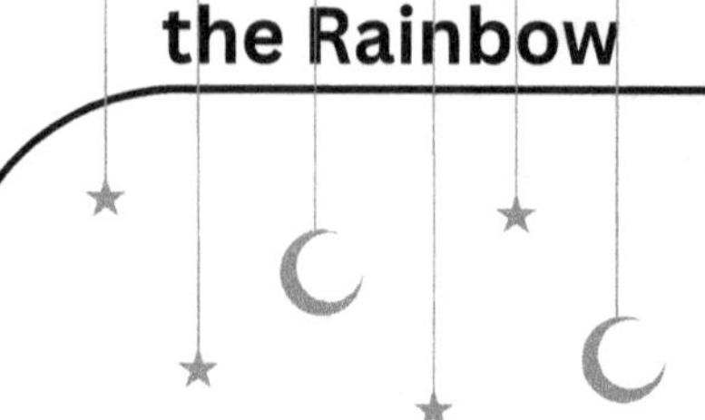



**Plot:**

The client, Kathleen Kilpatrick, who claims to be a leprechaun, wants to hire Blue Moon to protect her from men who she says are following her and are after her "pot of gold."

Maddie does not want to take the case, as she believes Kathleen needs psychiatric help, not a detective, but David decides to take the case anyway. After spending an evening with Kathleen, David discovers that there is some truth to men being after her, and Maddie and David try to protect her. Eventually, they track down her "pot of gold," which turns out to be money that was stolen from a bank in Ireland by the woman's father many years earlier.

Now Kathleen has to find a way to flee the country with her pot of gold, but soon a chase ensues through the airport and the gold is left in some other capable hands.

**Air Date:** November 19, 1985

**Teleplay by:**
Debra Frank
Carl Sautter

**Story by:**
Frank Dandridge
Debra Frank
Carl Sautter

**Director:** Peter Crane

## CAST CREDITS

**Alexandra Johnson** ... Kathleen Kilpatrick
**David Patrick Kelly** ... Ian McBride
**Robert Alan Browne** ... Ed O'Leary
**Sam Whipple** ... Young Man
**Billy Beck** ... Coroner
**Vivian Bonnell** ... Woman at Window
**Danny Dayton** ... Driver
**John Finnegan** ... Skycap (uncredited)

## CONTINUITY #1:
When David is walking outside with Kathleen, his arm changes positions between cuts.

## CONTINUITY #2:
Maddie's office bathroom magically becomes a closet in this episode!

## OUTFIT ROLE CALL:
- Maddie wears both the nightgown and pajama set again in s02e15, "Witness for the Execution."
- She wears the nightgown again in s03e01, "The Son Also Rises."
- She wears the purple pantsuit again in s02e12, "North by North Dipesto," and s02e15, "Witness for the Execution."

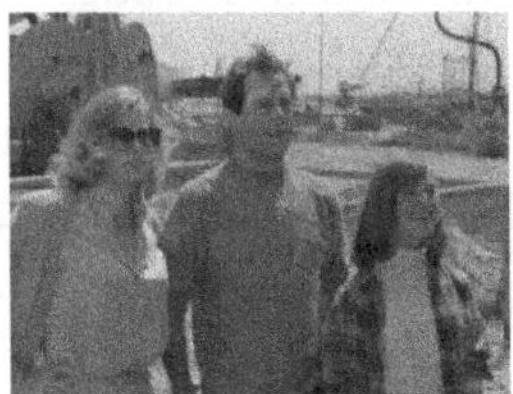

*"There it be!"*

## LOOK FOR #1:
Bruce laughing out of character in the outer office while discussing Kathleen's sanity.

## LOOK FOR #2:
Bruce Willis "going commando" in the opening scene in Maddie's office.



## GREAT LINES:
**David:** *He paints naked girls.*
**Maddie:** *Nudes.*
**David:** *Nudes right, nakes have staples in them.*

## CULTURAL REFERENCES:
~ Eugène Henri Paul **Gauguin** - French Postimpressionist artist.
~ **Godzilla** - Prehistoric reptilian monster.
~ **E. E. Cummings** - An American poet, painter, essayist, author, and playwright.
~ **Sylvia Plath** - An American poet, novelist, and short story writer.
~ **Leprechaun** - A diminutive supernatural being in Irish folklore.
~ **Tinker Bell** - A fictional character from *Peter Pan* (Play, 1904).
~ **Diana Ross** - An American singer and actress.
~ **"Barnacle Bill the Sailor"** - American drinking song.
~ **Tender Vittles** - Brand of pet food.

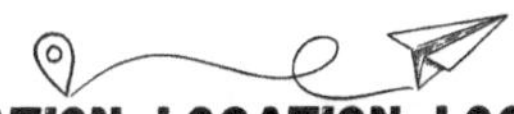

## LOCATION, LOCATION, LOCATION...
~ **Gerald Desmond Bridge** - Located at the southern end of State Route 710 in Los Angeles County/Long Beach, California, USA
~ **The Theme Building (LAX)** - 201 World Way, Los Angeles, California, USA

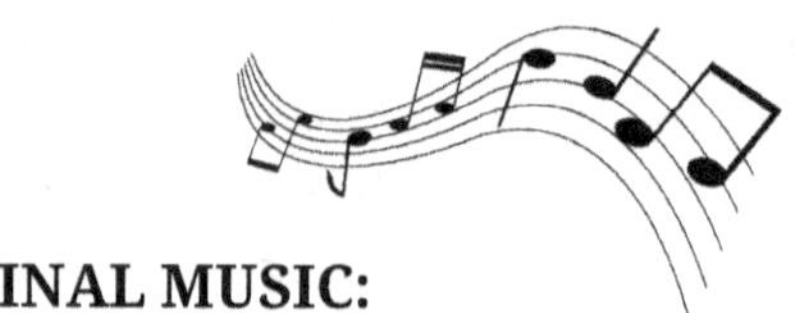

## ORIGINAL MUSIC:

**"Swing Low, Sweet Chariot"**
Written by Wallis Willis
Performed by Bruce Willis with original lyrics

<hr>

## WHAT'S YOUR TYPE?

Over the life of the series, we are served up an array of *Moonlighting* episodes that . . . according to our calculations . . . observations and other various aberrations, can be categorized into three distinct genres: "alternate universe," "fantasy," and "real life." Of course, *Moonlighting* being a show that would try anything and everything, more than one of these genres might be seen in a single episode! Let's dive in a bit deeper to see where some of our favorite episodes fall. Take the episode we're looking at here, s02e07, "Somewhere Under the Rainbow" – a leprechaun, a pot of gold, an office bathroom that magically becomes a closet? Clearly a fantasy episode, right? Another episode in the fantasy category would be s03e08, "It's a Wonderful Job" – while in s03e06, "Big Man on Mulberry Street," we've got a mix of real life and fantasy. As for alternate universes, we're lucky enough to witness "Maddie and David" living out many different lifetimes together over the five seasons . . . from Shakespeare to the 1940s. It's so satisfying for fans to know that these two always found each other . . . no matter where or when. The category of "real-life" episodes is pretty much everything else; these are the episodes that followed the everyday life of Blue Moon Detective Agency, the Wobblies, and the evolution of Maddie and David's complicated relationship. In the beginning, these were generally one-off episodes, but eventually, we get to story arcs in seasons three, four, and five. So, where does your favorite episode fall? What's your type?

# S02 E08
# Portrait of Maddie



**Plot:**

A struggling painter who is obsessed with Maddie Hayes completes a painting of her in his loft. His loft is surrounded with images of magazine covers of Maddie from her modeling years. The paint is still wet when he calls the gallery to let them know that it is ready to be collected, then commits suicide.

Maddie purchases the portrait from the gallery, using the recent profits from the business, only to gift it to the painter's brother, who shows up at her office the following day. The brother then dies the following day in the same manner and in the loft of his brother's apartment. The police now suspect Maddie of foul play, since she is in the portrait and purchases the painting only for it to show up at the loft where two men were murdered.

It transpires that the artist and the brother were part of a trio of international art thieves who had stolen a valuable painting from a museum in France three years earlier. Subsequently, the surviving accomplice shows up at Maddie's home and is convinced that the portrait of Maddie holds a clue to where it has been hidden and that Maddie knows more than she is letting on. A colorful climactic scene ensues when the real killer is revealed in an auto painting shop: Maddie and David, all covered in paint, use a car as a weapon to corner the killer, which covers him with paint as well.

**Air Date:**
November 26, 1985

**Written by:**
Ali Marie Matheson
and Kerry Ehrin

**Director:** Peter Werner

## CAST CREDITS

**John Calvin** ... Phillip/Charles Wright

**Dan Lauria** ... Detective Daroca

**Paul Rudd** ... Harry

**Gary Cervantes** ... Mechanic

**ART IMITATING LIFE:**
David suggests that Maddie has spent a lot of money on Elvis [Presley] memorabilia. Cybill Shepherd dated Elvis Presley in real life.

**LOOK FOR #1:**
When Maddie and David are taken back to the artist loft, Cybill alternates between wearing New Balance sneakers and heels.

**REVEALING MISTAKE:**
Phillip Wright's loft clearly has no windows. However, when Maddie discovers the location of the painting in the loft, she is looking through a window.

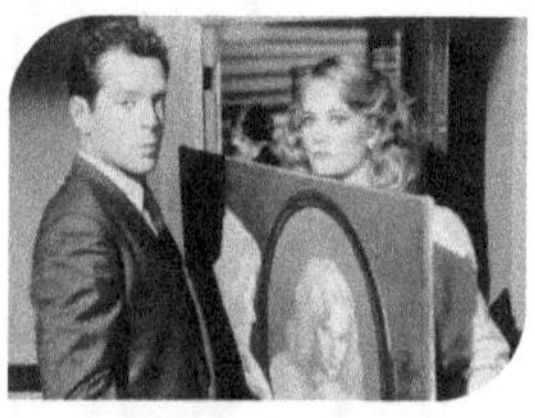



"You rang?" Is David's answer to Maddie's "men" or "David," here and in s02e11, "The Bride of Tupperman and s02e13, "In God We Strongly Suspect.

**FUN FACT (SPOILER ALERT):**
Actor Dan Lauria, who plays Detective Daroca, was asked to return to the set after completing his stint. The writers finished Act 4 of the script and decided that he was the killer.

**STATS:**

*Door Slams: 8*
*Feet out of Elevator: 1*
*Maddie's Outfit Changes: 6*
*Agnes Rhymes: 0*

**GREAT LINES:**

> **Maddie:** *David, my God!*
> **David:** *Isn't that redundant?*

**LOOK FOR #2:**
As John Calvin plays the roles of both Wright brothers, the film of when Phillip dies has been reversed to make it look like a different man.

**OUTFIT ROLE CALL:**
- Maddie wears the gray-blue dress at the end of s03e02, "The Man Who Cried Wife." and the beginning of s03e01 "The Son Also Rises."

**MISSING SCENE?**
Maddie beckons David down to the police station in the middle of the night. He shows up with a protective attitude and says a very sweet thing in the car about the "poor slobs who live for her," but by the time he sees her to her door, it's: **Maddie:** *"I have nothing more to say to you!"* **David:** *"Yeah, I know, for weeks now!"* What'd we miss?

**LOCATION...LOCATION...LOCATION**
~ **Portrait Gallery** - 275 S La Cienega Boulevard,Beverly Hills, California, USA

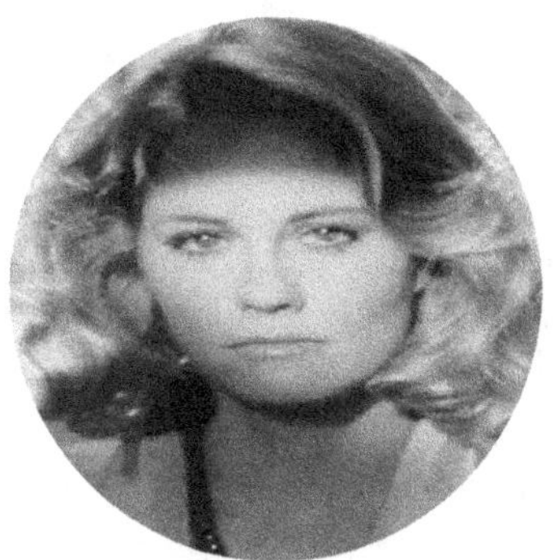

Another staple of *Moonlighting* is the lens filter used on Cybill, which was meant to soften her features and make her look younger and "more beautiful." When Jay Daniel joined Grace and Shawna on *Moonlighting the Podcast,* he talked about the care Jerry Finnerman took in lighting his leading lady. Jerry understood how important it was that Cybill look as good as she possibly could in every frame. The filter, which was made specifically for the Arri BL-3s camera they used on *Moonlighting,* slid in front of the camera lens when needed and produced a bit of a "Vaseline effect," which was much discussed in the media and parodied. *Moonlighting* even spoofed itself during s03e09, "The Straight Poop," when Cybill answered her office door for Rona Barrett holding a square of gauze over her face acting as a filter.

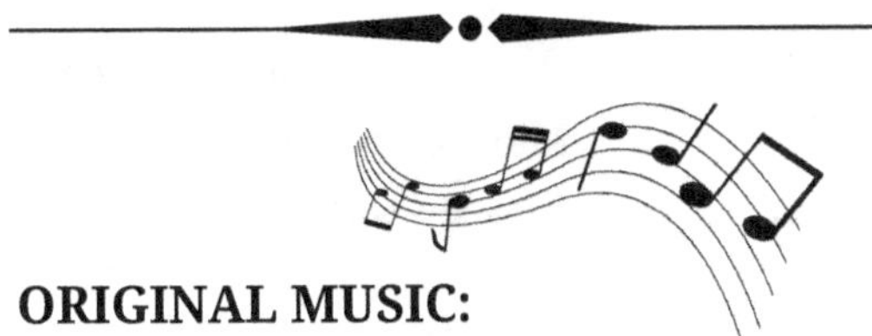

**ORIGINAL MUSIC:**

**"Something's Coming"**
Composed by Leonard Bernstein
Lyrics by Stephen Sondheim
Performed by Bruce Willis

# S02 E09
# Atlas Belched

Title Reference:
*Atlas Shrugged*
(Novel, 1957)

**Plot:**

The owner of a rival detective agency, Lou LaSalle, offers to buy Blue Moon, and Maddie accepts the offer. Maddie breaks the news to David by trying to butter him up and preparing breakfast in her office for the both of them.

The news of Maddie agreeing to sell the agency makes David extremely angry. He storms out and heads to a bar. While drowning his sorrows, David meets Phil (Mark Linn-Baker), who is about to be fired because his employer's prized Rolodex of celebrity phone numbers has been stolen on the one night that he didn't lock it in the safe. Once he finds out that the man's employer is a very wealthy and successful banker named Thornton Wellman, David decides to help Phil find the Rolodex.

He sees this as a way to save Blue Moon by acquiring Thornton Wellman as a client. He goes to Maddie's house in the middle of the night to give her the good news, but it's too late: Maddie informs him that she has already sold the agency. David decides to leave Blue Moon to set up his own agency. A series of madcap events occur, causing Maddie to have a change of heart about selling the agency. The episode ends with a confrontation with LaSalle, who now is feeling threatened because Thornton Wellman is HIS client, whom he fears losing. Does Maddie get her agency back? Well, you'll have to watch the episode to find out!

**Air Date:**
December 10, 1985

**Written by:** Roger Director

**Director:** Christian I Nyby II

### CAST CREDITS

**Mark Linn-Baker** ... Phil West

**George Coe** ... Lou LaSalle

**Sid Conrad** ... Thornton Wellman

**J.D. Hall** ... Pawnshop Owner

**Mindi Iden** ... Secretary

**Jeffery Lampert** ... Flower Messenger

**Gene Ross** ... Bartender

## OUTFIT ROLE CALL:

- Maddie wore the white striped suit in s02e02, "Lady in the Iron Mask," and in s02e17, "Funeral for a Door Nail."
- The purple suit she wore in s01e04, "The Next Murder You Hear."
- Maddie wears the pink dress/silky blazer combo again in s02e15, "Witness for the Execution," and s03e04, "Yours, Very Deadly."

### LOOK FOR #1:
That famous filter used on Cybill making her look slightly out of focus.

### LOOK FOR #2:
David downing his go-to drink, chocolate milk.

### CONTINUITY:
David's company name changes from "Addison Investigations" to "Addison & Associates" and back again.

## STATS:

*Door Slams: 4*
*Feet out of Elevator: 2*
*Maddie's Outfit Changes: 6*
*Agnes Rhymes: 1*

### GREAT LINES:


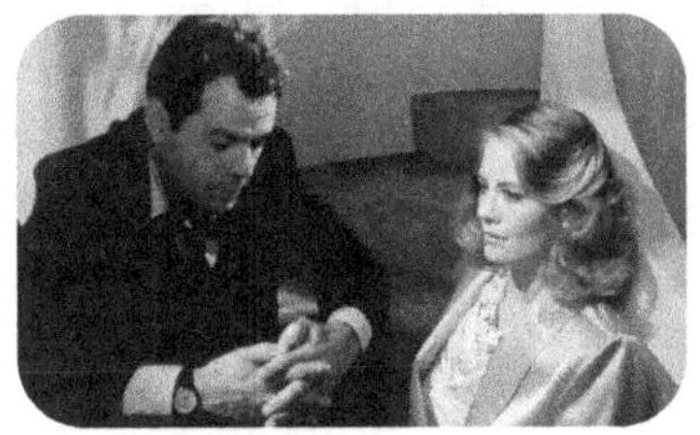

### REVEALING MISTAKE:
In the final scene, Cybill is wearing her watch on her right wrist, but the hand that reaches down to take a business card has the watch on the left wrist.

### FUN FACT #1:
Many *Moonlighting* guest stars went on to have their own shows. Dana Delany starred in *China Beach* (TV Series, 1988-1991); Mark Linn-Baker subsequently starred in *Perfect Strangers* (TV Series, 1986-1993).

### FUN FACT #2:
David drinks another Bloody Mary in s04e07, "Father Knows Last."

## *NOT* SO NICE TO MEET YOU

In much of the Western world, it is common courtesy to greet each other with a friendly handshake in business, but here in "Atlas Belched," David completely ignores Thorton Wellman's outstretched hand. However, for Maddie and David, it's usually the other way around. In s02e05, "My Fair David," Mrs. Greydon pointedly disregards the gesture of a handshake from both Maddie *and* David in quick succession. Alan Tupperman has no time for David's eager palm in s02e11, "The Bride of Tupperman," and Camille, in s02e18, "Camille," rebuffs the gesture too. Rude!

## TIMELINE ISSUE:

The story in this episode plays over a period of six days; however, there is a timeline issue in the plot. Phil West calls in sick on day three. David goes to see Thornton Wellman on day four, and Wellman informs David that Phil West called in sick "for the first time in six years" that day. So if it's the first time Phil has called in sick, this has to be day three, not four. On day five, Maddie and David meet Phil in the warehouse, and on day six, David is back to work.

## CULTURAL REFERENCES:

~ David refers to rivals **Hugh Hefner,** owner of **Playboy** magazine, and **Bob Guccioni,** the owner of **Penthouse** magazine.

~ Car Companies - **Ford Motor Company** and **General Motors**.

~ **Macy's** and **Gimbels** are American department stores.

~ The US Army's recruiting campaign song in the eighties, **"Be All That You Can Be."**

~ David called the **Pope (John Paul II)** and the president of the United States at the time, **Ronald Reagan.**

~ **"Que Sera, Sera,"** written by Jay Livingston and Jay Evans, sung by Doris Day in *The Man Who Knew Too Much* (Movie, 1955).

~ **Ed Meese** - American attorney, law professor, and author who served as attorney general in the Reagan Administration.

~ **Madonna** - An American pop star.

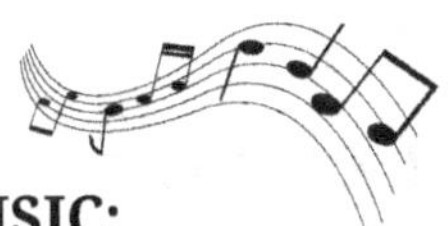

## ORIGINAL MUSIC:

**"William Tell Overture"**
Composed by Gioachino Rossini
Original lyrics performed by Bruce Willis
**"Be All That You Can Be"**
By Earl Carter (E. N. J. Carter)
Performed by Bruce Willis
**"Leaving on Your Mind"**
Written by Wayne Walker and Webb Pierce
Performed by Patsy Cline
*(Replaced with new music on Hulu streaming)*
**"Heigh-Ho"**
Music by *Frank Churchill*
Lyrics by Larry Morey
Performed by Bruce Willis and Mark Linn-Baker

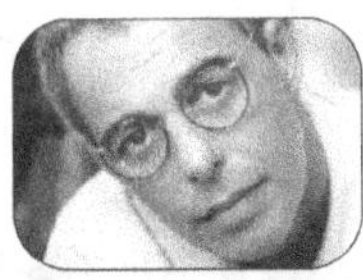

*Robert Turturice dressed Maddie impeccably all five seasons of* Moonlighting

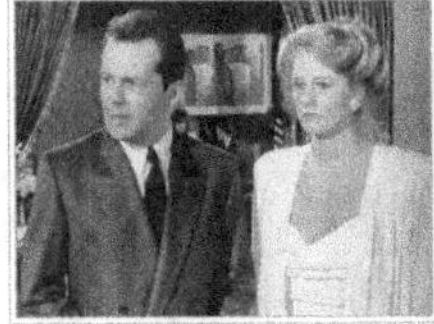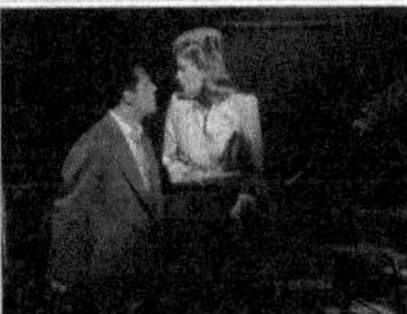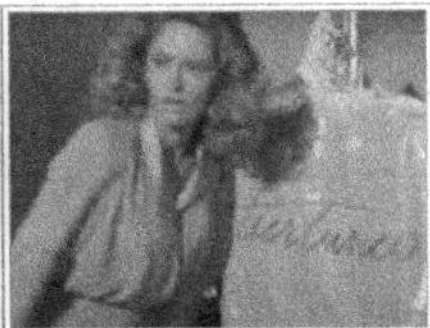

*He gave her a wonderful look. That gave another level of credence to the show. Those kinds of little things in a show like this make a big difference. You never know why they tune in. But when you dress her, you dress her as well as you possibly can, have her look as good as you possibly can. And you need somebody like Bob Turturice."*

**~ Jay Daniel**
**Moonlighting the Podcast**

# S02 E10
# 'Twas the Episode Before Christmas

> **Title Reference:**
> "'Twas the night before Christmas"
> (Line from Poem, 1823)

**Plot:**

Joseph Goodman, who is in the witness protection program, is asleep next to his wife and baby in their apartment, decorated for Christmas, when the man he testified against finds him and throws him over the balcony. His wife, Mary, manages to escape with their baby. To keep him safe, she leaves him in Agnes's apartment while Agnes is in the laundry room.

Maddie and David discover the next day that Agnes has brought the baby to work, and they set about trying to find the mother. Along the way, Maddie and David encounter the three "Kings," (three FBI Agents, all named King) at Agnes's apartment building, who are investigating the murder of Joseph to ensure that there was no foul play.

Meanwhile, Agnes and the baby stay at Maddie's home, and they both enjoy spending time with the baby under the Christmas tree. Eventually, the killer catches up with them at Maddie's home, but David makes a great entrance and impersonation of Santa Claus and comes down the chimney only to find the three Kings also dressed up as Santa. They have come to save the day by putting the killer under arrest. The episode ends with a break of the fourth wall while cast, crew, and their famlies sing "The First Noel."

**Air Date:** December 17, 1985

### CAST CREDITS

**Written by:**
Glenn Gordon Caron

**Director:** Peter Werner

**Leslie Wing** ... Mary Goodman
**Ralph Meyering, Jr.** ... Joseph Goodman
**Richard Belzer** ... Leonard
**James Avery** ... Reuben King
**Brian Libby** ... Leonard's Henchman
**John Hostetter** ... Jim King
**Daniel Chodos** ... Saul King

**Agnes Rhyme:**

Santa's Hotline Ho Ho Ho, we're here to listen so so so, tell me what you want, tell me what you'd like . . . a little baby doll or a shiny new bike, just tell me what it is, I'll tell you know who, and if you've been good, he'll bring it to you.

**Agnes's Rhyming Grocery List:**

Get us some lettuce,
grab us some steak,
remember the cheese please,
and a box of Frosted Flakes.

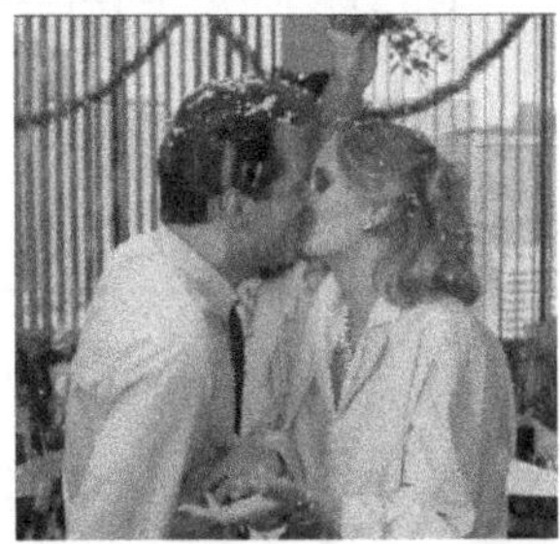

**BREAKING THE FOURTH WALL:**
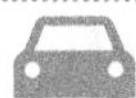
**Maddie:** "You know what we're gonna have to do, don't you?"
**David:** "Wrap this up in about twelve minutes; there's another show comin' on the air?"

## STATS:

*Door Slams: 2*
*Feet out of Elevator: 1*
*Maddie's Outfit Changes: 3*
*Agnes Rhymes: 2*

## GREAT LINES:

— 66 —
*Santa Claus Hotline.*
**~David Addison**
— 99 —

— 66 —
*Where's the little guy bunk?*
**~Leonard**
— 99 —

## FUN FACT:

Director Will Mackenzie mentioned in the DVD commentary for s02e05, "My Fair David," that he learned on *Moonlighting* that low camera angles make the "bad guys" look more sinister. We see this technique used to the extreme on Richard Belzer's character, Leonard.

---

## CAR TALKS:

"Car talks" are a staple of *Moonlighting*. In this episode we get three great car talks: Maddie and David discuss babies, contemplate "the right thing to do," and apologize for not having Christmas gifts to exchange. Perhaps they were also a bit behind on their filming schedule, as scenes in the car were a quick way to get through pages of dialogue in scripts that were twice as long as a normal one-hour show because they talked so fast!

# PAST THE CENSORS:

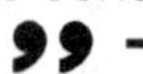

*That is the last time I jam myself into a tight hole with clothes on.*

Between the fast dialogue and episodes often being completed just before airtime, *Moonlighting* often slipped double entendre's past the censors.

---

**CULTURAL REFERENCES:**

~ **Steven Spielberg** - American film director who made classics such as *Close Encounters of the Third Kind* (Movie, 1977) and *E.T. the Extra-Terrestrial* (Movie, 1982).

~ **Camel** - An American brand of cigarettes.

~ The episode title is the first line in "Visit from St. Nicholas / The Night Before Christmas" by Clement Clarke Moore (Poem, 1823).

~ The song "I'm Gonna Wash That Man Right Outa My Hair" comes from *South Pacific* (Musical, 1949).

**LOOK FOR:**

Allyce Beasley's husband, Vincent Schiavelli, isn't standing behind her during "The First Noel" until the close-up of Bruce and Cybill saying "Merry Christmas, everybody."

**CONTINUITY:**

In the scene where Mary is in David's office, Cybill's hairstyle changes from one cut to the next.

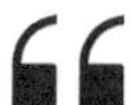

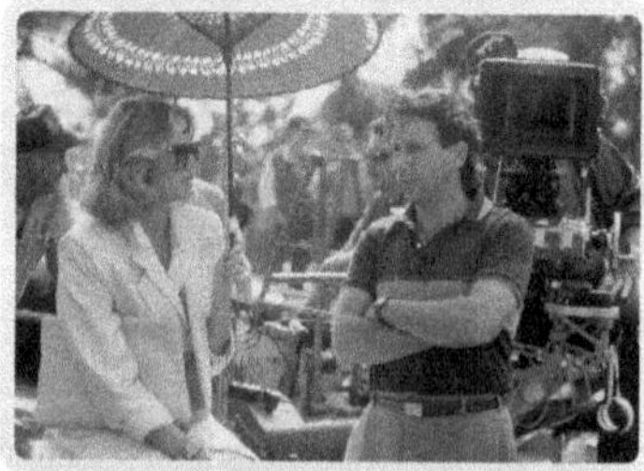

*Peter Werner probably directed the best episodes in those first couple years, and that was no accident. He understood the show.*

*~Glenn Gordon Caron*
*Moonlighting The Podcast*

## ORIGINAL MUSIC:

**"Santa Claus Is Coming to Town"**
Written by Haven Gillespie
and J. Fred Coots
Performed by the Crystals

**"Hush, Little Baby"**
Nursery Rhyme
Performed by Cybill Shepherd

**"I'm Gonna Wash That Man
Right Outa My Hair"**
Lyrics by Oscar Hammerstein II
Music by Richard Rodgers
Performed by Allyce Beasley

**"The First Noel"**
Traditional English Christmas Carol
with Cornish origins
Performed by Cast, Crew, and Family

## A Very Special Ending

The final minutes of this episode is another example of *Moonlighting* "breaking the fourth wall" as Cybill and Bruce walk out of the Blue Moon set and into the studio 20 soundstage, where all the cast, crew, and their families have gathered for a special segment singing "The First Noel" a cappella, to wish the viewers a very Merry Christmas as snow falls around them.

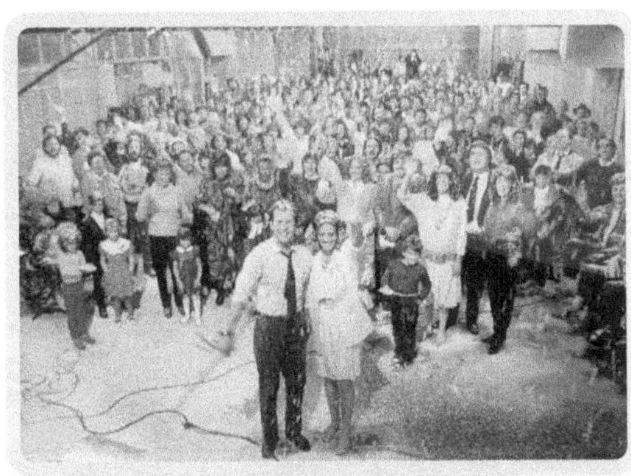

# S02 E11
# The Bride of
# Tupperman

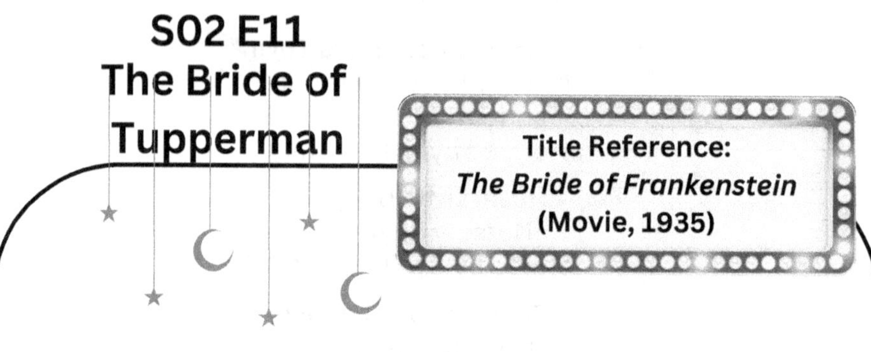

**Title Reference:**
*The Bride of Frankenstein*
(Movie, 1935)

**Plot:**

Alan Tupperman comes to Blue Moon with an "outside the box" idea, a twist on a missing person—one he's never met: he wants the detectives to find him a suitable wife. Of course, Maddie and David are a little confused because they are not a dating service, but he provides them with a description of his perfect mate and offers them a substantial sum of money. Although Maddie initially does not want to take the case, David loves the idea, and Maddie and David eventually decide to go their separate ways, each finding a candidate for Tupperman based on their own idea of what he's looking for.

Once the search is complete and the women are presented to Tupperman, he seems to choose the woman selected by David, but then it transpires that not only did he choose both women, but that he was already married. When they attempt to confront him, they find the woman chosen by David dead and the client in the hospital, which leads them to discover his true scheme. He is the biggest bigamist in bigamy history.

**Air Date:** January 14, 1986

**Written by:** Jeff Reno and Ron Osborn

**Director:** Will Mackenzie & Christian I. Nyby II

**#1 -** Blue Moon Detective Agency, get any strange calls in the middle of the night, strange notes in your mailbox by dawn's early light? Tell us about it, let us get involved, we'll find the perv and your problems will be solved. (She says this rhyme again but gets interrupted.)

**#2 -** Blue Moon Detective Agency, running a beauty pageant and need to know if any girls posed for photos that show more than a swimsuit competition would allow? Just give us a call and we'll find out now, we have sources at major men's magazines and we use them to keep your beauty pageant clean.

**REVEALING MISTAKE #1:**
Two boom mics and the film crew reflected in the Blue Moon window before Stevie comes in.

**REVEALING MISTAKE #2:**
First view of Stevie in the casket, her arms are crossed, but in the next shot they are straight.

**REVEALING MISTAKE #3:**
The hotel receipt is dated 12-1-86 (December 1st 1986), but the episode aired January of 1986.

**CONTINUITY #1:**
The hotel receipt says Tupperman is in room 311, but they knock on 319.

**CONTINUITY #2:**
In the second car talk David's foot alternates between being up on the dash and not.

## STATS:

*Door Slams: 11*
*Feet out of Elevator: 0*
*Maddie's Outfit Changes: 7*
*Agnes Rhymes: 2.5*

## GREAT LINES:

> *What do we do now?*
> **~Madolyn Hayes**

### *MOONLIGHTING* SPEAK:

David, David, David . . .
Maddie, Maddie, Maddie
Fine, Fine . . . Good, Good
Well... Well / So... So
Jealous, jealous, jealous
What are we going to do?
We are not taking this case!
What case? There is no case.

**CONTINUITY #3:**
Five men "don their goggles," but in the next shot there are only four men.

**LOCATION...LOCATION...LOCATION...**
~ **Los Angeles Tribune** - 7080 Hollywood Boulevard, Los Angeles, California, USA
~ **Il Cielo (En Brochette Restaurant)** - 9018 Burton Way, Beverly Hills, California, USA
~ **Hilton Universal City** - 555 Universal Terrace Parkway, Universal City, California, USA
~ **St. John's United Methodist Church (funeral)** - 4301 Cahuenga Boulevard, Toluca Lake, Los Angeles, California, USA

**~ Ripley's Believe It or Not** - (TV Show, 1982-1986)

**~ Rambo** - Character played by Sylvester Stallone.

**~ Lee Iacocca** - Lido Anthony Iacocca, Chrysler automobile executive.

**~ *The Color Purple*** - (Movie, 1985)



**Maddie:** *David, do you realize what we just did?*

**David:** *Found the climax.*

**Maddie:** *At the same time!*

**David:** *Should we have a cigarette now?*

## ART IMMITATING LIFE:

David wakes up laughing on the airplane, Bruce Willis often said that during this time of his life he "woke up laughing" everyday because he couldn't believe the situation he found himself in.

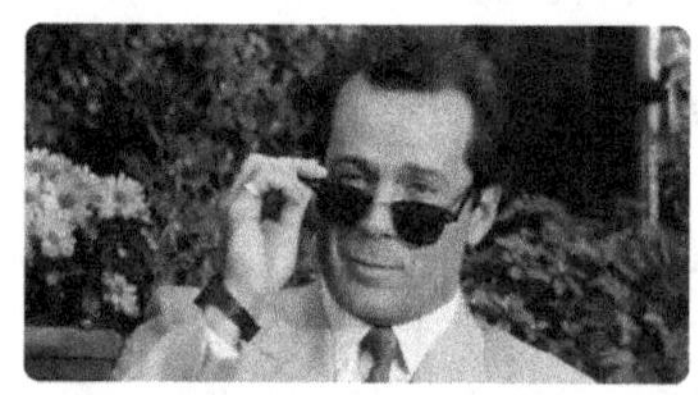

---

# WHAT IS BLUE MOON'S FEE?

- s02e02, "Lady in the Iron Mask"
  - ... Mrs. Wiley offers **$5,000**
- s02e05, "My Fair David"
  - ... Mrs. Greydon paid them **$50,000**
- s02e11, "The Bride of Tupperman"
  - ... Mr. Tupperman offers them **$30,000**
- s02e15, "Witness for the Execution"
  - ... Mr. Everett offers **$25,000**

**Blue Moon,** where the client names the fee!

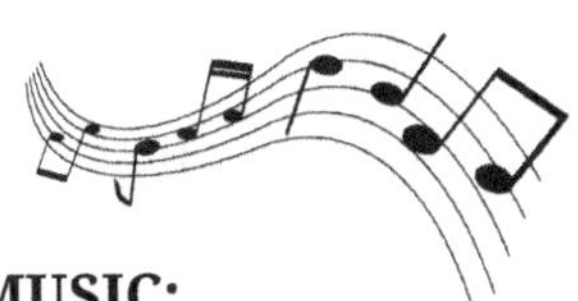

## ORIGINAL MUSIC:

**"I Was Made to Love Her"**
Written by Stevie Wonder,
Lula Mae Hardaway,
Sylvia Moy, and Henry Cosby
Performed by Stevie Wonder
*(Replaced with new music on Hulu streaming)*

**"I Like It"**
Written by Randy DeBarge,
El DeBarge and Bunny DeBarge
Performed by El DeBarge
*(Replaced with new music on Hulu streaming)*

**"Also Sprach Zarathustra"**
Theme song of *Space Odyssey* (1968)
Composed by Richard Strauss

**"The Skeleton Dance"**
**"Dem Bones" "Dry Bones" "Dem Dry Bones"**
Written by James Weldon Johnson
and J. Rosamond Johnson
Performed by Bruce Willis

———◄•►———

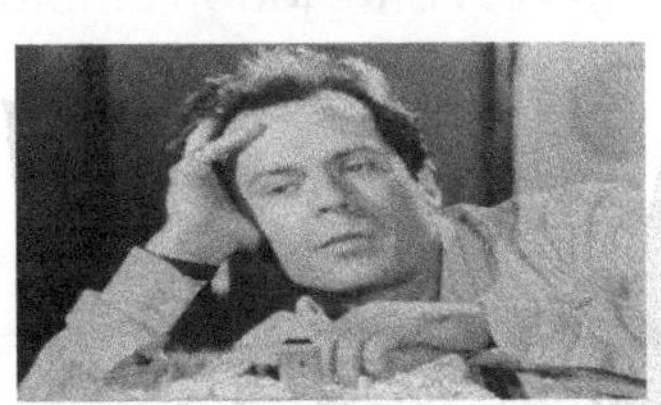

**"The scripts were, and the first one to figure it out was Bruce [Willis], frankly, the scripts are musical; they had a cadence."**

**~Glenn Gordon Caron**
*Moonlighting the Podcast*

**Special appearance by:**
**Guy Lloyd** ... Alan Tupperman
**Deborah Wakeham** ... Stevie
**Nora Heflin** ... Molly
**Sydney Lassick** ... Neighbor
**Lieux Dressler** ... Landlady
**Joe Howard** ... Doctor
**Tammy Brewer** ... Bridal Candidate
**Sue Bugden** ... Bridal Candidate
**Jensen Collier** ... Bridal Candidate
**Carole Tru Foster** ... Bridal Candidate
**Julie Hayek** ... Bridal Candidate
**Kelly Hine** ... Bridal Candidate
**Terri Lynn** ... Bridal Candidate
**Lorrie Marlow** ... Bridal Candidate
**Darrah Meeley** ... Bridal Candidate
**Jody Lee Olhava** ... Bridal Candidate
**Chris Rennolds** ... Bridal Candidate
**Bunny Summers** ... Bridal Candidate
**Robina Suwol** ... Bridal Candidate
**April Wayne** ... Bridal Candidate
**Christine Haber** ... Bridal Candidate
**Brenda McKinley** ... Bridal Candidate
**Bob Tzudiker** ... Blue Moon Employee
**Larry Stewart** ... Blue Moon Employee

"The scenes that people find most memorable are the scenes between Bruce and Cybill, and those scenes are duets."

*~ Glenn Gordon Caron*
*Moonlighting the Podcast*

# S02 E12
# North by North Dipesto

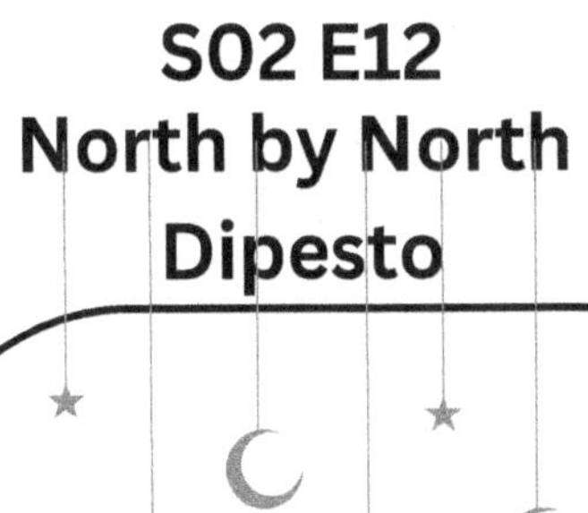



**Plot:**

Agnes is feeling blue; she feels like her life is the same day in and day out and needs some excitement. So Maddie and David give her their tickets to the Investigators Ball, which they weren't really looking forward to, with the hopes that Agnes has a good time. At the ball, Agnes meets a man who gives her a number to keep and says that he will be back for it. They meet up the next day at a bowling alley, where he is stabbed when she is called away to a phone call.

This leads to her involvement in an espionage operation that In turn leads her to being kidnapped and interrogated to find out where this number is. She manages to escape to a laundry facility, and discovers that it is being used by spies to hide stolen plans. But the bad guys need the number, as it is the number of the laundry bag where the plans are being hidden. Her adventures lead her to conclude that she is happy with her life after all.

**Air Date:** January 21, 1986

**Written by:**

Debra Frank and Carl Sautter

**Director:** Christopher Hibler

**CAST CREDITS**

**Douglas Warhit** ... Doug
**Marshall Teague** ... Kyle
**Jim Haynie** ... Chasing Man #1
**Joe Carafello** ... Lew
**Marc Christopher** ... Messenger
**John Durbin** ... Doug's Henchman
**Bob Goldstein** ... Limo Driver
**Bill Marcus** ... Bowling Alley Manager
**Charlie Stavola** ... Chasing Man #2
**Peter Trencher** ... Taxi Driver

## Agnes Rhymes:

**#1** - Blue Moon Detective Agency, if you're in trouble, if you're in a jam, don't tell me, I don't give a damn.

———◆———

**#2** - Blue Moon Detective Agency, say your pooch hasn't yet come home, called his name and bought him a new bone, just give us a shot, Mad and Dave will find Spot... (interrupted)

## OUTFIT ROLE CALL:
- Agnes wears the dress to the Investigators Ball that Maddie wore to Sawyer's casino in s02e03, "Money Talks, Maddie Walks."
- Maddie wears the purple pantsuit that she wore in s02e07, "Somewhere Under the Rainbow." She wears it again in s02e15, "Witness for the Execution."

## CONTINUITY #1:
Agnes is paged in the bowling alley under her real name, although the bad guys think her name is "Elaine."

## FUN FACT #1:
The bowling alley used in this episode is also used in s03e13, "Maddie's Turn to Cry."

## STATS:

*Door Slams: 3*
*Feet out of Elevator: 0*
*Maddie's Outfit Changes: 4*
*Agnes Rhymes: 1.5*

## — ❝ — GREAT LINES:
**David:** *The only thing that could liven up this shindig is a strip search demonstration with you as a volunteer.*

**Maddie:** *Thank you. . . . I think?*
——————— ❞ —

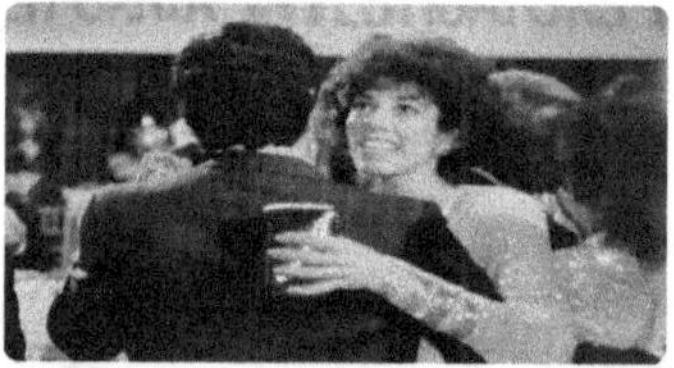

## BREAKING THE FOURTH WALL
**David:** "But we don't have any work."

**Maddie:** "Of course we do. We have to talk to the writers and get them to write bigger parts for next week's episode!"

## FUN FACT #2:
Marshall Teague, who plays Kyle, worked with Bruce Willis on *Armageddon* (Movie, 1998). He played Colonel Davis, the pilot on the *Independence*.

## LOCATION...LOCATION...LOCATION...
~ **Corbin Bowl (Bowling Alley)** - 19616 Ventura Boulevard, Tarzana, California, USA
~ **Park Plaza Hotel** - 607 South Park View Street, Los Angeles, California, USA

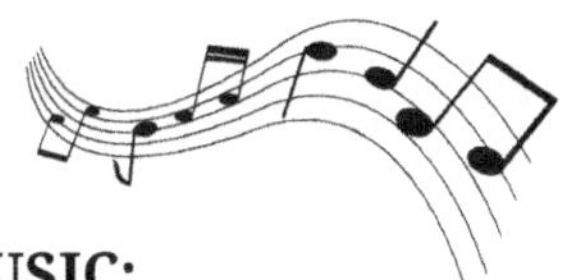

## ORIGINAL MUSIC:

### "Come See about Me"
Written by Lamont Dozier, Brian Holland,
and Eddie Holland
Performed by the Supremes
*(Replaced with new music on Hulu streaming)*

### "Object of My Desire"
Written by Ernesto Phillips,
Keith Diamond and Ky Adeyemo
Performed by Starpoint
*(Replaced with new music on Hulu streaming)*

### "Could It Be Magic"
Written by Barry Manilow and Frédéric Chopin
Lyrics by Adrienne Anderson
Performed by Barry Manilow
*(Replaced with new music on Hulu streaming)*

---

## Continuity #2: Dressing Agnes

In the scene where Agnes and Maddie go back to Maddie's house to pick out a dress for Dipesto to wear to the ball, there are many continuity issues. Maddie suddenly goes from wearing a pink outfit to a purple pantsuit. Also, Maddie shows Agnes the same dress twice—once Agnes shakes her head "no," the second time "yes." Finally, Maddie shows Agnes a dress and then throws it onto the pile of dresses, except it's a different dress that lands on the pile.

# S02 E13
# In God We Strongly Suspect



**Plot:**

Blue Moon is hired by Carolyn Kandinsky, who is afraid her dead husband might kill her. Mr. Kandinsky, a magician, died attempting to escape from a tank of water. Because Carolyn had cheated on her husband in the past, he often threatened to come back from the afterlife and kill her for all of her indiscretions.

The widow won't rest easy until he is cremated, so it is now Maddie and David's job to watch over the body and be sure he doesn't leave the casket. They spend the night in the morgue; sure, it's easy money, but in the morning they realize that the corpse has disappeared. Not long after this, the widow is found dead following a mysterious car accident. The plot twists when Maddie and David discover that the escape artist is in fact still alive and involved in a diamond heist, during which he seemingly dies again.

In the midst of all this, the Blue Moon workers organize a birthday party for Maddie for which they don't quite get the response they had hoped for. All is revealed in the final moments of the episode when Maddie and David corner the killer by knocking him out with a bull's-eye.

**Air Date:** February 11, 1986

**Written by:**
Scott Spencer Gordon

**Director:** Will Mackenzie

## CAST CREDITS

**K Callan** ... Carolyn Kandinsky
**Dominic Barto** ... Kandinsky
**J A Preston** ... Dr. Nealy
**Eddie Quillan** ... Abby Cadabra
**William Parker**
... Funeral Home Director
**Barry Cutler** ... Coroner
**David Ellzey** ... Coroner
**Hettie Lynne Hurtes** ... Reporter

## CONTINUITY #1:

The banner at the magic show reads, "The Great Kandinski," but when David and Maddie knock on Mrs. Kandinski's front door, the placard reads "Kandinsky."

## CONTINUITY #2:

When David is singing "Happy Birthday" to Maddie, he's not wearing shoes, but when he follows Maddie to her office, suddenly his shoes are on.

## OUTFIT ROLE CALL:

- Maddie wore the brown skirt/top outfit in s01e03, "Read the Mind . . . See the Movie," and s02e01, "Brother, Can You Spare a Blonde?"
- She wore the yellowish blouse/belt combo in s02e06, "Knowing Her."

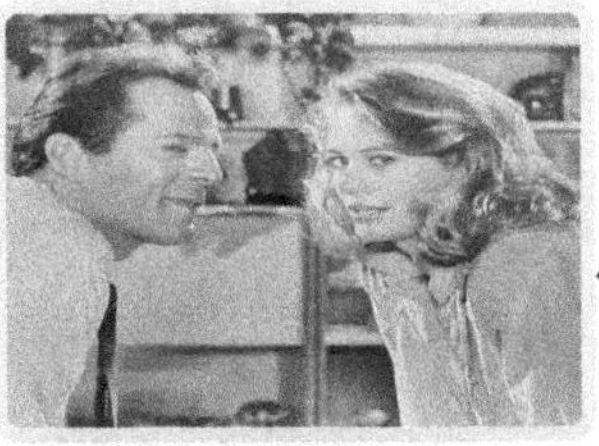

## BREAKING THE FOUTH WALL:

**David**: "I'm at a loss; I don't know what a flying fig is."

**Maddie**: "That's okay; they do" *(as they both look at the camera).*

## STATS:

*Door Slams: 7*
*Feet out of Elevator: 1*
*Maddie's Outfit Changes: 4*
*Agnes Rhymes: 0*

## GREAT LINES:

*David: Aren't you going to tell me we can't take this case?*
*Maddie: Why would I do that?*
*David: I dunno. That's what you always do.*

## LOOK FOR:

Obvious body doubles for Bruce and Cybill when the camera focuses on the melting candles.

· · ·

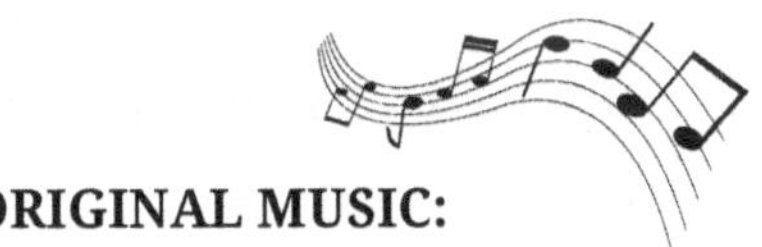

## ORIGINAL MUSIC:

**"Birthday"**
Written by John Lennon and Paul McCartney
Performed by Bruce Willis

**"The Skeleton Dance"**
**"Dem Bones" "Dry Bones"**
**"Dem Dry Bones"**
Written by
James Weldon Johnson and J. Rosamond Johnson
Performed by Bruce Willis

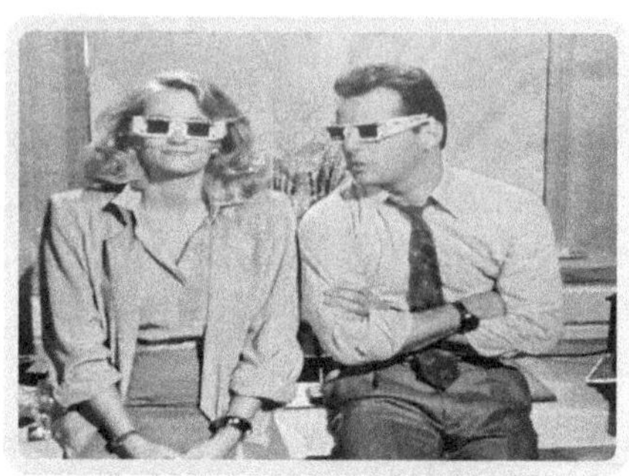

*A 3D episode was another experimental show Glenn Caron wanted to explore on Moonlighting, but it never materialized.*

## Origins of the Episode

Glenn Caron talked on *Moonlighting the Podcast* about his inspiration for "In God We Strongly Suspect." Caron said, "I was always fascinated with the business of *faith*. And while talking with the other writers on the show, I said, 'You know, my reflective instinct is to say that, well, Maddie must be fairly religious in the way that we typically think of religion... whereas David Addison clearly is an anarchist.'" Caron continued, "The more I thought about it. though, the more I realized it was really kinda the opposite. That the peculiar truth must be that Maddie, because she's a little cooler and colder and more analytical, she may have eschewed the idea of religion a long time ago. Whereas David, who, yes, he's an anarchist, but at the end of the day, he's a romantic." Which is how Maddie came to be the atheist and David the faithful.

# S02 E14
# Every Daughter's Father Is a Virgin



**Plot:**

Maddie's parents, Alexander and Virginia Hayes, arrive in town from Chicago to attend the wedding of one of her father's colleagues. Her mother confides that Maddie's father may be having an affair and that the woman may have followed them from Chicago. Maddie is determined to prove her mother wrong and wants to conduct an investigation of her own and follow him for a day to see where he goes. David offers to take the case and do it for her.

Unfortunately, David has to break the bad news to Maddie about what he witnessed—that her father is indeed having an affair. Maddie cannot bring herself to tell her mother the truth, so instead launches a furious attack on her father, who then tells her that the affair is over and it will never happen again. This episode reveals a close relationship between Maddie and her parents, something that had not been mentioned before.

The episode ends with David joking that given the situation with her parents, he could adopt Maddie so that he can bounce her on his knee and tell her stories at bedtime, though whether she'd have her own room or not is still unclear.

**Air Date:** February 18, 1986

**Written by:**
Bruce Franklin Singer

**Director:** Christopher Hibler

### CAST CREDITS
**Robert Webber** ... Alexander Hayes (Recurring Guest Star)
**Eva Marie Saint** ... Virginia Hayes (Recurring Guest Star)
**Rosanna Huffman** ... Woman in 458
**Kate Murtagh** ... Waitress
**Dante D'Andre** ... Hotel Desk Clerk
**Eduardo Ricard** ... Waiter
**Tammy Brewer** ... Blue Moon Staff
**Alain St. Alix** ... Blue Moon Staff
**Chris Rennolds** ... Blue Moon Staff
**Ben Hartigan** ... Blue Moon Staff

**LIGHTING DETAIL:**
Look for the shadow of a vase of flowers on the front door before "Father David" enters the Blue Moon office.

### FUN FACT #1:
The clip of Maddie lying in bed at the beginning of the episode is used again in s03e01, "The Son Also Rises."

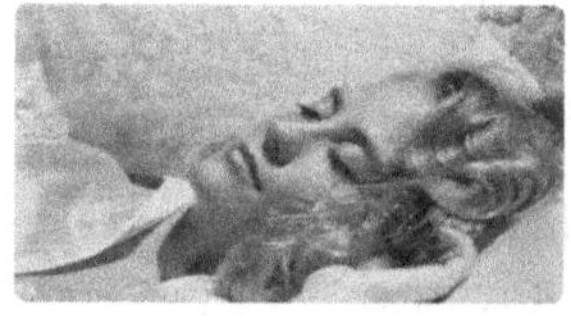

**CONTINUITY:**
David's black eye changes quite a bit throughout the episode.

### FUN FACT #2:
The waitress serving Maddie and her mother at the hotel is Kate Murtagh. She was on the front and back covers of Supertramp's 1979 album "Breakfast in America" holding a tall glass of orange juice. Kate also appears in s05e02, "Between a Yuk and a Hard Place," as a potential client.

**STATS:**

*Door Slams: 2*
*Feet out of Elevator: 0*
*Maddie's Outfit Changes: 6*
*Agnes Rhymes: 0*

### — 66 — GREAT LINES:

*David: [about Maddie's parents visiting] Maddie, don't worry. I'm not going to embarrass you.*
*Maddie: You leaving town?*
*David: I'm leaving your office.*
*Maddie: That's a start.*

### FUN FACT #3:
Bruce wears a headband in the cold open with "McMahon" written on it. This refers to Jim McMahon, who was a quarterback for the Chicago Bears American Football team.

**MISSING SCENE?**
After David says "We've known that for awhile now" to Ms. Dipesto, in the next cut they are unexplainably holding hands.

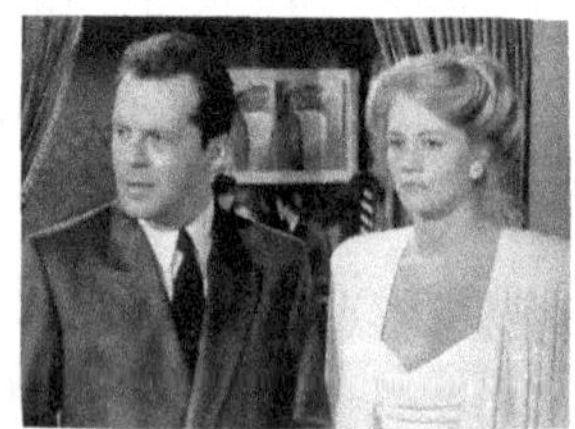

## LOCATION...LOCATION...LOCATION...

**~ Mr. and Mrs. Hayes stayed at the Radisson Wilshire Plaza Hotel -** 3515 Wilshire Boulevard, Los Angeles, California, USA

**~ David follows Mr. Hayes to the Sheraton Universal Hotel** - 333 Universal Hollywood Drive, Universal City, California, USA

**~ Dinner with Maddie's Parents - Wyndham Bel Age Hotel** - (no longer there) 1020 North San Vicente Boulevard, West Hollywood, California, USA

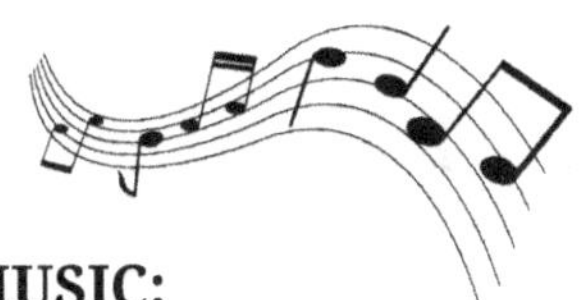

## ORIGINAL MUSIC:

**"Whistle While You Work"**
Written by Frank Churchill and Larry Morey
**"Tighten Up"**
Written by Archie Bell and Billy Buttler
Performed by Bruce Willis
**"Sweet Georgia Brown"**
Written by Ben Bernie and Maceo Pinkard
Lyrics by Kenneth Casey
Whistled by Bruce Willis
**"Papa Was a Rollin' Stone"**
Written by Barrett Strong and Norman Whitfield
Performed by the Temptations
**"Love Is a Many-Splendored Thing"**
Composed by Sammy Fain
*(Replaced with new music on Hulu streaming)*

---

# Imagining Maddie Hayes

The character of Maddie came from a "couple different places," Glenn Gordon Caron explained during his conversation with Shawna and Grace on *Moonlighting the Podcast.* "First of all, my mom was . . . a very strong person, so that was part of it. The other part was, I used to love Frank Capra [movies]. If you go back and look at his films, the women were always extraordinarily strong. . . . They planted their feet and weren't going to let some guy push them around. Their destiny wasn't tied to some guy. 'I will make my own destiny' was sort of their North Star, and to me, that's who Maddie was. Now, I was also a twenty-something-year-old kid. So I think there was a lot of fantasy or wish fulfillment in that, you know, you always want the person who won't have you."

# S02 E15
# Witness for
# the Execution

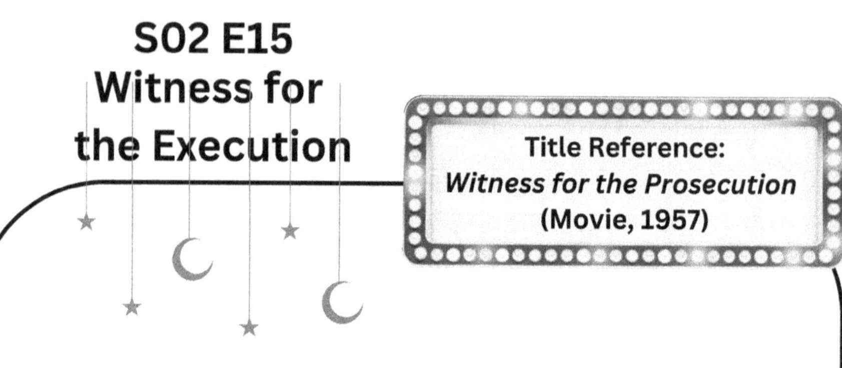



**Plot:**

Maddie and David are approached by an elderly man, Lawrence Everett, to assist him in witnessing a murder, his own. He says he has hired someone to murder him, but wants a witness to the murder to ensure that his family receives his life insurance money, since his policy does not pay out for suicide.

Of course, Maddie and David disagree on whether to take the case. Maddie decides that her agency will have nothing to do with it, since what Mr. Everett is trying to do is fraud, so David takes the case on his own.

Through a series of events, David is accused of murdering Mr. Everett and is forced to go underground. Maddie is left to solve the case, determined to clear David's name. The angst over David possibly leaving Los Angeles and Blue Moon indefinitely leads to some interesting developments in the detectives' relationship.

**Air Date:** March 11, 1986

**Written by**: Jeff Reno and Ron Osborn

**Director:** Paul Krasny

## CAST CREDITS

**Roberts Blossom** ... Lawrence Everett

**Ellen Geer** ... Amy Everett

**Michael MacRae** ... Lt. Tapia

**Maurice Sneed** ... the orderly

**Judith Searle** ... Nurse

**Corinne Carroll** ... Nurse

## OUTFIT ROLE CALL:

- Maddie wore the pink dress/ silky blazer combo in s02e09, "Atlas Belched."
- She wore the nightgown, pajama set, and purple pantsuit in s02e07, "Somewhere Under the Rainbow."
- The nightgown again in s03e11, "Blonde on Blonde," and in s03e01, "The Son Also Rises."
- The purple pantsuit in s02e12, "North by North Dipesto."
- The yellow outfit with stripes again later in s03e04, "Yours, Very Deadly."

### CONTINUITY #1:
When "Amy" takes the break off the wheelchair, she has bright red nail polish on, but in the next shot she is wearing clear nail polish.

### CONTINUITY #2:
David's shaving cream and the twisted strap of his undershirt change between cuts.

### CONTINUITY #3:
This show aired March of '86, but the date in the credits is 1985.

### LOOK FOR #1:
Bruce Willis has a scar on his right shoulder from a surgery he had to repair a broken arm as a teenager. He broke his collarbone on the left side during season three.

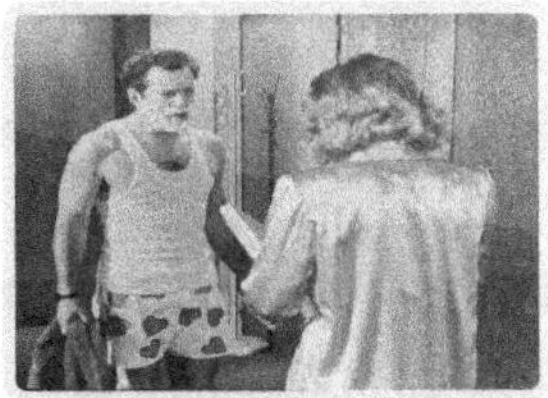

## STATS:

*Door Slams: 5*
*Feet out of Elevator: 0*
*Maddie's Outfit Changes: 9*
*Agnes Rhymes: 0*

### GREAT LINES:

" **Maddie:** *Don't go!*

**David:** *Gotta go...* "

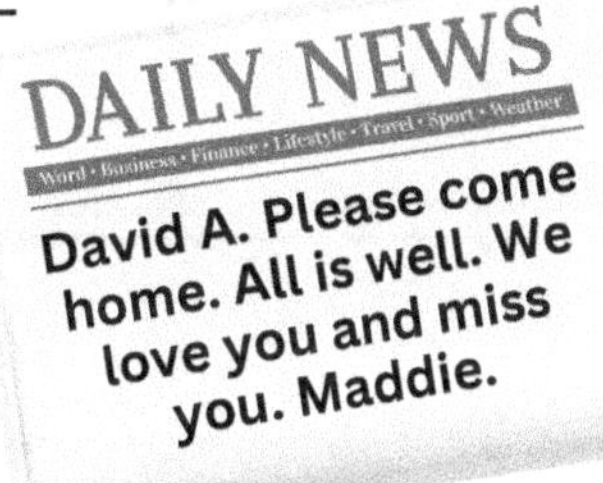


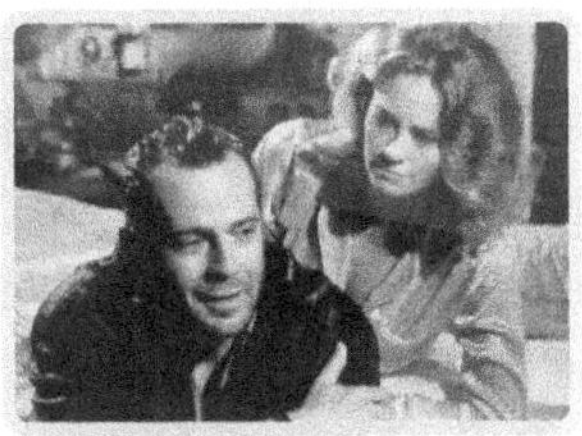

### LOOK FOR #2 (SPOILER ALERT):

Maddie and David's first real kiss outside a dream sequence, but the question is, who kissed whom?

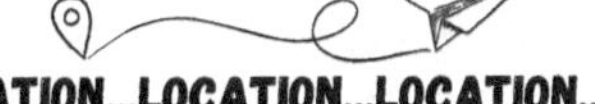

**LOCATION...LOCATION...LOCATION...**
~ **"Golden Hour" Rest Home** - South Boyle Avenue, Los Angeles, California, USA

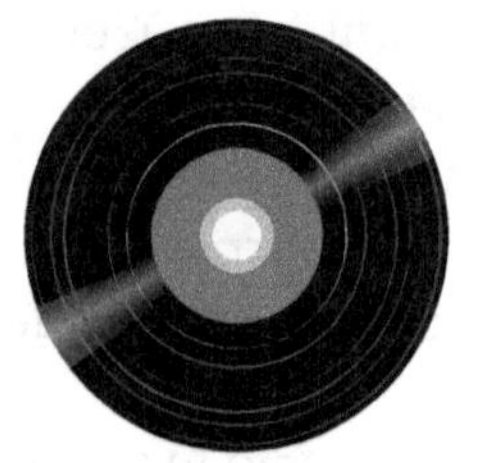

## ORIGINAL MUSIC:

**"Sympathy for the Devil"**
Written by Mick Jagger and Keith Richards
Performed by the Rolling Stones
*(Replaced with new music on Hulu streaming)*

**"Monday, Monday"**
Written by John Phillips
Performed by Cybill Shepherd

---

### GET OUT OF THE WAY!

Hurray! We've got our first *real* kiss here in "Witness for the Execution" . . . if only we could see it! What is with *Moonlighting* hiding the majority of the kisses? Kisses we waited a long time to see, and get so few of. Drop the squeaking handbag, Maddie! It's in the way of this ever so *spontaneous,* urgently passionate first kiss they share (outside of a dream). This is not the only kiss "hidden" from us. The kisses at the end of s03e08, "It's a Wonderful Job," can't see them. The kiss at the end of s03e09, "The Straight Poop," can't see it. The kiss in s04e10, "Tracks of My Tears" is cut off just as it's getting good, and in s03e07, "Atomic Shakespeare," between the angles and the sheet, *we cannot seeth those folk kisseth.* The sexy kisses in David's side of s02e04, "The Dream Sequence Always Rings Twice" are mostly in shadow. So are *both* the kisses at the end of s03e02, "The Man Who Cried Wife," with the addition of Maddie's hand covering most of the kiss she initiates with David. Please . . . people, objects, bedding, and shadows . . . would you get out of the way!

# S02 E16
# Sleep Talkin' Guy

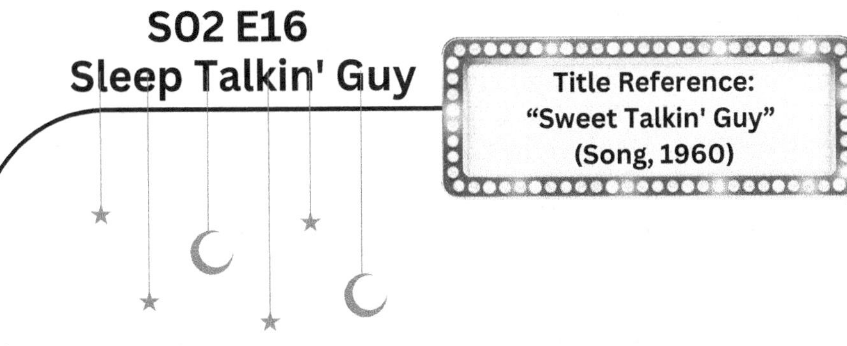


**Plot:**

After asking for a raise and learning that Maddie questions his skills as a detective, David has something to prove. He is approached by a prostitute, Toby, who has a client who talks in his sleep, spilling the beans about murders he's about to commit. David begins to make a name for himself when he solves several big cases in quick succession with the "sleep talking guys" information. Maddie is impressed, unaware that he is using information passed to him by a prostitute with a mobster client who talks in his sleep about people who are due to be murdered.

Everything is going well for David until he is told by his lady of the night that there is now a contract out on him due to his notoriety.

He ends up in a fistfight with the mobster at a nightclub. When Maddie arrives and finds out that David is not as good as a detective as she thought after all, she becomes livid.

**Air Date:** April 1, 1986

**Written by:** Debra Frank and Carl Sautter

**Director:** Christopher Hibler

## STATS:

*Door Slams: 12*
*Feet out of Elevator: 0*
*Maddie's Outfit Changes: 6*
*Agnes Rhymes: 1*

## CONTINUITY:

Maddie takes the glass of champagne with her left hand, but in the next cut, the glass is in her right hand.

## REVEALING MISTAKE #1:

When David confronts Jerry in the bar, Jerry should know David Addison because David is on his hit list.

— • • • —

## CULTURAL REFERENCES:

~ **Spinks and Holms** - Boxers
~ **Sears, Roebuck and Co.,** - American department store
~ **Heckle and Jeckle** - Cartoon characters
~ **Culligan** - Water company
~ **D. B. Cooper** - Hijacked a plane in 1971 and parachuted out and was never found.

## GREAT LINES:

— 66 —

***David:*** *One year ago today you slithered into my office and pleaded with me to go into business.*

***Maddie:*** *A year, huh? Why does it seem so much longer?*

— 99 —

## REVEALING MISTAKE #2:

When Jerry chokes David, his thumbs are nowhere near his neck.

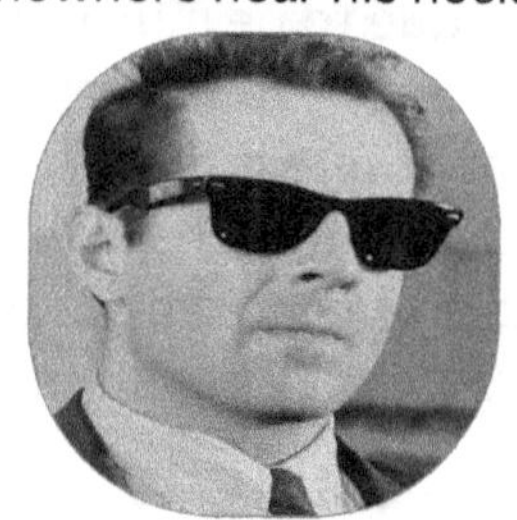

## WHAT A KNOCKOUT!

Starting from the Pilot episode, Maddie Hayes was as feisty as she was beautiful. David received a slap and a punch during their first few days together, but that didn't stop him from coming back for more. In subsequent episodes, Maddie found many good reasons to kick, stomp on, and push David around, but it's not until this episode that he's earned another punch. Stay tuned, folks, there are many more slaps, pulls, pushes, and punches to come—some even lead to some fun things. She certainly was a knockout!

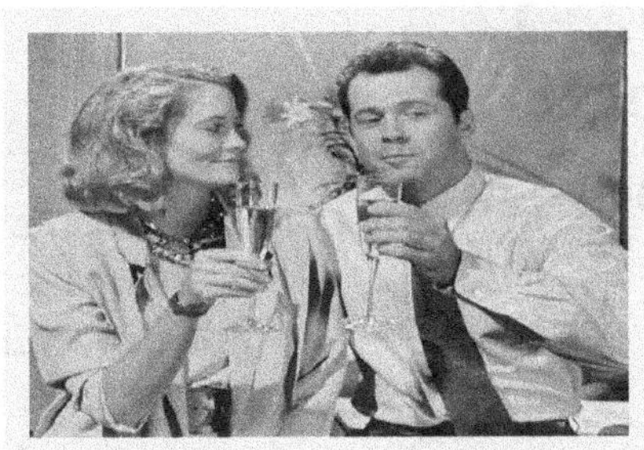

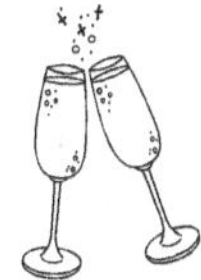



## TINY BUBBLES

Any time there is an occasion to pop bottles on *Moonlighting*, their bubbly of choice is almost always Perrier-Jouët champagne (though it's Dom Pérignon '76 in s02e03, "Money Talks, Maddie Walks"). You can recognize the Perrier-Jouët bottle by the signature floral design that encircles the label. Keep an eye out for this fine champs being served in the following episodes, and let us know if you spot it in any others!

- **s02e16, "Sleep Talkin' Guy"** - To celebrate Maddie and David's first anniversary,  and David sends a bottle to Toby and her date
- **s02e18, "Camille"** - Being delivered by room service
- **s03e02, "The Man Who Cried Wife"** - To celebrate Macgillacudy getting married
- **s03e03, "Symphony in Knocked Flat"** - In the limo
- **s05e01, "A Womb With a View"** - Maddie's baby shower
- **s05e13, "Lunar Eclipse"** - Celebrating Bert and Agnes's wedding

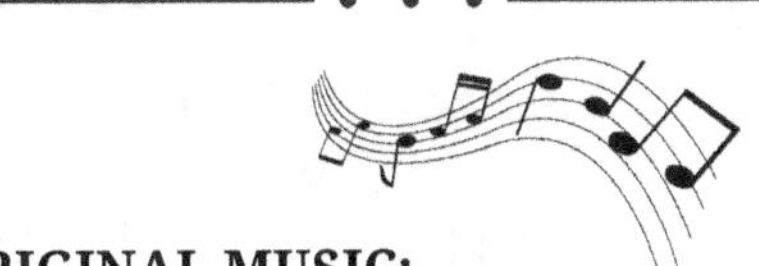

**ORIGINAL MUSIC:**

**"Baby Talk"**
Composed by Gregg Brown
Performed by Alisha
**"West End Girls"**
Written by Neil Tennant and Chris Lowe
Performed by Pet Shop Boys

# S02 E17
# Funeral for
# a Door Nail

**Title Reference:
(to be as) "dead as a
doornail" (English Idiom)**

**Plot:**

Roger Clements is distraught over the apparent death of his wife, but unable to commit suicide. He decides to hire a hitman to kill him—but asks for a few days so that he can get his affairs in order. While he is at his lawyer's office to amend his will, he sees his wife, Celia, walking down the street toward the building. But by the time he runs down to the street to confront her, she's gone.

Knowing that Celia is alive, Roger then hires Blue Moon to find her and to also stop the hitman from murdering him. Unfortunately, the client dies anyway in a car bombing, which leads Blue Moon's investigation in a different direction and toward a new suspect.

In the midst of all this, Maddie invites David to be her date to her cousin's wedding in Chicago. He says he would be delighted to escort her, but Maddie is not happy with his enthusiasm. David has to think quickly, so he suggests that they make it a business proposition: he suggests Maddie pay him to be her escort. David is very disappointed when they have to cancel going to the wedding due to events that occur solving this very interesting case.

**Air Date:** April 29, 1986

**Teleplay by:**
Jeff Reno & Ron Osborn
and Charles H. Eglee

**Story by:**
Jonathon Lempkin

**Director:** Allan Arkush

### CAST CREDITS

**Jeffrey DeMunn** ... Roger Clements
**Granville Van Dusen** ... Allen Margalese
**Teri Hafford** ... Celia Clements
**Leslie Ackerman** ... Woman In Porn Shop Booth
**Allan Arkush** (Cameo) ... Adult Bookstore Customer
**Charles Walker** ... Man
**Patty Lotz** ... Porn Shop Attendant

### Agnes Rhyme:

> Blue Moon Investigations, are you being watched? Are you being bugged? Just give us a call and we'll find the thug, whoever is your peeping Tom, Dick, or John, we won't quit until he is gone.

### FUN FACT #1:
Director Allan Arkush makes a cameo appearance in this episode as the guy in the porn shop who tells David which booths are the best.

### FUN FACT #2:
Guest star Teri Hafford can also be seen in a 1986 ad for Seagram's wine coolers alongside Bruce Willis.

### OUTFIT ROLE CALL:
- Maddie wore the white stripped suit in s02e02, "The Lady in the Iron Mask," and s02e09, "Atlas Belched."

### CULTURAL REFERENCES:
~ **Jordan Almonds** - Sugar-coated almonds traditional at Greek and Italian weddings.
~ **Avon Lady** - cosmetics and skin care company.
David imitates **Elvis,** an American singer and actor.
~ **Lindbergh baby** - Abducted from his crib in 1932.
~ **John Houseman** - Actor who was in an ad with the catchphrase "They Earn It."
~ **Jimmy Hoffa** - American labor union leader who disappeared in 1975.
~ "Failure to remunerate" - ***Cool Hand Luke*** (Movie, 1967: "What we have here is a failure to communicate").

### STATS:

*Door Slams: 4*
*Feet out of Elevator: 1*
*Maddie's Outfit Changes: 2*
*Agnes Rhymes: 1*

### GREAT LINES:
— " —
***Clements:*** *I really don't know how to thank you.*
***David:*** *Money works.*
— " —

### LOOK FOR:
When Maddie and David step out of the elevator, the name on the first office window says "*Horace D. Fennermann,*" an homage to cinematographer Gerald P. Finnerman

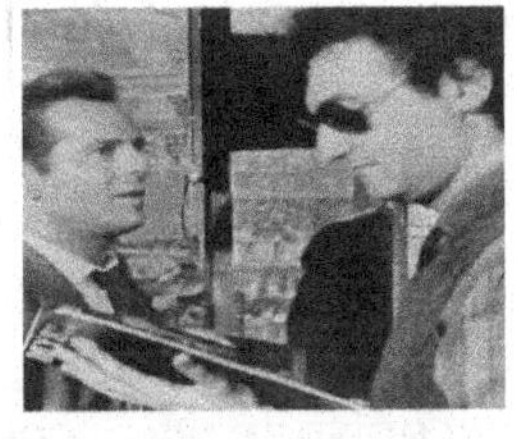

**MOONLIGHTING MENTION:**
*Sledge Hammer!* "The Spa Who Loved Me" (TV Episode, 1987)

**"The terrorists also demand that a new episode of *Moonlighting* be broadcast each week."**

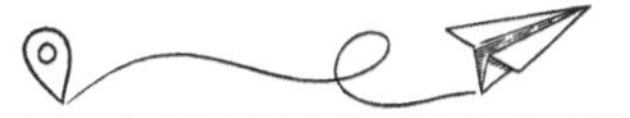

## LOCATION...LOCATION...LOCATION...
~ **Stan's Books & Video** - 1117 North Western Avenue, Los Angeles, California, USA

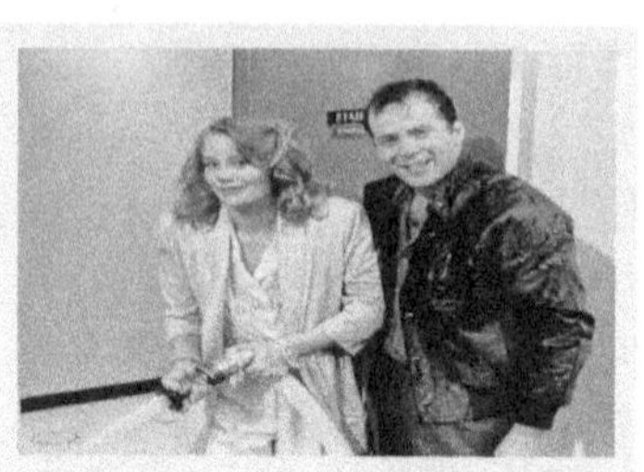



**ORIGINAL MUSIC:**

**"Star Wars"**
Theme song of *Star Wars* (Movie, 1977)
Written by John Williams

**"Jaws"**
Theme song of *Jaws* (Movie, 1975)
Written by John Williams

**"Psycho (The Murder)"**
Theme song of *Psycho* (Movie, 1960)
Written by Bernard Herrmann
*(All replaced with new music on Hulu streaming)*

## GREAT WAITERS

The first season of *Moonlighting* (the first six episodes) was a mid-season replacement. For seasons two to five, ABC ordered twenty-two episodes per season, but that never happened. Season two has a total of eighteen episodes, season three has fifteen episodes, season four has fourteen episodes (it was put on hiatus due to the 1988 writers' strike), and season five completed thirteen episodes before the series was canceled. So according to our calculations, there should have been ninety-four-ish episodes of *Moonlighting* over the five seasons. There are sixty-six episodes in total (sixty-seven when the Pilot is split into two episodes, as was done for syndication). So much of the discussion, curiosity, and interest in the show at the time surrounded the fact that one never knew if a new episode of *Moonlighting* was actually going to air or not. The second *TV Guide* landed in the mailbox each week, fans flipped directly to Tuesday night's schedule to check if a new episode or a repeat was listed. But even that wasn't always reliable; at least once a new episode was scheduled to air but a repeat ran instead. Fans and media alike wondered, *What was the trouble?* Over the years, through DVD commentary and interviews, some of those reasons have become clear. First, *Moonlighting* took its time making episodes that were done right and avoided sacrificing shots to make a deadline. Second, it was a single-camera, one-hour show with the two leads in almost every scene and twice the normal pages of dialogue, quite an exhausting undertaking, and after a while, they needed breaks. Third, all pages went through Glenn Caron's typewriter, and production could not move forward without a script. When Glenn joined Grace and Shawna on *Moonlighting the Podcast*, he talked about how the pages would come very late, and it wasn't something he was proud of, but he was "waiting for the truth." So in the eighties, we waited! Weeks, sometimes months for new episodes. *Moonlighting* fans are great waiters . . . head waiters. But, hey, we'll take quality over quantity any day. Thanks, Glenn!

# S02 E18
# Camille

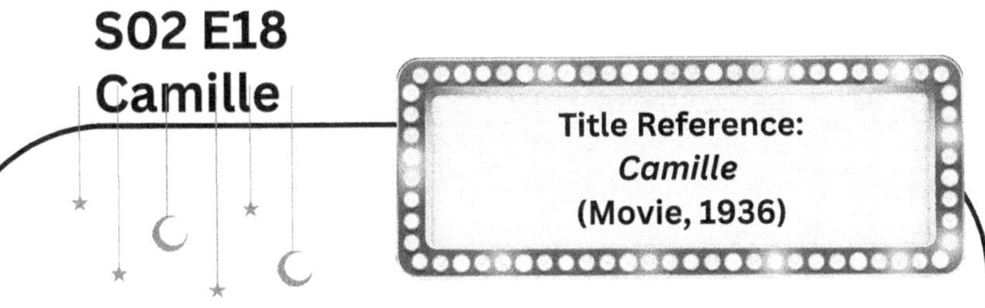


**Plot:**

Camille Brand (Whoopi Goldberg) is a con woman who becomes a national hero after accidentally preventing the assassination of a politician. David convinces Maddie  that it would be wise to cash in on the publicity by giving Camille a job at Blue Moon as a detective, hoping to attract some attention to the agency.

Meanwhile, a crooked policeman (Judd Nelson) spends much of the episode pursuing and attempting to arrest Camille.

The episode ends with an extended chase that breaks the fourth wall and blurs lines between characters and actors, in which the players wander right off the show's set into other parts of the studio lot. Several members of the show's production crew appear on camera as the chase commences and ends, leaving Maddie and David (Cybill and Bruce) to explain the plot resolution.

**Air Date:** May 13, 1986

**Written by**: Roger Director

**Director:** Peter Werner

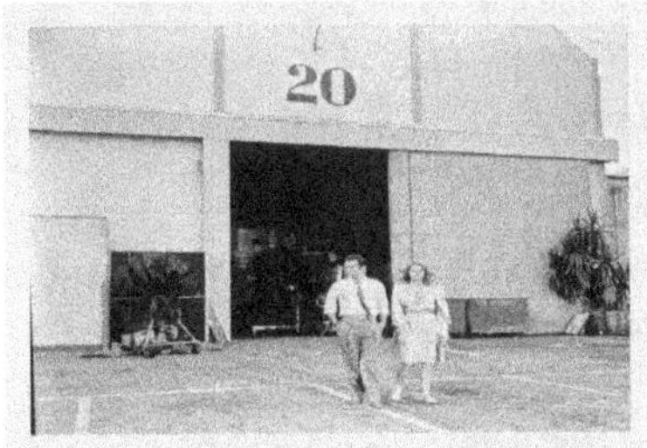

*To end season two, Maddie and David leave Studio 20, where the Blue Moon offices were located.*

Blue Moon Investigations, if you're in trouble, if you're in a fix, we're the people to turn to, we make things right quick, we're effective 'cause we listen, listen, listen to all you say, we listen, listen, listen and send help on the way. (Agnes says this rhyme again later, but gets interrupted.)

## STATS:

*Door Slams: 3*
*Feet out of Elevator: 1*
*Maddie's Outfit Changes: 7*
*Agnes Rhymes: 1.5*

## REVEALING MISTAKE:

When Agnes gives Camille the welcome card, she says, "We all signed it." Yet the card only has six signatures, including David's and Maddie's (but not Ms. Dipesto's), and the office has many more people.

## LOOK FOR:

Maddie's heels magically turn into sneakers in the last chase scene.

## OUTFIT ROLE CALL:

- Maddie wears the purple dress again in s03e08, "It's a Wonderful Job."

## CULTURAL REFERENCE:

When Maddie and David try to convince Camille to come work for Blue Moon, David says the line "6-2 and even, over and out," which is apparently a line used in old **Dick Tracy** cartoons (TV Series, 1961- present) and also a term a bookie would use in horse racing. This line is used again by Maddie and David at the end of s05e13, "Lunar Eclipse."

## GREAT LINES:

**David:** *I just had a thought.*
**Maddie:** *How is that possible?*

## FUN FACT:

Camille asks if *The Color Purple* (Movie, 1985) is on cable yet, a movie Whoopi Goldberg starred in. The movie is also mentioned in s02e11, "The Bride of Tupperman."

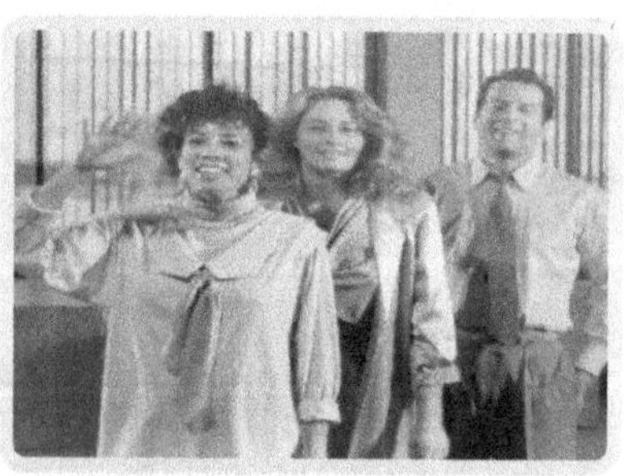

*The "Blue Moon" set is dismantled around them as the illusion between the characters and the actors dissolves.*

## LOCATION...LOCATION...LOCATION...

~ **Park Plaza Hotel** - 607 South Park View Street, Los Angeles, California, USA

# Whoopi Goldberg

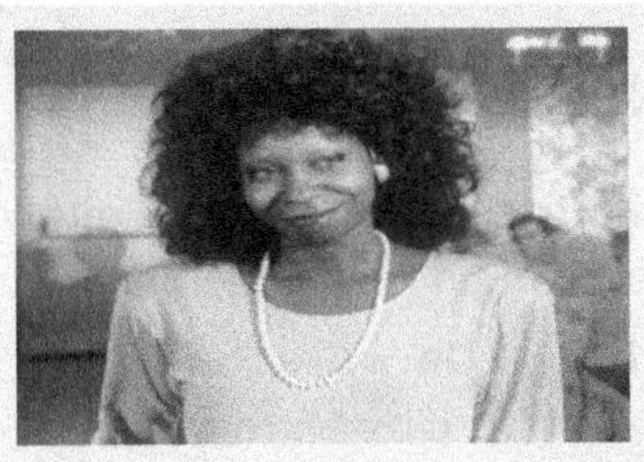

Whoopi Goldberg asked Glenn Gordon Caron if she could guest star on the show, but also asked if she could star with her friend Judd Nelson. Of course, Glenn obliged. Whoopi is an American actor who has been in over 150 films. She is also a comedian, television personality, and author.

She has been the recipient of numerous accolades and is one of only eighteen entertainers to win the EGOT, (Emmy, Grammy, Academy, and Tony awards.)

Her breakthrough year was in 1985 when she received a Golden Globe Award for Best Actress in a Motion Picture for her role as Celie in *The Color Purple* (Movie, 1985). In 1990, Whoopi received an Academy Award for Best Supporting Actress for her role as the eccentric psychic in the romantic fantasy film *Ghost* (Movie, 1990), (which also starred Bruce Willis's wife at the time, Demi Moore). She starred in the hit comedy *Sister Act* (Movie, 1992) and in the sequel, *Sister Act 2: Back in the Habit* (Movie, 1993), becoming the highest-paid actress at the time.

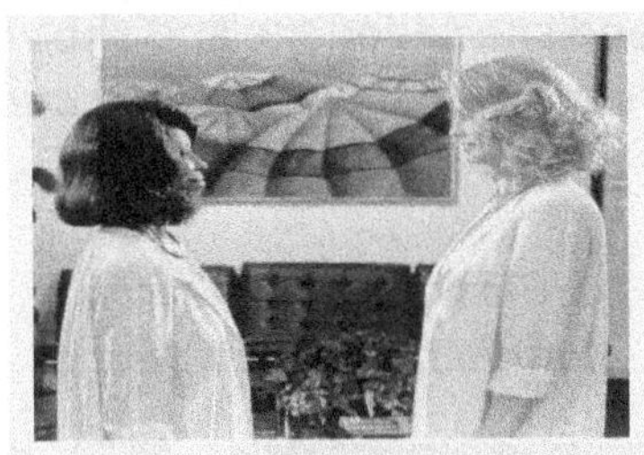

*Camille trying her best to fit in around Blue Moon.*

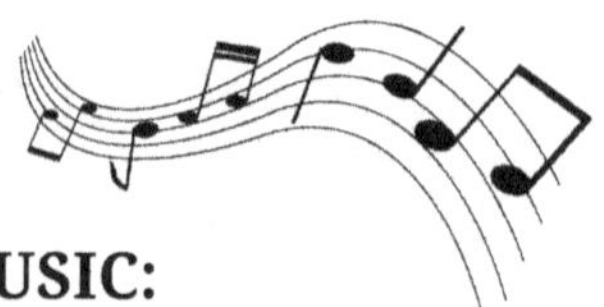

## ORIGINAL MUSIC:

**"For He's a Jolly Good Fellow"**
French origin from the 18th Century

**"Happy Days Are Here Again"**
Music by Milton Ager
Lyrics by Jack Yellen
*(Replaced with new music on Hulu streaming)*

**"Devil with a Blue Dress On"**
Written by Shorty Long and William "Mickey" Stevenson
Performed by Mitch Ryder & the Detroit Wheels

**"Good Golly Miss Molly"**
Written by Bumps Blackwell and John Marascalco
Performed by Mitch Ryder
*(Replaced with new music on Hulu streaming)*

**"Hooray for Hollywood"**
Music by Richard A. Whiting,
Lyrics by Johnny Mercer
*(Replaced with new music on Hulu streaming)*

**"The Magnificent Seven"**
Theme song of *The Magnificent Seven* (Movie, 1960)
Music by Elmer Bernstein
*(Replaced with new music on Hulu streaming)*

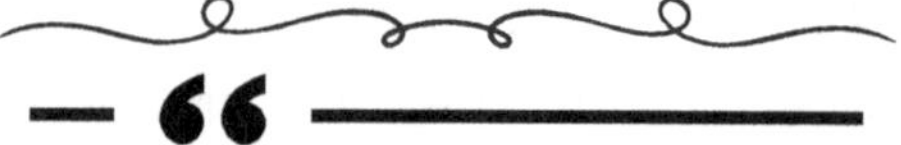

**I still remember Whoopi Goldberg had just been nominated for an Oscar for *The Color Purple,* and she called me and she went, *"I'd like to be on your show. Oh, and can I bring my friend Judd Nelson?"***

*~Glenn Gordon Caron*
*Moonlighting the Podcast*

## CAST CREDITS

**Whoopi Goldberg** ... Camille Brand/Herself

**Judd Nelson** ... The Bad Cop/Himself

**Monty Ash** ... Mordecai "Mordy" Mishienski

**David Paymer** ... Camille's Agent

**Edie McClurg** ... Beauty Parlor Customer

**Gerry Gibson** ... Minister

**Leigh Webb** ... The Assistant Director

**Eve Smith** ... Resident

**Sid Kane** ... Resident

**J.P. Bumstead** ... Stage Manager

**Michael Francis Clarke** ... Senator

**Marianne Muellerleile** ... Beauty Salon Customer

**Danna Hansen** ... Beauty Salon Customer

**Betty Bunch** ... Beauty Salon Customer

**Billy Barty** ... Himself

**Mik One** ... Scar-faced man

**Lawrence Trimble** ... Prop Man

**Ray O'Connor** ... Bad Cowboy

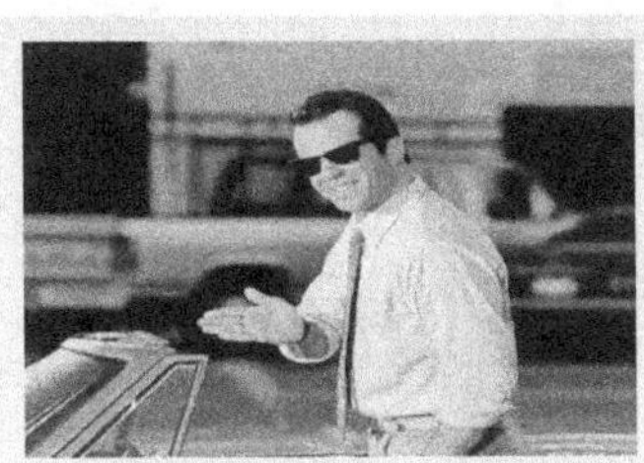
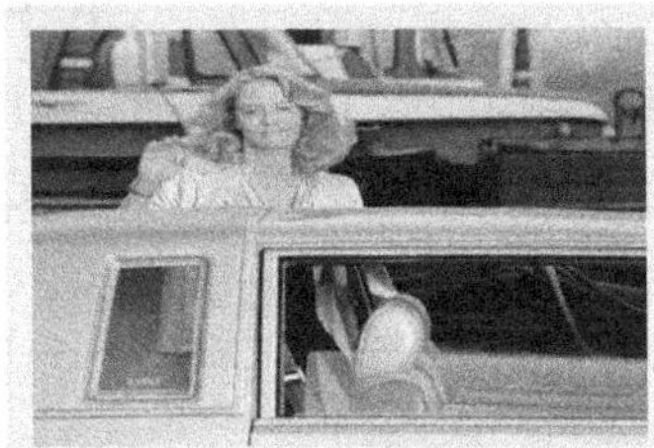

*After deciding "it'll keep 'til the Fall," Maddie and David get into Cybill and Bruce's real-life cars and drive off the studio lot...blurring the lines yet again between the characters and the stars.*

# S03 E01
# The Son Also Rises

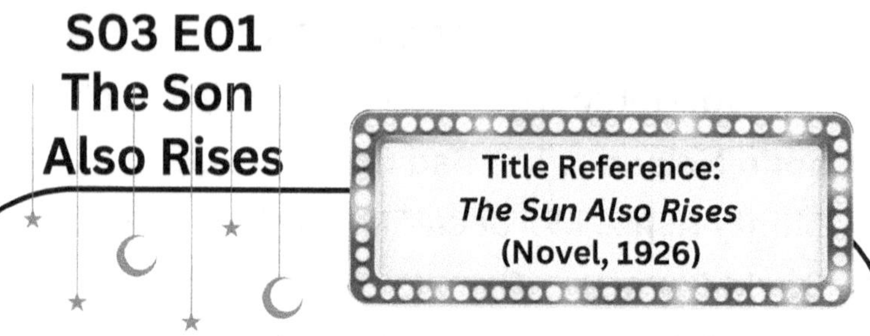

**Title Reference:**
*The Sun Also Rises*
(Novel, 1926)

**Plot:**

Blue Moon has been on a two-week break for the holidays, and everyone has returned from their vacations. David arrives still in holiday mode from Mexico. Sensing the workers' dismay at being back at work, he immediately gets the Wobblies in a festive mood by singing "La Bamba" before paying Maddie a visit in her office. David's father, David Addison Sr. (Paul Sorvino), arrives in town to tell his son that he is getting married and he would like David to be his best man.

David is very happy for him until he finds out that he knows his father's bride to be. David had a one-night stand (actually a three-night stand) with this woman several years ago and goes all out to avoid coming face-to-face with her. This causes friction between father and son, so David Sr. asks Richie (Charles Rocket) to be best man instead of David. David decides to interrupt the ceremony to speak to Stephanie, the bride to be, in private. During this conversation, David is surprised to learn that after all this, she does not remember him at all.

**Air Date:**
September 23, 1986

**Written by:**
Jeff Reno and
Ron Osborn

**Director:** Allan Arkush

## CAST CREDITS

**Paul Sorvino** ... David Addison Sr.

**Charles Rocket** ... Richard Addison

**Brynn Thayer** ... Stephanie

**F.J. O'Neill** ... The Minister

**Duncan McLeod** ... Stephanie's Father

**Edith Fields** ... Dolores

**Susan Brabeau** ... Miss Parrish

**Agnes Rhyme:**
Blue Moon Detective Agency, have things gone awry? Is it solutions you seek? We're eager to help, but we're closed a few weeks, so if you're despondent and your life's out of whack, we hope you're still troubled when we all get back.

**Landlord:** I am not amused by your trip out of state, this is your landlord, the rent's two week's late, your toilet's backed up, and the place smells like heck, if you want me to fix it, then send me a check.

## CONTINUITY #1:
David tells Maddie he "won" Stephanie *three* years ago . . . but then, a few minutes later, Maddie says, *"But David, that was four years ago . . . "*

## CONTINUITY #2:
When David enters Maddie's office, one of the furry dice falls off his sombrero. Yet when he takes the hat off and puts it on a chair a moment later, it has two dice again.

## CONTINUITY #3:
At the party, Maddie calls a cab, leaving David with the car. When she leaves work the next day, she goes to the car in the garage (even though David had the car and she hasn't seen him all day). She gets in the car and doesn't question why music is blaring from the stereo.

**STATS:**

*Door Slams: 6*
*Feet out of Elevator: 2*
*Maddie's Outfit Changes: 8*
*Agnes Rhymes: 1*

**GREAT LINES:**

**Maddie:** *Missed you.*

**David:** *What was that?*

**Maddie:** *You heard me.*

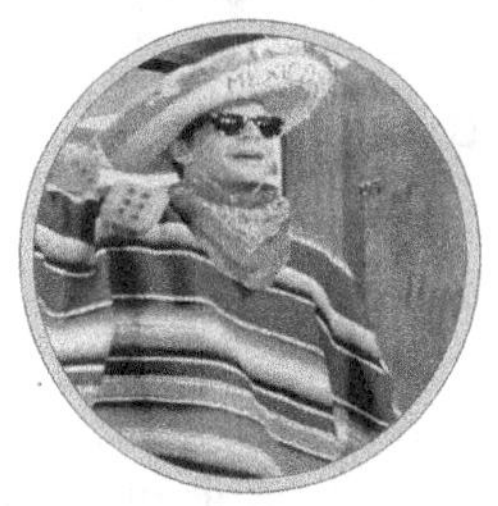

**TITLE (SPOILER ALERT):**
"The Son Also Rises" also refers to the idea of father and son sleeping with the same woman.

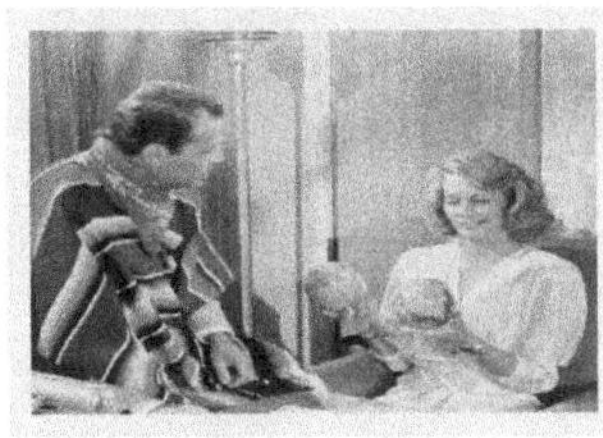

*"I told the saleslady you already had nice maracas, but . . . [knock on door] word must be out; bet that's somebody that wants to see you shake 'em."*

**LOOK FOR #1:**
Blue Moon has a new front door with a mail slot.

**REVEALING MISTAKE #1:**
The answering machine message stops playing while Maddie isn't pressing any buttons.

**REVEALING MISTAKE #2:**
At Stephanie's mom's house, David crawls/runs right to the bathroom, although he's never been to this house before!

**REVEALING MISTAKE #3:**
David punches Richie, and a moment later his eye is black and blue.

**FUN FACT #1:**
Allan Arkush directed the most episodes of *Moonlighting*, starting with s02e17, "Funeral for a Door Nail," and ending with s05e04, "Plastic Fantastic Lovers." He directed twelve episodes total.

**FAMILY TIES:**
This is the first time we meet David's father, David Addison Sr., played by Paul Sorvino.

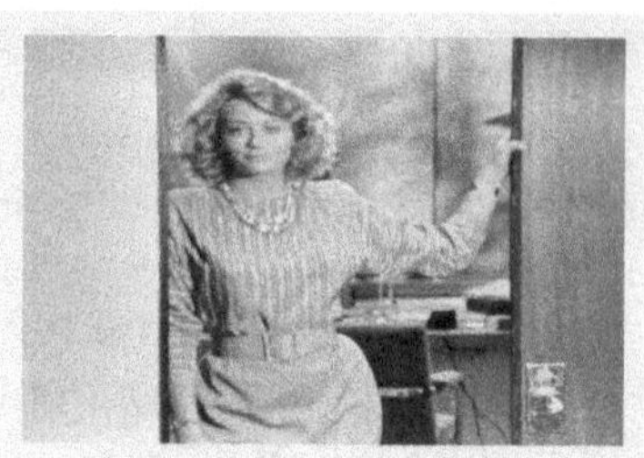

*Grace's favorite of Maddie's outfits.*

**OUTFIT ROLE CALL:**
- Maddie wears the gray skirt and striped blouse again in s05e11, "In 'n Outlaws."
- The blue dress she wore in s02e08, "Portrait of Maddie," and again in s03e02, "The Man Who Cried Wife."
- The nightgown she wore in s02e07, "Somewhere Under the Rainbow"; s02e15, "Witness for the Execution"; and later in s03e11, "Blonde on Blonde."
- She wears the pink robe in s03e11, "Blonde on Blonde."

**FUN FACT #2:**
This is the first episode in which Jamie (Jamie Taylor) is part of the Blue Moon staff!

**CONTINUITY #4:**
During the wedding, the priest calls "Stephanie," "Stephen."

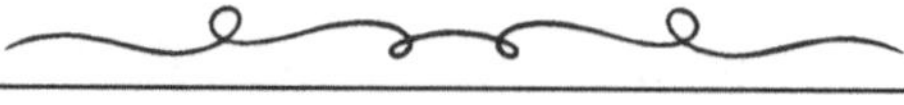

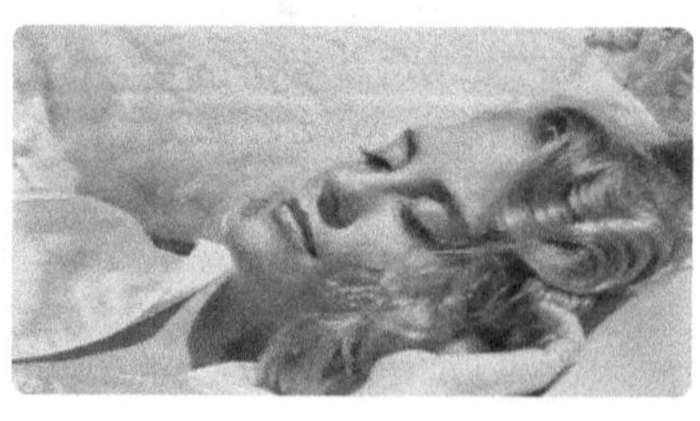

**LOOK FOR #2:**
The clip of Maddie lying in bed was taken from s02e14, "Every Daughter's Father Is a Virgin."

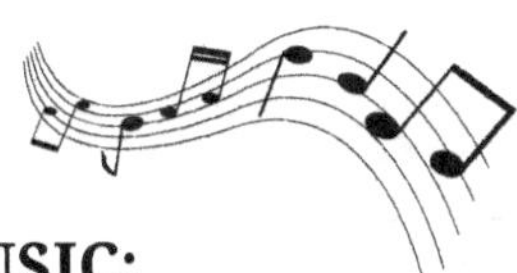

## ORIGINAL MUSIC:

**"La Bamba"**
Written by Ritchie Valens
Performed by Ritchie Valens

**"It's a Small World (After All)"**
Written by Robert B. Sherman
and Richard M. Sherman

**"Whistle While You Work"**
Written by Frank Churchill and Larry Morey

**"Yankee Rose"**
Written by David Lee Roth and Steve Vai
Performed by David Lee Roth
*(Replaced with new music on Hulu streaming)*

**"Sweet Love"**
Written by Anita Baker,
Louis A. Johnson and Gary Blas
Performed by Anita Baker
*(Replaced with new music on Hulu streaming)*

**"Powerhouse"**
Composed by Raymond Scott
Whistled by Bruce Willis

**"(They Long to Be) Close to You"**
Written by Burt Bacharach and Hal David

**"Moon River"**
Written for *Breakfast at Tiffany's* (Movie, 1961)
Written by Johnny Mercer
Music by Henry Mancini

**"Ave Maria"**
Composed by Franz Schubert

**"The Bridal Chorus"**
Composed by Richard Wagner

**"Tequila"**
Written by Chuck Rio
Performed by Bruce Willis

# S03 E02
# The Man
# Who Cried Wife

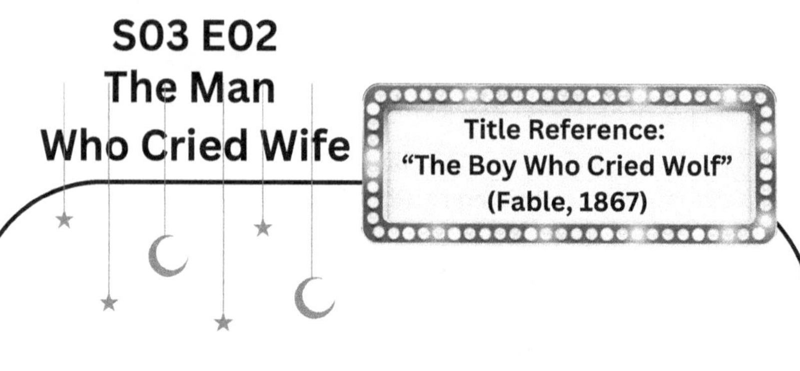


**Plot:**

James Bower "spontaneously" kills his wife in the heat of the moment during an argument. He buries her near their log cabin in the woods. But the next day, she begins harassing him with threatening phone calls. Bower goes back to the woods to check on the body but it's gone. So he decides to approach Blue Moon to help him find her.

However, he doesn't tell Maddie and David that he killed her (or thought he killed her) during an argument. After some heated debate about whether or not to take on the case of a man who would strike his wife, and a fight of their own, Maddie and David track down the woman. However, during a car chase she seemingly drives over a cliff and dies again.

**Air Date:** September 30, 1986

**Written by:** Kerry Ehrin

**Director:** Christian I. Nyby II

**CAST CREDITS**

**Jack Blessing** ... MacGillicudy (recurring character)
**Stephen Godwin** ... James Bower
**Alley Mills** ... Claire
**Patricia Duff** ... Melissa Dower
**Richard Tyson** ... Daniel
**John Bower** ... Funeral Man
**Read Morgan** ... Funeral Man
**Constance Pfeifer** ... Funeral Woman
**Jensen Collier** ... Funeral Woman

**REVEALING MISTAKE #1:**
Visible string lifting the newspaper as David snores.

**REVEALING MISTAKE #2:**
In the last scene of the episode, when David and Maddie walk into Blue Moon, David never inserts his key into the lock; he just wiggles it against the doorknob.

**REVEALING MISTAKE #3:**
The crew lights are reflected in David's sunglasses.

**REVEALING MISTAKE #4:**
Obvious body doubles for Bruce and Cybill in the front seat of the car during the chase when the camera focuses on Bower in the back.

**CONTINUITY:**
In the opening scene when everyone in the office is toasting with champagne, Maddie has two Styrofoam cups (stacked); then, in the next cut, there is only one.

**PHRASE THAT REPEATS:**
The phrase "for the love of Mike" is used here in "The Man Who Cried Wife" as well as in s05e07, "I See England, I See France, I See Maddie's Netherworld"; s04e01, "A Trip to the Moon"; and s03e10, "Poltergeist III— Dipesto Nothing." Keep an ear out for it in these episodes!

**STATS:**

*Door Slams: 5*
*Feet out of Elevator: 0*
*Maddie's Outfit Changes: 4*
*Agnes Rhymes: 0*

**GREAT LINES:**

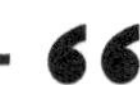

*Maddie:* No.
*David:* No?
*Maddie:* No! Yes, I mean no. Putting my foot down, standing my ground, digging my heels in.
*David:* Gonna create a lot of wear and tear on the old pumps.

**OUTFIT ROLE CALL:**
- Maddie wore the gray-blue dress in s02e08, "Portrait of Maddie," and s03e01, "The Son Also Rises."

**LOOK FOR #1:**
Cybill questioned if she was wearing a bra in s02e14, "Every Daughter's Father Is a Virgin," we question if she's wearing a bra when running back to the car at the motel?

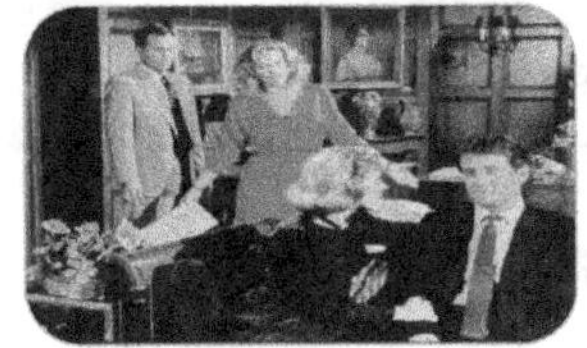

**LOOK FOR #2:**
Bruce's lips say, " . . . while you and the Mrs. were headboard **banging**," but it's been overdubbed to **bouncing**.

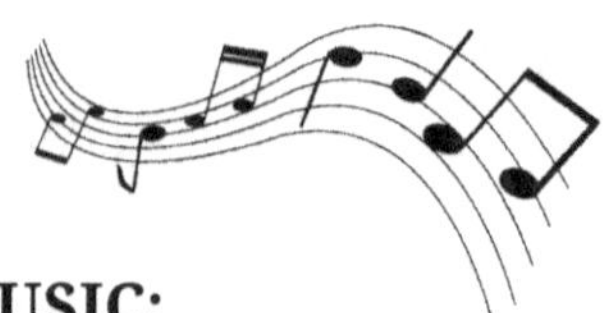

## ORIGINAL MUSIC:

**"Dedicated to the One I Love"**
Written by Ralph Bass and Lowman Pauling
Performed by the Shirelles
*(Replaced with new music on Hulu streaming)*

**"Waiting For a Girl Like You"**
Written by Mick Jones and Lou Gramm
Performed by Foreigner
*(Replaced with new music on Hulu streaming)*

---

## '80s ITEMS IN *MOONLIGHTING*

- Beepers
- Men wearing suits for every occasion
- Women wearing heels and dresses for every occasion
- Shoulder pads
- Boxy TVs & tiny computers
- Sony Walkman
- Oversized cellphones
- Answering machines
- Paper maps
- Phone booths
- Calculators with paper rolls
- Smoking indoors
- Dot matrix printing paper
- Cassettes
- VHS tapes
- Phone books

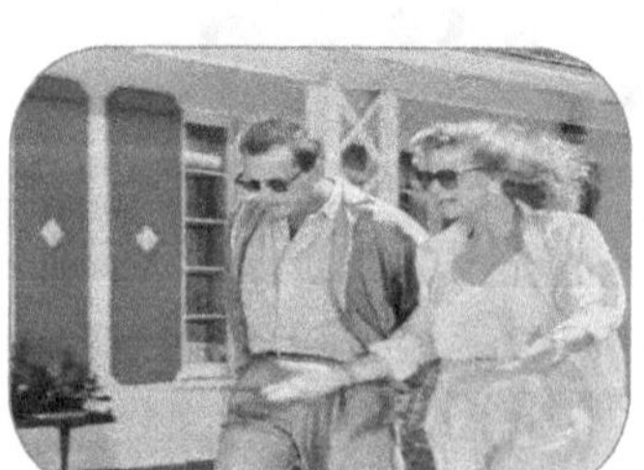

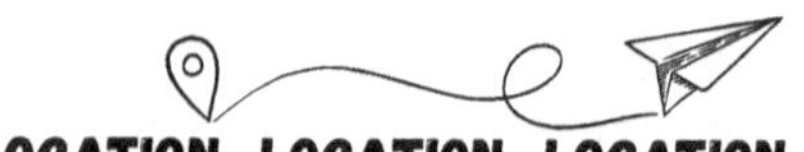

**LOCATION...LOCATION...LOCATION...**
~ **Sierra Pelona Motel** - 12117 Sierra Highway, Santa Clarita, California, USA

# S03 E03
# Symphony
# in Knocked Flat

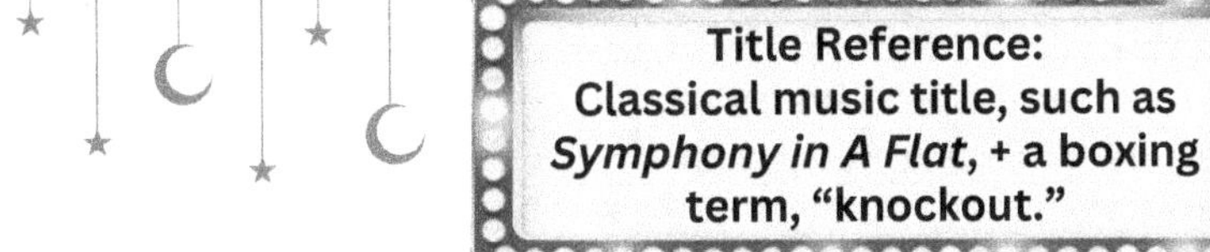

**Title Reference:**
Classical music title, such as
*Symphony in A Flat*, + a boxing
term, "knockout."

**Plot:**

Maddie's had it with dating—she has expectations that her suiters can't seem to meet. Upon hearing this, David challenges Maddie to take him out on a "fun" evening, and in return, he'll show her a "fine" evening. Later that day, David is desperate for theater tickets. He drives all around town looking for tickets but finds that they are all sold out.

He thinks his luck has changed when a scalper approaches him with two tickets to the symphony. Unfortunately for David, these tickets were robbed from a man who was involved in an assassination plot, and unbeknown to David, the tickets are not together—which affects their "fine evening" out.

Along the way, Maddie and David discover that there is an assassination plot that in a few hours will cause an international incident. The episode culminates with David being forced to take the place of one of the participants in a boxing match promoted by Don King, who makes a guest appearance.

This episode includes yet another "breaking the fourth wall" cold open, this one including the Temptations singing their hit song "Psychedelic Shack" as well as David talking Maddie into singing and dancing to the same song.

**Air Date:** October 14, 1986

**Written by:** Dale Gelineau and Pauline Turboff Miller

**Director:** Paul Lynch

## SPOOF:

*Rocky IV* (Movie, 1985)

The final scene, which involves a boxing match between David and the Russian boxer, Gabinov, mirrors the Balboa-Drago fight. The Rocky anthem can be heard, and there's even a Stallone look-alike cheering David on.

## REVEALING MISTAKE:

The ticket scalper sells David tickets that say C-2 and D-3 but at the theater, David is told his seat is 9-A by the usher.

## LOOK FOR #1:

When Maddie runs from the rental car, you can see a piece of paper taped underneath the steering wheel—possibly a script, as they used to catch up on time with car scenes. With the car on a tow car and the pages of the script taped to the dashboard, Cybill and Bruce could get through pages of dialogue quickly and in a controlled environment.

## LOOK FOR #2:

The full-length mirror in Maddie's room is sitting on bricks—possibly so that it was the right height for Cybill in the scene.

## CONTINUITY:

Maddie's handbag is suddenly no longer with her as the two walk toward the American dressing room.

## STATS:

*Door Slams: 12*
**Including the limousine door slam*
*Feet out of Elevator: 1*
*Maddie's Outfit Changes: 5*
*Agnes Rhymes: 0*

## GREAT LINES:

> **David:** *Where's the Russian dressing?*
>
> **Security:** *In the kitchen.*

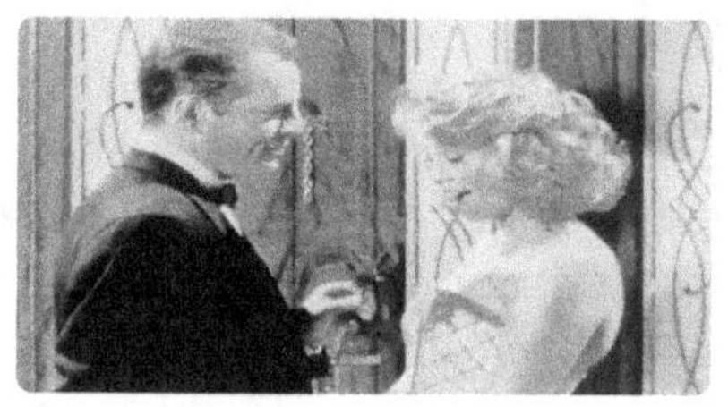

## OUTFIT ROLE CALL:

- Maddie wears the purple and white dress again in s05e05, "Shirts and Skins."

## BREAKING THE FOURTH WALL:

" . . . either somebody's lying or the writers just xeroxed the other scene."

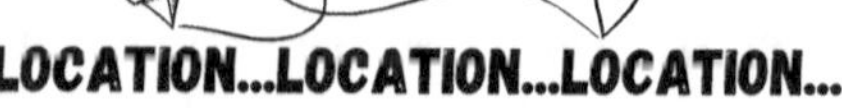

## LOCATION...LOCATION...LOCATION...

~ **Trinity Auditorium, Embassy Hotel (Symphony Venue)** - 851 South Grand Avenue, Los Angeles, California, USA

~ **Joe's Auto Parks (Murray's Parking)** - 812 South Grand Avenue, Los Angeles, USA

~ **Grand Olympic Auditorium (boxing ring)** - 1801 South Grand Avenue, Los Angeles, USA

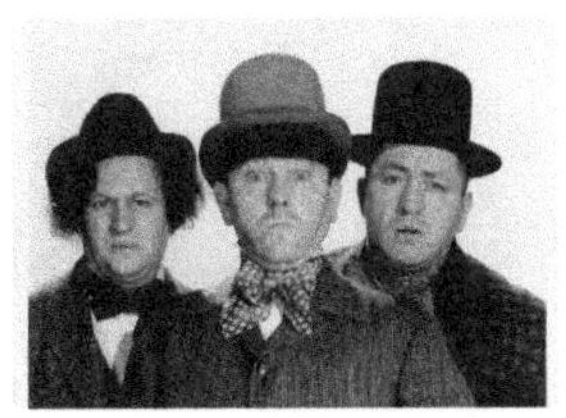

*The Three Stooges were a major influence on the comedy of the show.*

*The Three Stooges* obviously had a huge influence on the comedy of the show, as sound effects, references, and imitations are peppered throughout all five seasons. *Moonlighting the Podcast* asked Glenn Caron about this when he visited. Glenn shared with us that although the actors remained true to the pages of the script for the most part, these types of sound effects were something that they might ad-lib in the moment. During the commentary for s04e01 "A Trip to the Moon" Glenn and Bruce mention that *The Honeymooners* (TV Series, 1955-1956), *The Three Stooges* (TV Series, 1960-1972), and Bob Hope (American comedian and actor) were their "comedy touchstones." Bruce even credited The Three Stooges as three of the four people who inspired him to be an actor (along with Al Pacino) in the acceptance speech for the Primetime Emmy Award he won in 1987! Look for nods to the Stooges in s02e01, "Brother, Can You Spare a Blonde"; s02e09, "Atlas Belched"; s02e11, "The Bride of Tupperman"; s03e02, "The Man Who Cried Wife"; 03e07, "Atomic Shakespeare"; s04e11, "Eek! A Spouse!"; s05e03, "The Color of Maddie"; s05e08, "Those Lips, Those Lies"; and s05e09, "Perfetc," to name just a few!

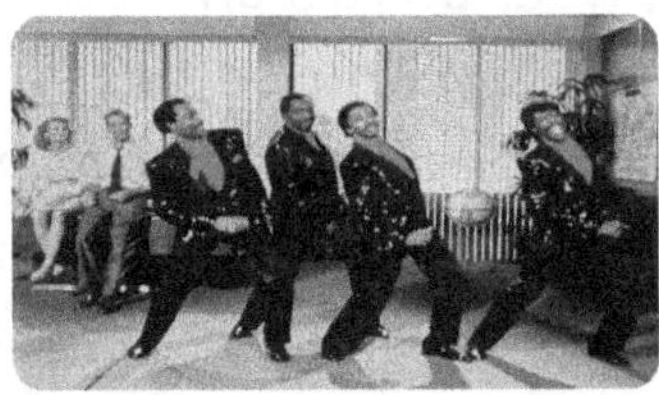

**The Temptations**
*Getting funky on* Moonlighting *with Maddie and David.*

---

### Art Mirroring Life

In January 1987, Bruce Willis put out his first studio album, titled *The Return of Bruno* (along with a mockumentary of the same name), on Motown Records. The Temptations sang background vocals on "Under the Boardwalk" on this album. So in true *Moonlighting* fashion, the cold open blurs the lines between the star's real life and the Blue Moon world, where David Addison is making a "funk video."

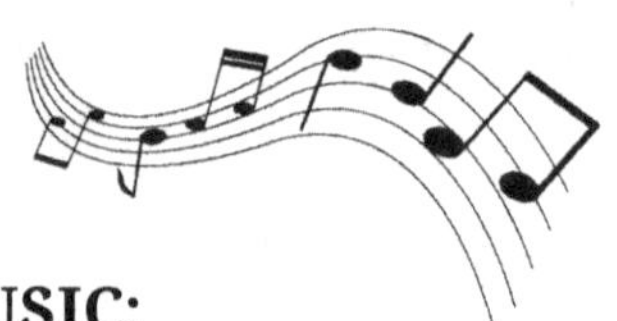

## ORIGINAL MUSIC:

**"Psychedelic Shack"**
Written by Barrett Strong and Norman Whitfield
Performed by the Temptations

**"Close to You"**
Written by Burt Bacharach and Hal David
*(Replaced with new music on Hulu streaming)*

---

## ON SCOUTING LOCATION...LOCATION...LOCATIONS FOR MOONLIGHTING...

*"You have a boxing scene, well, there's only so many places in LA you can go that's gonna be believable. Olympic Theatre is the first thing that comes to mind because that's where wrestling and boxing went on and whatnot, and that's what we ended up shooting, and it worked great. But that could have been a situation where it didn't work great or they wouldn't let you shoot there, and now where do you go? You'd probably end up having to create something onstage, which would be more expensive."*

*~Executive Producer Jay Daniel*
*Moonlighting the Podcast*

## CAST CREDITS

**Jan B. Daley** ... Agent Bellow

**Linda Thorson** ... Agent Gregory

**Will MacMillan** ... Agent Dayton

**Steve James** ... Mohammed "Boogaloo" Brown

**Tom McFadden** ... Agent Gibson

**Mario Roccuzzo** ... Ticket Seller

**Allan Kolman** ... Ticket Buyer

**Xander Berkeley** ... Scalper

**Jon Menick** ... Guard

**Ernie Banks** ... Boogaloo's Trainer

**E. Hampton Beagle** ... Theater Usher

**Lou Filippo** ... Referee

**Mae Marmy** ... Woman at Symphony

**Jade Roberts** ... Sly Stallone Impersonator

**Roderick Vann** ... Parking Attendant

### Special Guest Star

**Don King** ... Himself

## CONJURING UP DAVID ADDISON

We've all heard the story about how three thousand actors auditioned for the part of David Addison, but what was it that made Bruce Willis stand out and nab the role? Glenn Caron answered this question on *Moonlighting the Podcast*: "What we were looking for were two things. You had to be really good with language because the part was all about language. There's just tons of language, and as I said, Bruce immediately understood that it was musical, that there was a cadence to it because he's musical. And I could write a three-page monologue for him, and often did, at 6:30 in the morning, he'd come into work at 7:00, and by 7:45 he'd have it word perfect. Bruce also had this unbridled sexuality; he just was . . . a guy! Unapologetically a guy."

# S03 E04
# Yours,
# Very Deadly

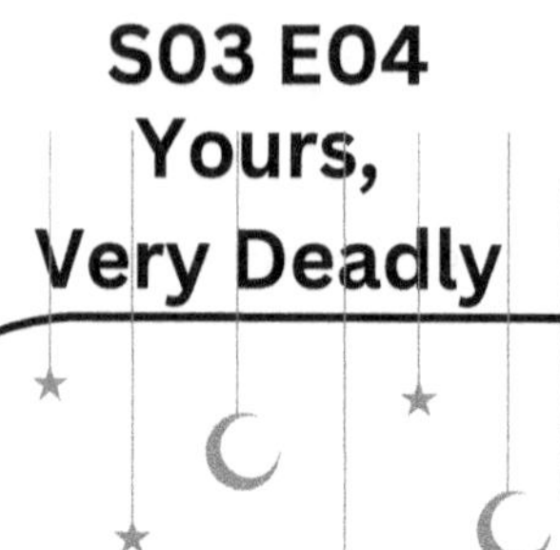



## Plot:

Gail Woodley approaches Blue Moon to help find a man whom she has been corresponding with behind her husband's back. Gail confesses that at first, getting attention from this man was fun, but now he's gotten serious and controlling. Woodley wants Maddie and David to contact this man and inform him that the letter writing must now stop.

While Maddie and David are investigating the case, Gail and her admirer, Peter Macy, die. She is murdered, and Macy jumps out of the window of his apartment. However, Maddie and David believe there is more to this "murder-suicide" than first appears.

This episode introduces a new character to the *Moonlighting* Team, Herbert Viola, played by Curtis Armstrong (uncredited in this episode), who will become the love interest of Miss Dipesto.

**Air Date:** October 28, 1986

**Written by:** Roger Director

**Director:** Christian I. Nyby II

### CAST CREDITS

**Paul Roebling** ... Ken Woodley
**Brooke Bundy** ... Gail Woodley
**Curtis Armstrong**... Herbert Viola (Uncredited)
**Martin Ferrero** ... Peter Macy
**John Kassir** ... Detective
**Chino "Fats" Williams** ... Postal Worker
**Mike Narz** ... Blue Moon Staff
**C. Thomas Howell** ... Postal Worker

### Maddie's "Last Will and Testament"

*(Written while sitting in the post office)*

*"I being of sound mind execute this last will and testament on this 24th day of October 1986. I leave my house to my husband David and my six children. My car I leave to my mother in the hope that she will not get as many speeding tickets as I have gotten . . . "*

*(David interrupts her and she stops writing.)*

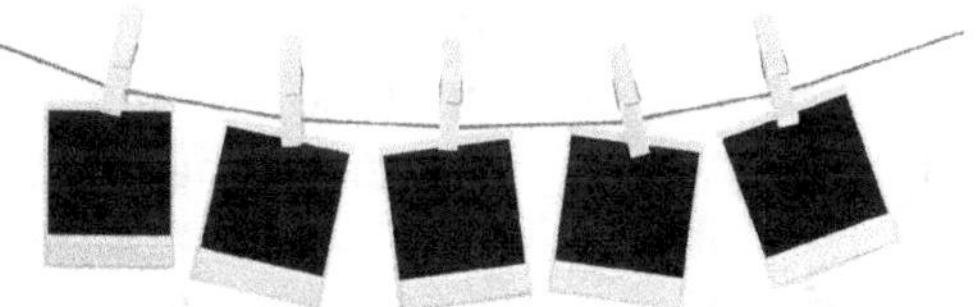


**OUTFIT ROLE CALL:**

- Maddie wore the pink dress/silky blazer combo in s02e09, "Atlas Belched," and s02e15, "Witness for the Execution."
- She wore the striped yellow dress in s02e15, "Witness for the Execution."

## On location: from our personal photo archive

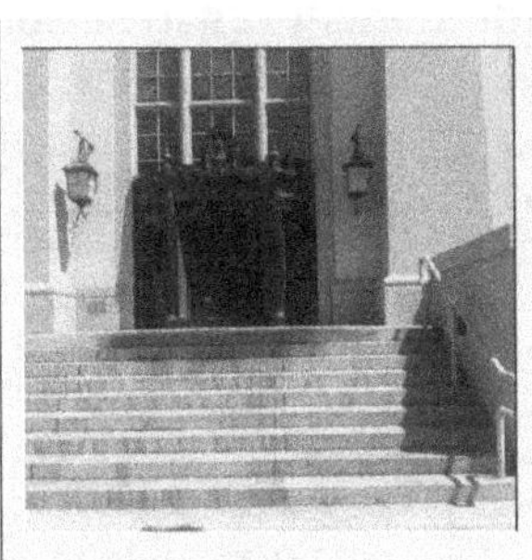

*Post Office: Exterior*

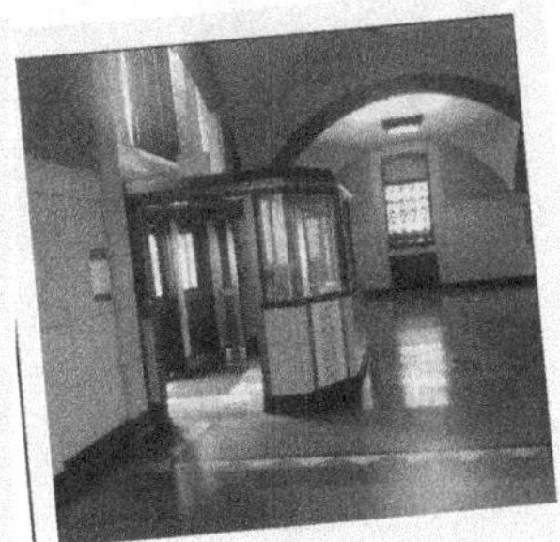

*Post Office: Interior*

## CONTINUNITY:

The car scene on the way to the post office was obviously filmed at two different times. Maddie's hair changes midway through the scene, and on David's line "All right, I give up, what's with you today?" the camera angle changes slightly (as evident by the headrest behind him), his tie is done up higher, and he's chewing gum.

**LOOK FOR #1:**
Actor C. Thomas Howell makes a cameo appearance in this episode as a postal employee.

**LOOK FOR #2:**
The clock insert is an analogue clock, not Blue Moon's usual digital clock.

**LOOK FOR #3:**
Bruce's and Cybill's stunt doubles run from behind the pillar to take over the chase scene at the post office.

**FUN FACT:**
Guest star Paul Roebling, is the great-grandson of John Roebling, designer of the Brooklyn Bridge.

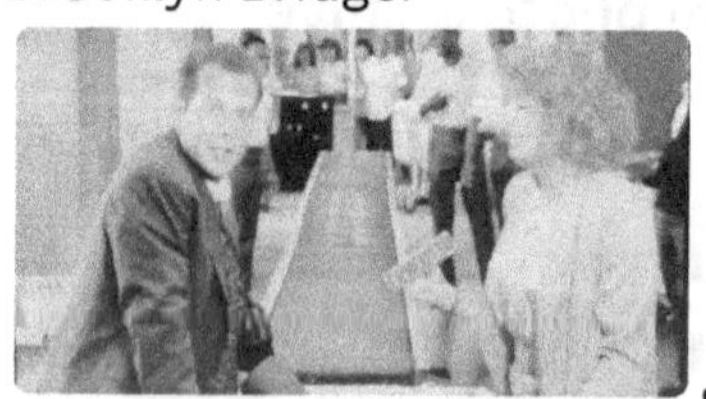

*"I'd still rather end the show with her legs in the air."*

**LOOK FOR #4:**
Cybill is holding the *cancelled* stamp backwards, yet when she stamps Mr. Woodley's behind, it's stamped correctly.

## STATS:

*Door Slams: 6*
*Feet out of Elevator: 1*
*Maddie's Outfit Changes: 7*
*Agnes Rhymes: 0*

### GREAT LINES:

**Maddie:** *Kick it or I'll kick you!*

*(David kicks door in)*

**David:** *(to camera) Easy choice.*

### BREAKING THE FOURTH WALL:
David admits to the audience that he had to go to Mrs. Woodley's with Maddie because they *"still have half a show left."*

**LOOK FOR #5:**
Bruce Willis affectionately touching the face of one of the Blue Moon workers as he walks down the hall at the beginning of the episode. This girl is also the "zounds, what mounds" girl in s03e07, "Atomic Shakespeare," and is quite possibly also the girl inside the church in s03e01 "The Son Also Rises," who points David in the right direction. Her final appearance is in s03e11, "Blonde on Blonde," during the strip poker scene.

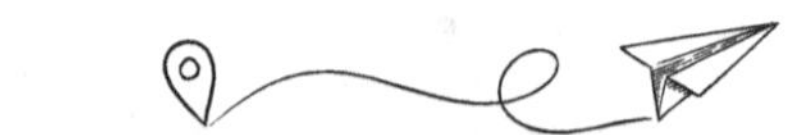

**LOCATION...LOCATION...LOCATION...**
**~ USPS Terminal Annex -**
900 North Alameda Street, Los Angeles, California, USA

# BURT/BERT—WHAT'S IN A NAME?

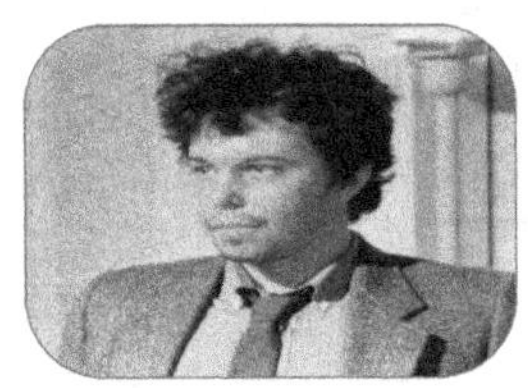

There's a bit of a continuity issue with Herbert's shortened name when he begins getting credit for his role on *Moonlighting* (he is not credited here, in his first appearance on the show). However, in s03e05, "All Creatures Great and . . . Not So Great," he's credited as Burt Viola, but in s03e07, "Atomic Shakespeare," it's spelled Bert Viola, though it's again spelled Burt Viola in s03e08, "It's a Wonderful Job." In subsequent episodes, everyone seemed to settle on Bert Viola. Welcome, Burt or Bert!

---

### GETTING TO KNOW YOU

As they had never met before, Allyce Beasley and Curtis Armstrong held up production for forty-five minutes in this episode, because their first scene was a kissing scene. They decided to go out for a little while to get to know each other first, before returning for the first cut.

---

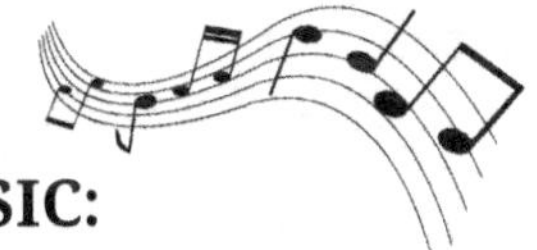

## ORIGINAL MUSIC:

### "Shake, Rattle and Roll"
Written by Charles F. Calhoun
Performed by Bruce Willis

### "The Syncopated Clock"
Composed by Leroy Anderson

### "Please Mr. Postman"
Written by Georgia Dobbins,
William Garrett, Freddie Gorman,
Brian Holland, and Robert Bateman
Performed by the Marvelettes
*(Replaced with new music on Hulu streaming)*

# S03 E05
# All Creatures Great and ... Not So Great



**Plot:**

Father McDonovan, a Catholic priest, falls in love with a woman who comes to confession on a regular basis. In her last confession, she informs McDonovan that she thinks she wants to die. Worried, he chases after her when she leaves, but he is unable to catch up with her, seeing only her heels as she climbs into a taxi cab and drives away. McDonovan decides to hire Blue Moon to find this woman even though he doesn't know her name or even what she looks like.

During their investigation, Maddie and David track down the woman but are surprised to find that on the surface she seems to be happily married, which totally contradicts what the priest said. They are now in a dilemma about whether to tell McDonovan that she is married.

The woman apparently commits suicide, but Maddie solves the crime when she realizes that the woman couldn't have killed herself due to the length of the shotgun. So as always, Maddie and David are on the case to find the killer.

**Air Date:** November 11, 1986

**Teleplay by**:
Charles H. Eglee

**Story by:**
Eric Blakeney
Gene Miller
Charles H. Eglee

**Director:** Christian I. Nyby II

**Working Title**
**"Our Father, Who's Not in Heaven"**

**CAST CREDITS**

**Brad Dourif** ... Father McDonovan

**Richard Beymer** ... Ray Adamson

**Jessica Harper** ... Janine Dalton

**Stan Ross** ... Homeless Man

**Santos Morales** ... Father Estevez

**John Gallogly** ... Father

## FUN FACT #1:

The conniving husband in this episode is Richard Beymer, who played 'Tony' in the movie *West Side Story* (Movie, 1961).

## FUN FACT #2:

This episode was filmed after s02e06 "Big Man On Mulberry Street," but aired before it.

## CULTURAL REFERENCES:

~ *Rebel Without a Cause* (Movie, 1955) - Maddie calls David "a rebel without a clue."

~ *The Exorcist* (Movie, 1973) - David mentions "projectile vomiting" from this movie.

## REVEALING MISTAKE #1:

While Father McDonovan is explaining his problem, he mentions that because of his vow, he cannot disclose why it is important he finds the location of the woman. Later on, Maddie and David discuss the woman's desire to commit suicide, although we never saw them obtain this information.

## REVEALING MISTAKE #2:

In the end scene, the priest calls Mrs. Adamson Alisse instead of Alicia.

## OUTFIT ROLE CALL:

- Maddie wears the pink/peach-colored dress again in s05e05, "Shirts and Skins."
- She wears the white raincoat (from the end of the episode) again in s03e13, "Maddie's Turn to Cry," and s03e14, "I Am Curious . . . Maddie."

## STATS:

*Door Slams: 2*
*Feet out of Elevator: 2*
*Maddie's Outfit Changes: 5*
*Agnes Rhymes: 0*

## " GREAT LINES:

*David:* Oh, ho ho ho ho . .

*Maddie:* What oh ho ho ho ho? "

## FUN FACT #3:

The church used in this episode is also used in s03e07, "Atomic Shakespeare."

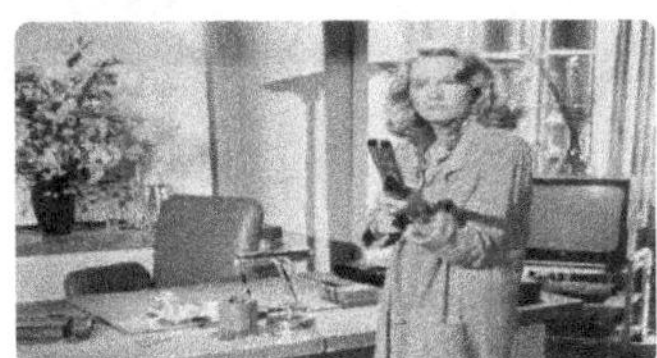

*Shawna's favorite Maddie outfit of the series.*

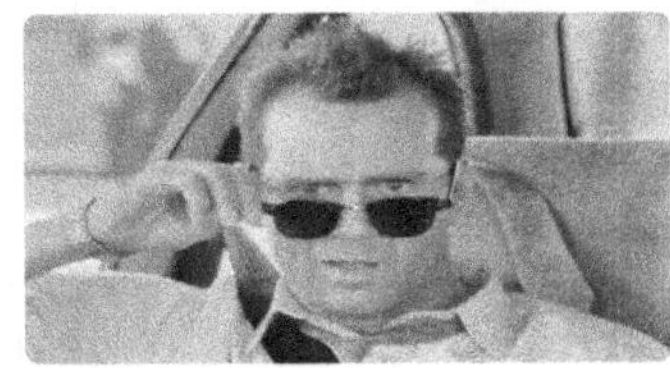

## CONTINUITY:

The sign at the beginning says the mission/church is called Our Lady of Sorrows, but the priest and Maddie later call it Our Lady of Sorrow.

## LOCATION...LOCATION...LOCATION...

~ **St. John's Episcopal Cathedral** - 514 West Adams Boulevard, Los Angeles, California, USA

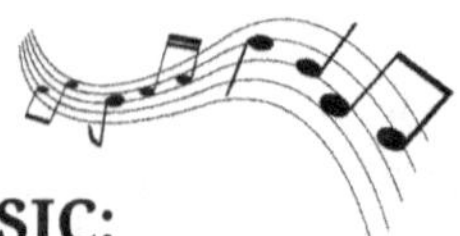

# ORIGINAL MUSIC:

**"All Creatures of Our God and King"**
Hymn written by William Henry Draper
**"Girl Watcher"**
Written by Ronald B. Killette and Wayne Pittman
Performed by Bruce Willis

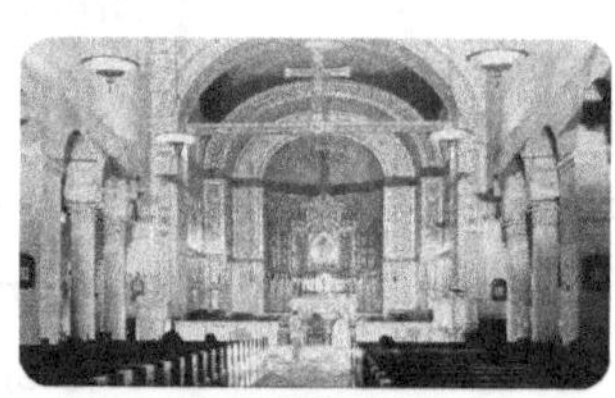

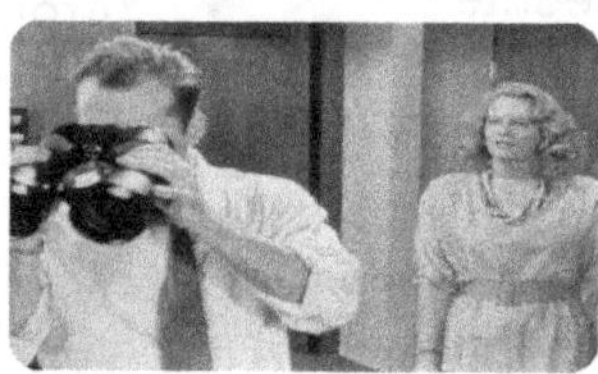

*On Robert Turturice*
*Moonlighting Costume Designer*

Turturice gave [Cybill] a wonderful look. Again, that gave another level of credence to the show. Those kinds of little things in a show like this can make a big difference. You never know why they tune in, but when you dress her, you dress her as well as you possibly can, have her look as good as you possibly can. You need somebody like Bob Turturice who can tell her, "You look better in that than in that, so you're gonna wear *that*." That was him; they had that relationship, and that worked great. She trusted him.

*~Jay Daniel*
*Moonlighting the Podcast*

# S03 E06
# Big Man on Mulberry Street



**Plot:**

Maddie is furious when David shows up late, hung over, and without the picture they promised a client in hand. Back at Blue Moon, they get into an argument about Maddie not being able to depend on David.

Later, David informs Maddie that he has to leave town for a few days for a funeral, and drops a bomb on her—he's been married before. Maddie, shocked by the news David told her before he left, has a dream depicting how she thinks the events in David's past life unfolded.

Maddie decides to follow him to New York; David is happy to see her but does not want to take her to the funeral. She decides to attend anyway. Once there, she finds that David never showed up to the funeral, but she does meet his ex-wife, who gives Maddie some conflicting information about why their relationship ended.

This is one of *Moonlighting*'s most iconic episodes and includes a lengthy dance number set to Billy Joel's song "Big Man on Mulberry Street." The dance sequence depicts Maddie's dream about the relationship between David and his ex-wife; however, she includes herself in it too. The dance number, featuring the talents of accomplished dancer Sandahl Bergman, took four days to shoot, with choreography by Jacqui and Bill Landrum.

**Air Date:** November 18, 1986

**Written by:** Karen Hall

**Director:** Christian I. Nyby II

**REVEALING MISTAKE #1:**
The timeline doesn't work for Maddie to leave LA in the middle of the night and be in David's NYC hotel room by the time he returns from the bar.

**REVEALING MISTAKE #2:**
The hotel clerk wouldn't give Maddie the room next to David's until he says it's okay, but she's somehow inside his room on the bed.

**LOOK FOR:** 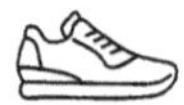
When Maddie runs toward David's office, she's wearing heels, but once inside she has sneakers on. She's also in sneakers on the fire escape with Tess.

## LOCATION...LOCATION...LOCATION...

~ **High's Restaurant** - Century City, California, USA  (now closed).
~ **New York, New York**



**GREAT LINES:**
— 66 —
*I was sorta related to him for a while. I was sorta married to his sister.*
**~David Addison**
— 99 —

**CONTINUITY:**
The position of Maddie's hand changes from one angle to another while she is lying in bed just before the dream.

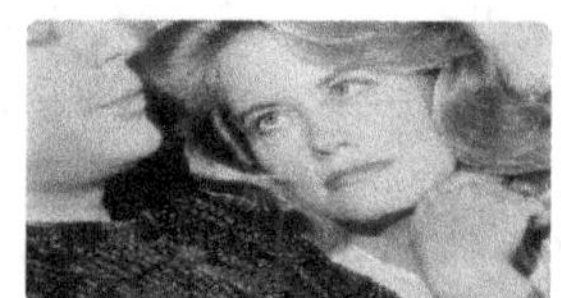

*Maddie ponders returning David's shoulder twenty or thirty years from now.*

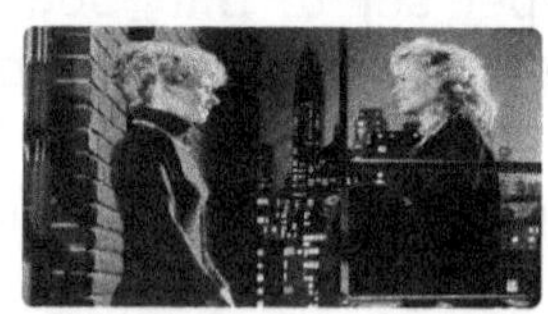

## Beginning of the end?

Cybill works her way through the scene above after a well-documented spat on the set between her and Glenn. Agents and lawyers were summoned the next day, and lines were drawn. Eventually, the network was forced to choose between the creator and the star. The network did not want to lose the star of Its hit show. Therefore, after the fourth season, Glenn moved on to other projects and had less involvement with *Moonlighting.* "And the Flesh Was Made Word," s04e14, was the last episode Glenn executive produced, and "A Womb with a View," s05e01, was the last episode he wrote.

**REVEALING MISTAKES #3:**
When Maddie leaves her bathroom and presses the light switch, the light turns off just before she fully touches the switch.

**OUTFIT ROLE CALL:**
- Maddie wore the gray top with the pink flowers in s01e05, "Next Stop Murder."
- She wears the pink pajama set again in s03e12, "Sam and Dave."

## CULTURAL REFERENCES:

- **Broyhill Dinette Set** - David acting as host of the game show in which you might win furniture from this company.
- **Sunoco** - A chain of American gas stations.
- **Greenwich Village** - A neighborhood in New York City.
- **Bruce Springsteen** - American singer-songwriter and guitarist.
- **Charlie Brown** - Character in the "Peanuts" comic strip.
- **Abraham Lincoln** - Tess calls David "honest Abe," a reference to U.S. President Abraham Lincoln.
- **Dolly Parton** - An American singer-songwriter and musician.
- **Groucho Marx** - One of the Marx Brothers comedy team.

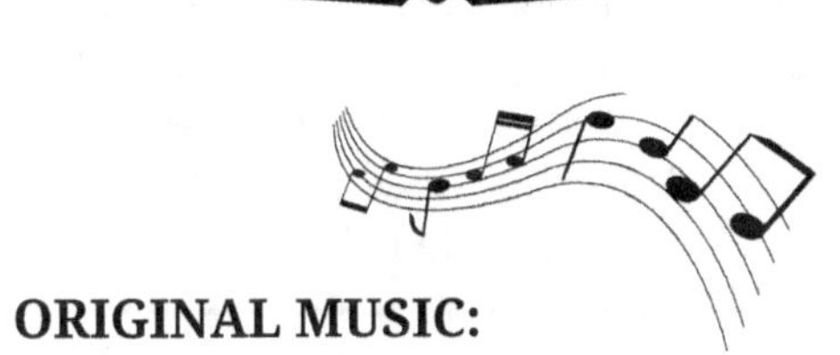

## ORIGINAL MUSIC:

**"Big Man on Mulberry Street"**
Written and performed by Billy Joel
Produced by Phil Ramone

**"New York State of Mind"**
Written and performed by Billy Joel

**"Good Morning"**
Music by Nacio Herb Brown
*(Replaced with new music on Hulu streaming)*

**"Top Cat"**
Theme song of *Top Cat* (TV Series, 1961–1962)
Composed by Hoyt Curtin
Performed by Bruce Willis,
Allan Katz (II), Bill Applegate and friends

# "THE DANCE SHOW"

Glenn Caron and Jay Daniel referred to this episode as "The Dance Show" and began planning it in July 1986. Glenn had already approached Jay about doing a show of this type at the end of season two. With no scripts in the pipeline at this time, production had to shut down for a week, so they used the time to rehearse the dance sequence. The first scene in the restaurant was the first scene shot. The production designer James Agazzi, designed the set by giving it a 50s look. His inspiration came from the dance sequences of Cyd Charisse, where she would dance in front of painted backgrounds. If you watch the dance sequence between Cyd Charisse and Gene Kelly in "Singing in the Rain" you will see the similarities between this episode and the movie, especially in relation to the painted background. The episode took nine days to shoot, and when it aired, it was ranked number seven for the week.

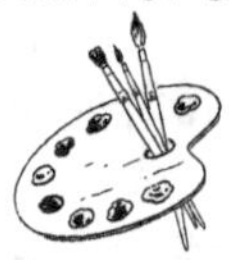

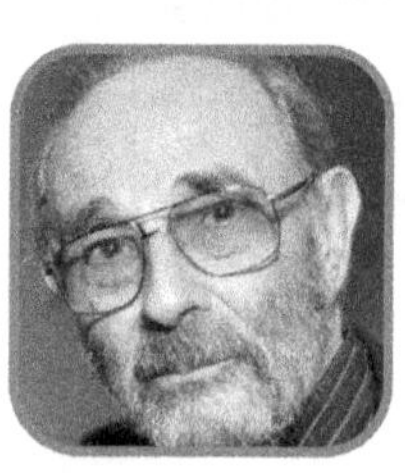

The legendary Stanley Donen directed the seven-minute dance in Maddie's dream, which brings to life her ideas about David's marriage and divorce. The number is accompanied by an extended version of the Billy Joel song of the same name as the episode title.

— ● —

## CAST CREDITS

**Andra Akers** ... Mrs. Kendrick
**Sandahl Bergman**
...David's Ex-wife (in the dream dance sequence)
**Marilyn Jones** ... Tess
**Rick Ducommun** ... Rick
**Betty McGuire** ... Rosemary
**Radu Gavor** ... Cab Driver
**Michael Laskin** ... Dancer
**Allan Katz (II)** ... David's Friend
**Bill Applegate** ... Bill (David's Friend)

**Special guest director:**
**Stanley Donen**

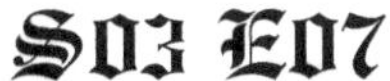
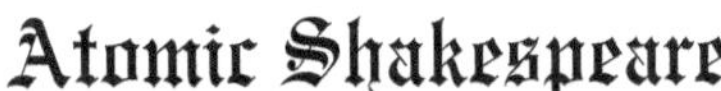

# S03 E07
## Atomic Shakespeare

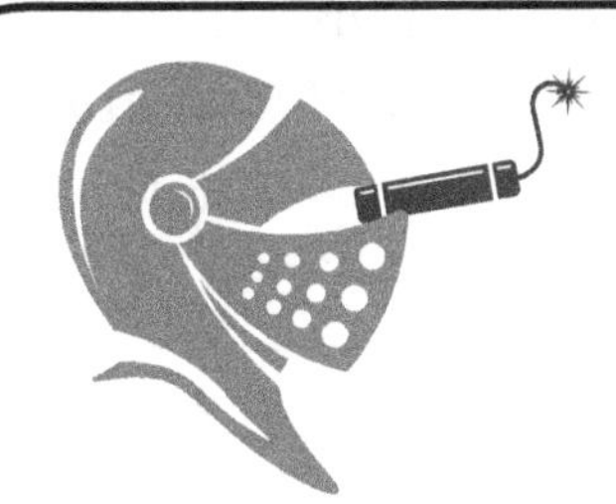



**Plot:**

At the beginning of this episode, a teenage "Moonlighting" fan is forced by his mother to do his homework rather than watch the show. His homework is to read William Shakespeare's "The Taming of the Shrew."'

As he is reading the book, the show transforms back in time to a day in Padua, Italy, in 1593. The main characters of "Moonlighting" enact the remainder of the show with their version of William Shakespeare's play "The Taming of the Shrew" in period costume and setting.

Katherina's father is in search of a suitor for his feisty daughter. Along the way, there are many in-jokes that refer to the real show, such as when Petruchio, played by David Addison, arrives in town on horseback with a BMW logo clearly visible on the saddle.

Eventually, Petruchio forcibly marries Katherina while she is tied up in a church, after which he sings a rockin' version of "Good Lovin'." He marries her for her dowry. But Katherina's father's terms of the marriage are that Petruchio must tame his bride into a dutiful and well-trained wife.

The couple fight, slam doors, and provide us with the usual fast-paced dialogue, but finally fall in love. Petruchio tames Katherina, but Katherina also tames Petruchio, as shown in a touching scene in the town square.

Writers:
Jeff Reno and Ron Osborn

Air Date: November 25, 1986

Director: Will Mackenzie

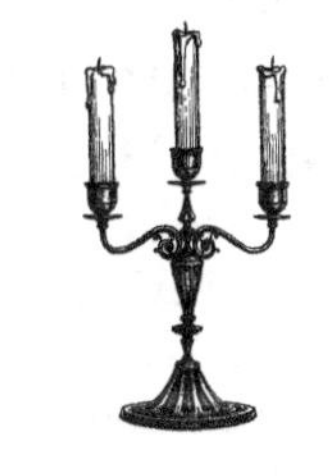

**Sterling Holloway** ... Narrator
**Kenneth McMillan** ... Baptista
**Curtis Armstrong** ... Lucentio
**Colm Meaney** ... Suitor
**Ralph Drischell** ... Minister
**Joseph G. Medalis** ... Second Townsman
**Hap Lawrence** ... The Bishop
**Daniel Frishman** ... Suitor
**Danny Stone** ... Suitor
**Frank Collison** ... Padua Resident
**Raymond Guth** ... Townsman
**Rob Wickstrom** ...
Western Union Messenger

**FUN FACT #1:**
"Atomic Shakespeare" took eleven days to film (a typical episode was filmed in seven to eight days.)

**FUN FACT #2:**
The episode was narrated by Sterling Holloway, the voice of many Disney animated films.

**FUN FACT #3:**
The blue costume Cybill wore weighed thirty-five pounds! She requested that the inside linings be changed as they itched. So moleskin was sewn into all her costumes.

**FUN FACT #4:**
Ranked number forty-eight in TV Guide's Top 100 Episodes of All Time (TV Special, 2009)

**LOOK FOR #1**
Cybill trying not to laugh out of character when Bruce pins her down underneath the piano and when he kisses her in the church.

**LOOK FOR #2:**
Did they make New Balance shoes in sixteenth century Padua? Because Cybill is wearing a pair with her beautiful blue dress.

**LOOK FOR #3:**
When Petruchio flicks the switch as he enters his home, the candles light up.

**REVEALING MISTAKE:**
Boom mic visible behind Bruce on the line "like so much overstuffed furniture."



## GREAT LINES:



**MOONLIGHTING MENTION:**
***Perfect Strangers*** - "Snow Way to Treat a Lady: Part 2" (TV Episode, 1987)

**Mary Anne:** "I think that's Shakespeare . . . or *Moonlighting*."

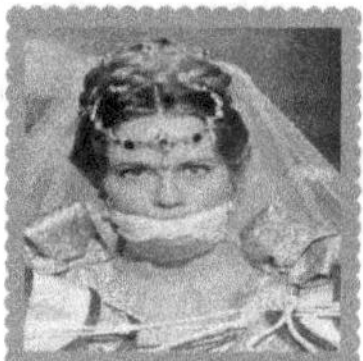

*Cybill loved being tied up.*

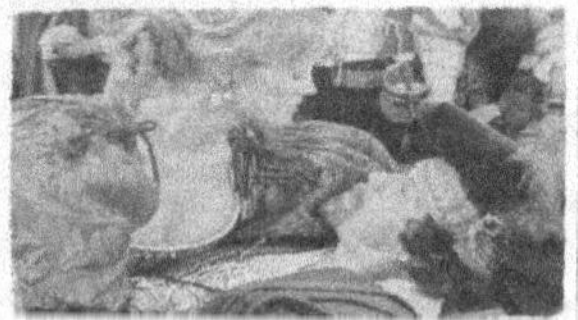

*"We hate iambic pentameter!"*

## Location...location...location...

~ Universal Backlot, Hollywood - Court of Miracles Stage 747, Los Angeles, California, USA
~ St. John's Episcopal Cathedral - 514 West Adams Boulevard, Los Angeles, California, USA

# AWARDS:

## Atomic Shakespeare:

- Robert Turturice; Emmy Award for Outstanding Costume Design

- Kathryn Blondell (Cybill Shepherd's Hairstylist) Josee Normand (Hairstylist); Emmy Award for Outstanding Achievement in Hairstyling

- Roger Bondelli and Neil Mandelberg; Emmy Award for Outstanding Editing for a Series—Single Camera Production

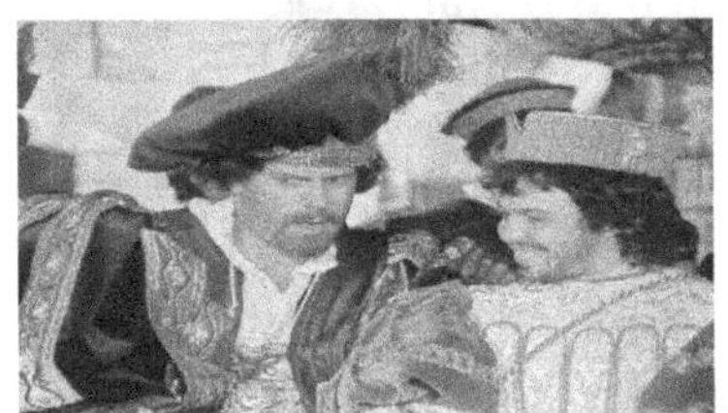

*Bruce and Curtis are great together in any scene . . . in any century.*

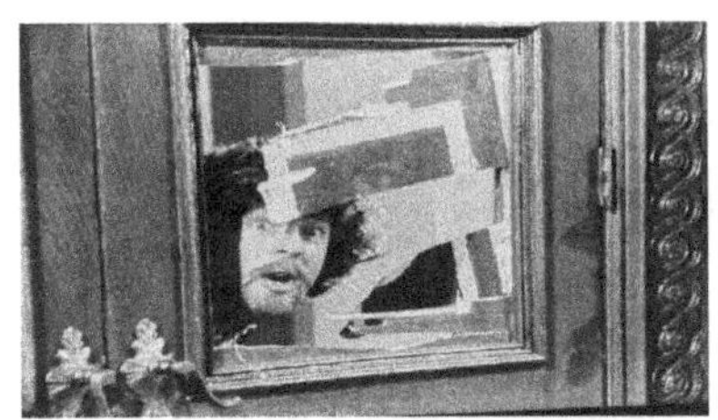

"Here's Petruchio!" is a reference to the "The Shining" (Movie, 1980) when Jack Nicholson says, "Here's Johnny!" This is repeated in s05e02, "Between a Yuk and a Hard Place," when David says, "Here's David!"

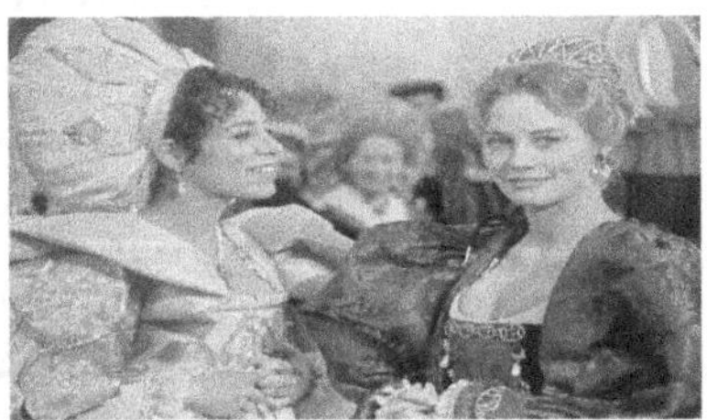

*Cybill's "Daisy Miller" look.*

> ZOUNDS. What MOUNDS!
> -Petruchio

---

**On Location:**
**from our personal archive**

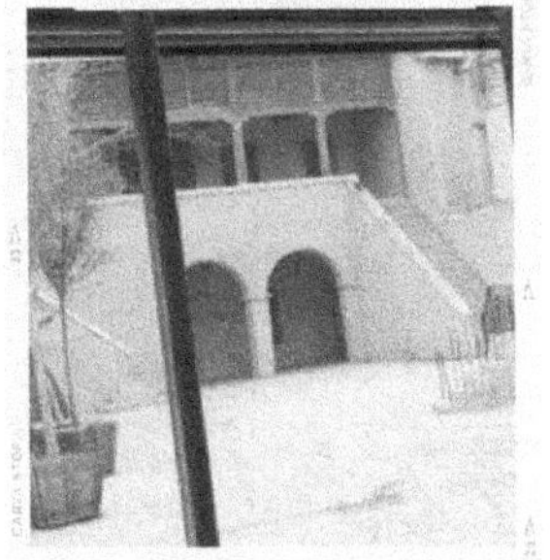

**Universal Backlot Tour, Staircase from Atomic.**

## FUN FACT #5:

Raymond Scott's "Powerhouse," (Song, 1937), otherwise known as the "Bugs Bunny / Looney Tunes assembly line music," plays as Petruchio tries to "kill Kate with kindness." The song is whistled by David in at least three other episodes' s02e02, "The Lady in the Iron Mask"; s02e04, "The Dream Sequence Always Rings Twice"; and s03e01, "The Son Also Rises."

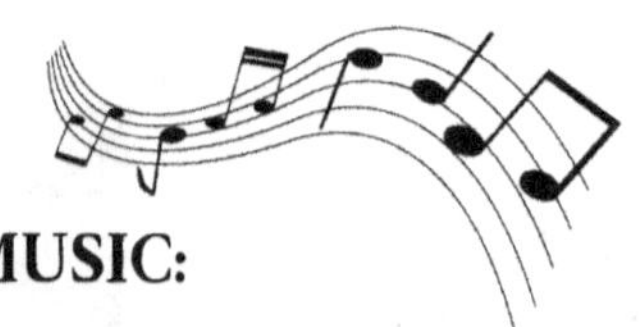

## ORIGINAL MUSIC:

**"Good Lovin"**
**Written by Rudy Clark and Arthur Resnick**
**Performed by Bruce Willis with harmonica**

**"I'm an Old Cowhand"**
**By Johnny Mercer**
**(Replaced with new music on Hulu streaming)**

**"The Name Game"**
**Written by Shirley Ellis and Lincoln Chase**
**Performed by Bruce Willis**

**"Greensleeves"**
**Traditional English Folk Song**
**Sixteenth Century**

**"Close to You"**
**Written by Burt Bacharach and Hal David**
**(Replaced with new music on Hulu streaming)**

**"Powerhouse"**
**Composed by Raymond Scott**

**Wedding March (Here Comes the Bride)**
**Written by Richard Wagner**

---

## TO BE . . . OR NOT TO BE

When executive producer Jay Daniel joined Shawna and Grace on *Moonlighting the Podcast*, he talked about filming this episode. Jay said, "You know, we did the Shakespeare show, and I directed half of it and another director directed the other half because it was a ten-day shoot. And we shot on the back lot at Universal. There was a courtyard there with a fountain in it, very Shakespearean. Curtis Armstrong was a fun little actor in *Moonlighting,* and I thought did a really good job for what he was hired for. He had done quite a lot of Shakespeare, so one of the scenes I shot, it opened with him walking across this crowded courtyard with all these Elizabethan costumes and whatnot spouting Shakespearean-like dialogue, and God, he really was good, so I said, "Maybe we've got something here!"

# S03 E08
## It's a
## Wonderful Job



**Plot:**

This classic episode, very popular with Moonlighting fans, is an homage to the movie *It's a Wonderful Life,* made in 1946 and starring Jimmy Stewart and Donna Reed. In the movie, an angel is sent down from heaven to show a frustrated businessman what life would have been like if he never existed.

Maddie is forced to make her employees work over Christmas due to one of their client's court cases being moved up to December 28. After a lively and angry discussion with the employees and David, Maddie snaps and says, "I wish I'd never kept this place open. Then we'd see how cocky you'd be; then we'd see." While sitting in a bar, she meets a man. Unbeknown to her, this man is an angel sent down from heaven to show her what life would be like without her.

The angel begins to take her to see people and places she knows, showing her what paths they took and how successful they are because Maddie never existed. Maddie now wants her agency back. She wants everything back to the way it was now that she has seen the life of her friends without her. The episode ends with another passionate kiss between Maddie and David (which is what *Moonlighting* fans love!). They then turn to the camera and say, "To all a goodnight."

**Air Date:**
December 16, 1986

**Written by:**
Debra Frank and
Carl Sautter

**Director:** Ed Sherin

### CAST CREDITS

**Jack Blessing** ... MacGillicudy
**Charles Rocket** ... Richie Addison
**Cheryl Tiegs** ... Herself
**Richard Libertini** ... Albert
**Lucy Lee Flippin** ... Julie
**Wally Taylor** ... The Bartender
**Lionel Stander** ... Max
**Patti Cohoon-Friedman** ... Hart Agency Receptionist

> Blue Moon Detective Agency, if your stocking gets stolen and your tree can't be found, you may as well call us 'cause we'll be around, we have to work Christmas, so if you're in a pinch, just give Blue Moon a jingle and ask for the Grinch.

## OUTFIT ROLE CALL:

- Maddie wore the purple dress in s02e18, "Camille."

## FUN FACT #1:

Max from *Hart to Hart* (TV Series, 1979–1984) appears. The Harts bought the Blue Moon Detective Agency.

## FUN FACT #2:

It's been said that the plot was chosen to remind Cybill, who was quite unhappy at the time with the long working hours, that this really was "a wonderful job."

## LOOK FOR:

Maddie's outfit turns from purple to blue when she returns to Blue Moon after running from Albert.

## REVEALING MISTAKE #1

The same women walk by twice when Maddie tells the first Santa she doesn't have time for the tree trimming.

## REVEALING MISTAKE #2:

Maddie asks Max about Blue Moon Detective Agency. Max tells her that they came in and fired everyone 2 1/2 years ago. But since City of Angels Investigations was renamed Blue Moon, Max should have had no idea what she's talking about.

## STATS:

*Door Slams: 2*
*Feet out of Elevator: 1*
*Maddie's Outfit Changes: 2*
*Agnes Rhymes: 1*

## GREATLINES:

> **Maddie:** *Ms. Dipesto, I'd like you to call Mr. Hamilton in the morning and tell him that we just can't have his casework by the twenty-eighth, doesn't he know it's Christmas!?*
>
> **Ms. Dipesto:** *I'll make that call right now.*

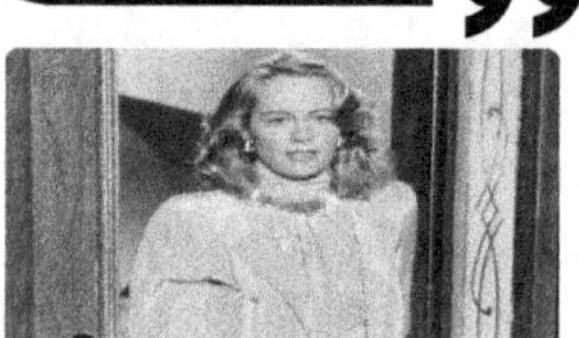

## CONTINUITY:

Maddie's coat disappears from her arm when she opens the door to step outside in the opening shot.

## REVEALING MISTAKE #3:

When Maddie's life flashes before her eyes, the memory from s02e04, "The Dream Sequence Always Rings Twice," is from David's dream.

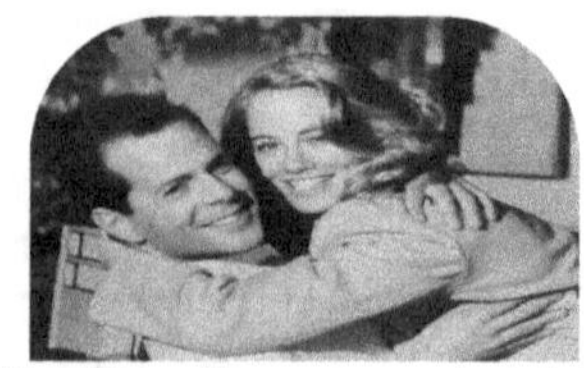

*"And to all . . . a good night!"*

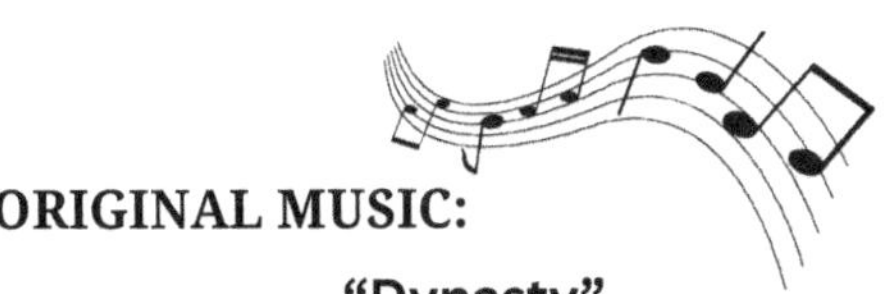

**ORIGINAL MUSIC:**

**"Dynasty"**
Theme song of *Dynasty* (TV Series, 1981-1989)
Composed by Bill Conti
*(Replaced with new music on Hulu streaming)*
**"Silent Night"**
Composed by Franz Xaver Gruber
**"It's Beginning to Look Like Christmas"**
Written by Meredith Willson
**"Sleigh Ride"**
Music by Leroy Anderson
Lyrics by Mitchell Parish
Performed by the Ronettes
*(Replaced with new music on Hulu streaming)*
**"White Christmas"**
Written by Irving Berlin
Performed by the Ronettes
*(Replaced with new music on Hulu streaming)*
**"Jingle Bells"**
Written by James Lord Pierpont

• • •

## MAD FOR MADDIE

What can we say about Cybill Shepherd? She was already a major motion picture star by the time she got to *Moonlighting* and will always be remembered for her roles in such classics as *The Last Picture Show* (Movie, 1971), *The Heartbreak Kid* (Movie, 1972), and *Taxi Driver* (Movie, 1976). Yet we maintain that some of her best acting work was done on *Moonlighting*. Her vulnerability in s02e14, "Every Daughter's Father Is a Virgin"; her monologue in s03e06, "Big Man on Mulberry Street"; and everything about her performance in s03e08, "It's a Wonderful Job." Cybill pulls off Shakespeare and shines as a 1940s small-town singer. She's been described as a woman who is "up for anything," and she proves it many times over in *Moonlighting*, whether taking a pie to the face or being folded into a bed, hung from a clock, tied to an altar, or doused in everything from paint to champagne — not to mention the verbal cliff diving she and Bruce delivered each week. . . . oh, and a whole lot of physical comedy thrown in there too. Thank you, Cybill, for being Madolyn "Maddie" Hayes; she was ahead of her time and the sexiest sexist there ever was.

# S03 E09
# The
# Straight Poop

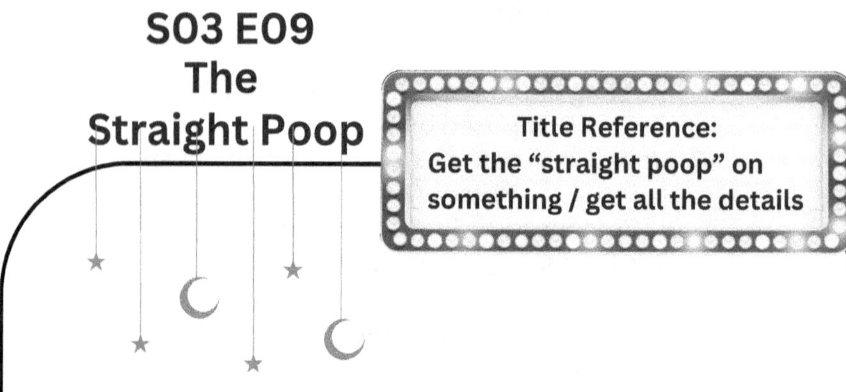


**Plot:**

Many other programs have done clip shows that look back on the best moments of past seasons. But *Moonlighting* liked to do things differently. Would we have it any other way?

This episode begins with gossip columnist Rona Barrett, who has arrived at the studio to ask why there is no new episode of *Moonlighting* (as was so common). Rona enters the offices of Blue Moon to get "The Straight Poop." She finds out that Maddie and David have not been talking to one another and have locked themselves in their offices.

As Rona talks with Maddie, David, Miss Dipesto, and Bert Viola, clips from previous episodes provide examples of the cast's answers to her questions.

The episode ends with Maddie and David promising that there will be a new episode next week—and they "kiss and make up."

**Air Date:** January 6, 1987

**Written by:** Glenn Gordon Caron

**Director:** Jay Daniel

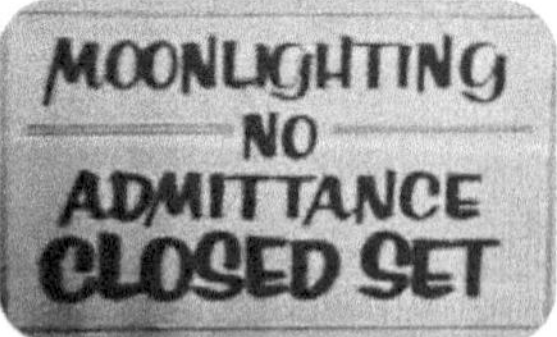


**Guest Appearances**

**Rona Barrett**

**Pierce Brosnan**

**Peter Bogdanovich**
as themselves

## FUN FACT #1:
On the DVD release, Aretha Franklin's "(You Make Me Feel Like) A Natural Woman" plays instead of Patti LaBelle's "If Only You Knew" when Maddie and Richie dance in s02e01, "Brother, Can You Spare a Blonde." *(However, both have been replaced with new music on Hulu streaming).*

## FUN FACT #2:
The first of two of the show's "blooper reels" appears during the end credits. The second appears at the end of s05e05, "Shirts and Skins."

### GREATEST LINES:

> *Rona: Well, America, so much for Maddie and David, and so much for me. I'm Rona Barrett. Sleep tight*
> *(looks at Maddie and David, who are kissing)*
> *Not you two.*

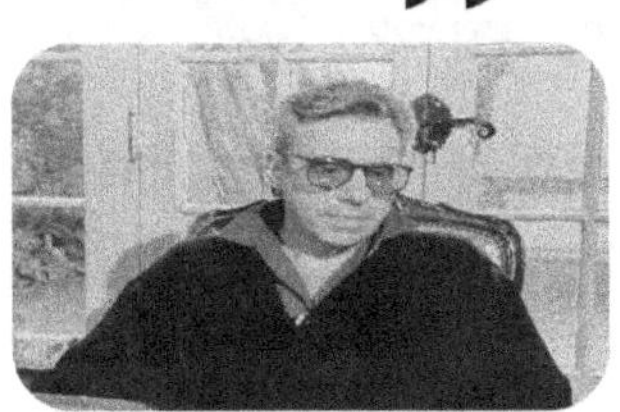

## STATS:

*Door Slams: 0*
*Feet out of Elevator: 0*
*Maddie's Outfit Changes: 1*
*Agnes Rhymes: 0*

## OUTFIT ROLE CALL:
- Maddie wears this pink dress again (with a different belt) in s05e07, "I See England, I See France, I See Maddie's Netherworld."

## FUN FACT #3:
This marks the fourth episode in a row in which Maddie and David kiss.

### *MOONLIGHTING* MENTION:
*Head of the Class* - "I Am the King" (TV Episode, 1989)

*Dr. Samuels: "I have nothing against moonlighting."*

*Charlie: "I'm sure Bruce and Cybill would be pleased to hear that."*

## ART IMITATING LIFE:
Cybill Shepherd's former lover, The late Peter Bogdonovich appears and discusses how he and Maddie dated in the past.

## THE ONE AND ONLY
"The Straight Poop," *Moonlighting's* only clip show, was created in response to the many real-life tabloid stories written about the rumored "trouble" on the *Moonlighting* set, as well as the much-discussed "contentious" (Sometimes? Maybe? Yes? No?) relationship between Bruce Willis and Cybill Shepherd. This episode is one of the many examples of how *Moonlighting* blurred the lines between real life and the show - addressing rumors about Cybill and Bruce through the characters of Maddie and David.

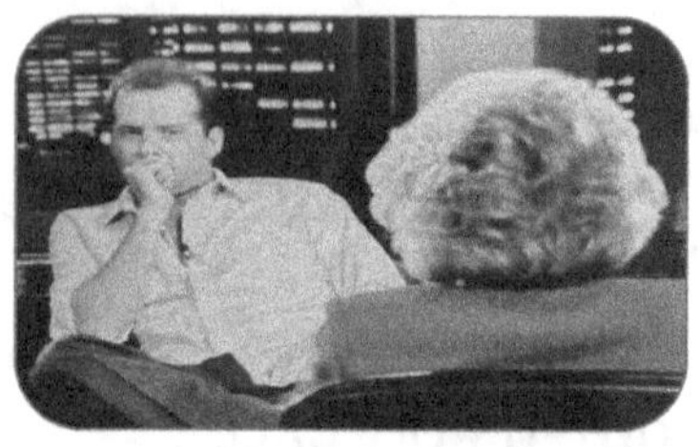 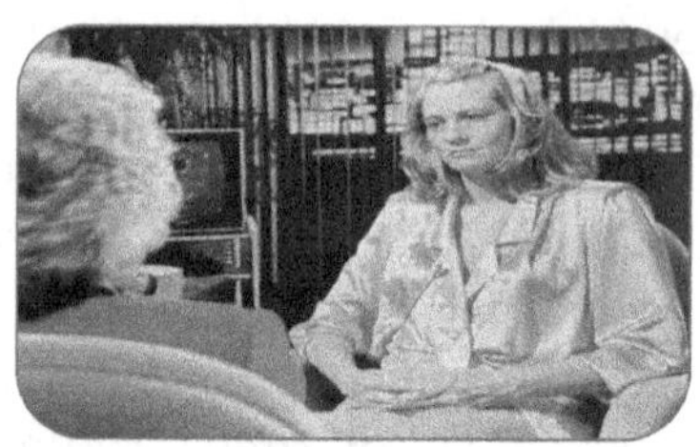

The idea for the "The Straight Poop" happened spontaneously. As Glenn Caron tells it, he saw Rona Barrett, a popular gossip columnist at the time, standing in a valet parking line outside a restaurant in Los Angeles and asked her to come to the *Moonlighting* set the next day to film the show.

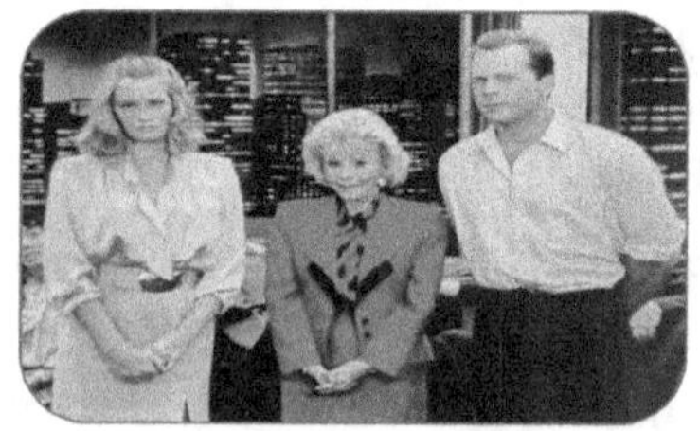 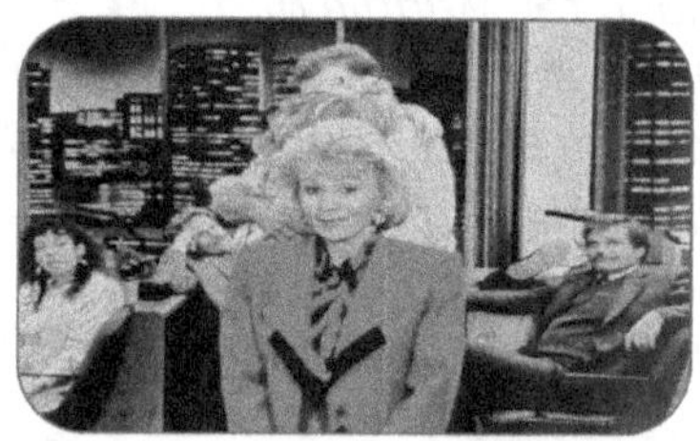

## ARE THEY REALLY KISSING?

In the DVD Commentary for s03e07, "Atomic Shakespeare," Cybill Shepherd and Bruce Willis seem to disagree about whether they always "really kissed" when Maddie and David had a kissing scene together in the show. Bruce's memory was that they "always kissed"; Cybill responded with "I don't think we did." What do *you* think? Are they always *really* kissing?

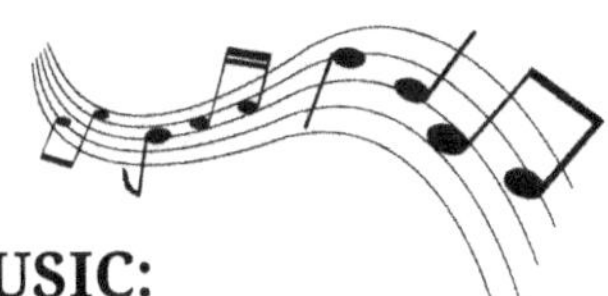

## ORIGINAL MUSIC:

**"Limbo Rock"**
Written by Kal Mann
and Billy Strange
Performed by Chubby Checker

**"I Told Ya I Love Ya, Now Get Out"**
Written by Lou Carter, Herb Ellis, and Johnny Frigo
Performed by Cybill Shepherd

**"Blue Moon"**
Written by Richard Rodgers and Lorenz Hart

**"The Hokey Pokey"**
**"The Hokey Pokey" Hokey Cokey"**
Written by Taft Baker,
Roland Lawrence LaPrise and Charles Macak
Performed by Bruce Willis

**"This Old Heart of Mine (Is Weak for You)"**
Written by Brian Holland, Lamont Dozier,
Eddie Holland and Sylvia Moy
Performed by the Isley Brothers
*(Replaced with new music on Hulu streaming)*

**"(You Make Me Feel Like) A Natural Woman"**
Written by Gerry Goffin, Carole King, and Jerry Wexler
Performed by Aretha Franklin
*(Replaced with new music on Hulu streaming)*

**"Take Me Out to the Ball Game"**
Written by Jack Norworth and Albert Von Tilzer
*(Replaced with new music on Hulu streaming)*

**"Hooray for Hollywood"**
Written by Johnny Mercer
*(Replaced with new music on Hulu streaming)*

# S03 E10
# Poltergiest III—
# Dipesto Nothing



**Plot**:

Maddie and David have decided to give Herbert Viola more responsibility by putting him in charge of more cases. Agnes is not happy to hear this, as he has been at Blue Moon for only two and a half months and she has worked for Maddie and David for five years. A very feisty Agnes goes to Maddie's office and tells them both that in those five years she's had only one day off and has been late just three times, only one of which was her fault. She has also taken pay cuts in bad times and has never asked for a raise. Maddie and David try to weasel their way out of it by downplaying Herbert's role.

Margaret Renbourn arrives at Blue Moon to hire the detectives to find proof that her house is haunted. Unbelievably, Maddie and David actually agree that they should not take this case. Upon hearing this, and without informing her bosses, Agnes decides to take the case on her own. Bert tells Agnes that he didn't just fall off a turnip truck and that he knows what she's up to. Agnes and Bert end up joining forces and solve the case.

**Air Date:** January 13, 1987

**Written by:**
Karen Hall and
Charles H. Eglee

**Director:** Christopher Hibler

**CAST CREDITS**

**H. Richard Greene** ... Jake Renbourn
**Ian Abercrombie** ... Ludwig
**John Lehne** ... Dr. Beddows
**Karen Kondazian** ...
Margaret Renbourn
**Rhoda Gemignani** ... Emily

### Agnes Rhyme:

Blue Moon Detective Agency, if your spouse is a louse, or your kid has been napped, you've misplaced your fortune, your phone's being tapped . . . we'll solve any problem. Can you hold please?

## STATS:

*Door Slams: 1*
*Feet out of Elevator: 0*
*Maddie's Outfit Changes: 2*
*Agnes Rhymes: 1*

## GREAT LINES:

**Bert:** *It's our fault. We heard you turn down the Renbourn case and we went after it.*
**Maddie:** *And you solved it.*
**Agnes:** *Well, yes, I guess so.*
**Bert:** *We caught the murderer.*
**David:** *And everybody lived happily ever after.*
**Agnes:** *Well, no, almost everybody died.*
**David:** *Well, you gotta start somewhere.*

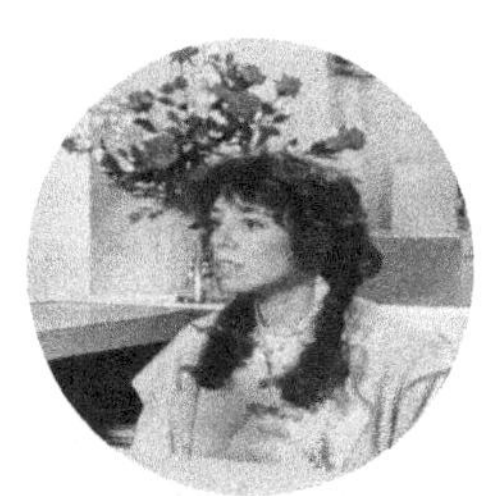

*Agnes investigates the case on her own*

**Bert:** *"Black Gold?"*

**Agnes:** *"Texas Tee?"*

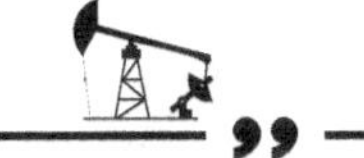

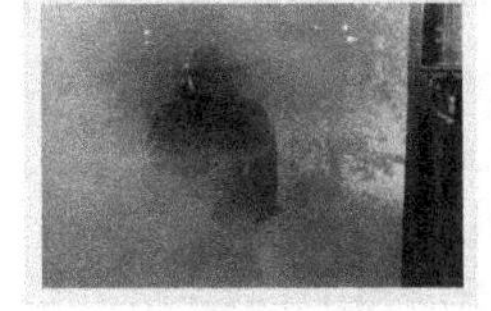

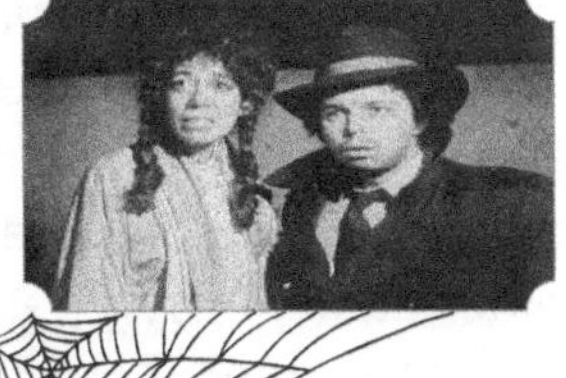

### SPOOF:
When Herbert arrives at the front door of the haunted house, the theme music from *The Exorcist* (Movie, 1973) is playing in the background.

## ORIGINAL MUSIC:
**"Tubular Bells"**
Written by Mike Oldfield
*(Replaced with new music on Hulu streaming)*
**"Black Bottom"**
Composed by Gus Horsley and Perry Bradford
Performed by Gertrude "Ma" Rainey
**"Twilight Zone"**
Theme song of *The Twilight Zone* (TV Series, 1959-1964)
Composed by Marius Constant
*(Replaced with new music on Hulu streaming)*

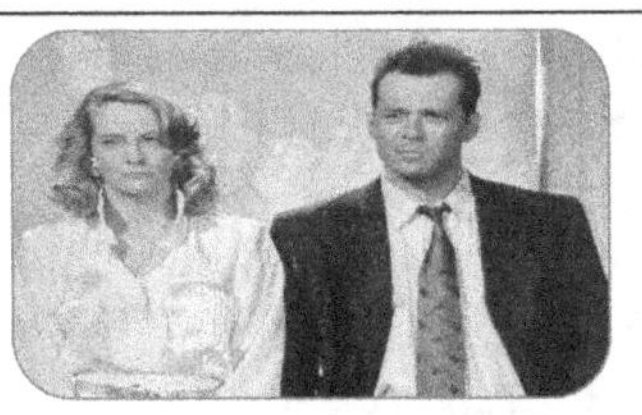

**FUN FACT:** Cybill and Bruce appear for approximately seven minutes in this episode.

# S03 E11
# Blonde on Blonde



**Plot:**

When Maddie does not react after walking in on a strip-poker game David is playing with the employees, he realizes that there is something wrong. After some coaxing, Maddie confides in David that she has been having urges lately to go out "find a man and be bad." For obvious reasons, he is extremely worried about her, so he decides to follow her.

Later, a woman steals Maddie's coat and hat in the ladies' room, and David mistakenly follows the wrong woman from a club. After a crazy turn of events, David is implicated in a murder. While he is in police custody, David comes to the realization that he is in love with Maddie. Once he is released from jail, some cops drive him over to Maddie's house at four o'clock in the morning. It's a rainy night when he shows up at her doorstep. He rings the bell and knocks on the door yelling her name, but he gets the surprise of his life when he sees who answers the door.

**Air Date:** February 3, 1987

**Written by:** Kerry Ehrin

**Director:** Jay Daniel

### The Working Title
**"The Night of the Zipless Dave"**

### CAST CREDITS

**Mark Harmon** ... Sam Crawford (recurring guest star)

**Donna Dixon** ... Joan Tenowich

**Sam McMurray** ... Moe Hyland

**Andrew Masset** ... Ed Sherlock

**Robert Wuhl** ... Crazy Guy in Cell

**Jeff Osterhage** ... Mr. Goodbar

**John McCook** ... Robert ... Married Man in Bar

**Abraham Alvarez** ... Bartender

**Steve Eastin** ... Bakery Clerk

**Wendee Winters** ... Waitress

### Agnes Rhyme:

> Blue Moon Investigations, we'd love to speak to you, that would be keen, but since we're not here, talk to this machine, when you hear the beep, leave your name and number, don't hang up, that would be a bummer.

**FUN FACT:**

Maddie only wears a hat three times in the series. In the pilot episode, in "s01e03, "Read the Mind ... See the Movie" and here.

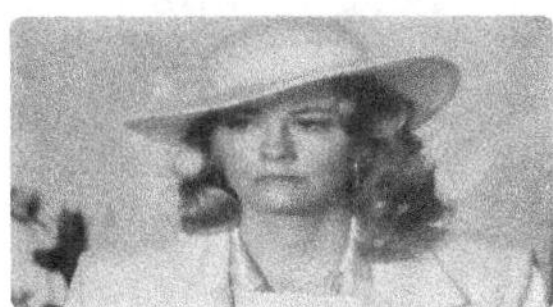

**CULTURAL REFERENCES:**
~ **In Cold "Mud"** - Play on title *In Cold Blood* (Novel, 1965) by Truman Capote.
~ **Disneyland** - Kids have souvenirs from Disney park.
~ **Mr. Goodbar** - American crime drama *Looking for Mr. Goodbar* (Movie, 1977, based on 1975 novel).
~ **Dragnet:** - Crime Drama (TV Series, 1967)
~ **Niagara Falls (slowly I turned)** - Comedy bit done by the likes of *The Three Stooges*.

### STATS:

*Door Slams: 3*
*Feet out of Elevator: 2*
*Maddie's Outfit Changes: 5*
*Agnes Rhymes: 1*

### GREAT LINES:

**Joan Tenowich:** *Does she know you love her?*

**David:** *What?*

**Joan Tenowich:** *I'm sorry, It's just so clear.*

**LOOK FOR:**
It seems David was such an influence on the Blue Moon workers that they even emulated his choice in underwear. When the strip poker players are re-dressing after Maddie walks in, one Wobbly is wearing a pair of boxers with red hearts, just like David wore in s02e15, "Witness for the Execution." David wears yet another pair of these boxers in s05e02, "Between a Yuk and a Hard Place." Richie even wore a pair in s05e08 "Those Lips, Those Lies!"

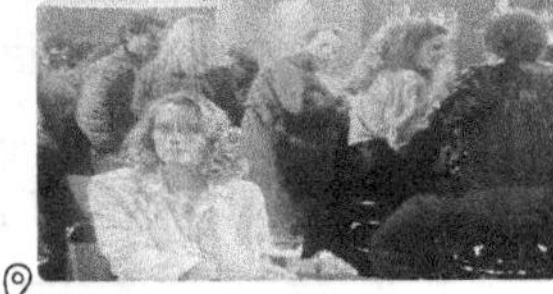

## LOCATION...LOCATION...LOCATION...

~ **(Exterior) Sheraton Town House** - 2959 Wilshire Boulevard, Los Angeles, California, USA

~ **(Interior lobby) Hollywood Roosevelt Hotel** - 7000 Hollywood Boulevard, Hollywood, California, USA

~ **Hollywood Walk of Fame** - Hollywood, Los Angeles, California, USA

~ **Cafe St. Laurent** - 7013 Hollywood Boulevard, Los Angeles, California, USA

~ **Metropolis Nightclub** - Los Angeles, California, USA (Now Closed)

**OUTFIT ROLE CALL:**
- Maddie wears the nightgown with the lace straps in s02e07, "Somewhere Under the Rainbow," and s02e15, "Witness for the Execution."
- She wore the pink robe in s03e01, "The Son Also Rises."

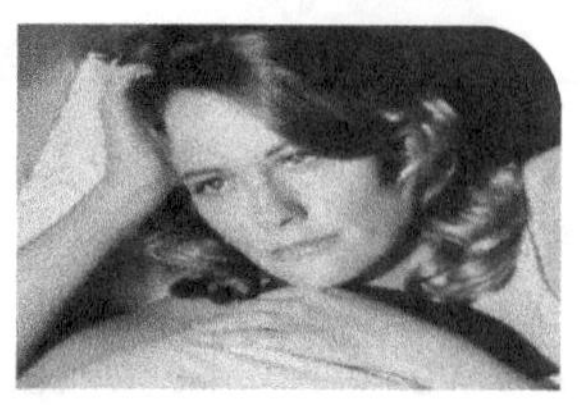

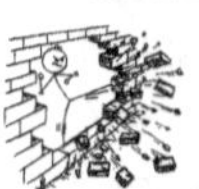

**BREAKING THE FOURTH WALL:**

"Police? This might be a good time for a station break. But then again, I'm just an actor. What do I know?"

**CONTINUITY:**

David makes his way into Maddie's house in s01e02, "Gunfight at the So-So Corral"; s02e09, "Atlas Belched"; and s02e15, "Witness for the Execution," so why can't he get inside her house without pounding on the door here in "Blonde on Blonde"?

---

**MOOD:**

Rain was often used as an effect to signify a change in mood. We see it here when thunder is heard crackling in the background as Maddie discusses her *urges* with David. Look for a similar effect in episodes such as s01e04, "The Next Murder You Hear" and s02e15, "Witness for the Execution."

---

# THEIR SONG

Listen to the lyrics of "Since I Fell for You" and it's clear why it's *their* song. Do you remember, they first danced together in the pilot episode to the Lenny Welch version of this song? Here in "Blonde on Blonde," the Al Jarreau version is fitting for the shock David gets when Maddie's door flies open at the end of the episode and that unfamiliar face appears — talk about misery and pain! It's one of those unforgettable moments for fans. And, in a *Moonlighting* first, the song even plays over the end credits.

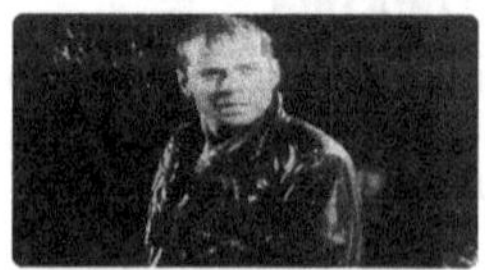

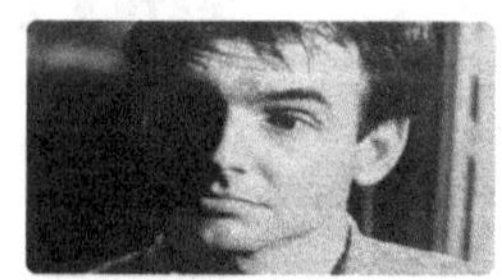

*Mark Harmon's sudden appearance as astronaut and pretty boy Sam Crawford throws a monkey wrench into David's plans.*

# JAY DANIEL

Jay Daniel was not only the executive producer of *Moonlighting,* but he also directed multiple episodes (and parts of multiple episodes), and was the all-around "go-to guy." He was there from the Pilot episode straight through to the finale, s05e13, "Lunar Eclipse." Jay was the calm figure amid all the chaos that surrounded *Moonlighting.* He saw to it that everything was done correctly and smoothly. Of course, that wasn't always easy! He was the man who thought ahead; he even kept a journal of all the daily activities on the set (wouldn't we love to get a hold of that!). Jay was the glue that held it all together, and he acted as a referee when there was tension between the two leads (or star and creator!) He would talk to each of the parties individually in their trailers and convince them (in his logical, calm manner) that it was in their best interest to get back to work. Jay directed several episodes in season three, including s03e09, "The Straight Poop," and s03e11, "Blonde on Blonde," and directed the second unit on s03e07, "Atomic Shakespeare." In season five, he directed s05e01, "A Womb with a View," and s05e12, "Eine Kleine Nacht Murder." To this day, the cast and crew still talk about Jay with great affection and maintain that he was an integral part of making *Moonlighting* what it was. His attention to detail, such as reshooting a scene the next day even when under a time crunch, helped preserve the high quality of the production. Thank you, Jay, for your immense hard work and love for *Moonlighting.* You and the rest of the crew put a wonderful show together that was ahead of its time and is still enjoyed today by fans all around the world.

---

## ORIGINAL MUSIC: 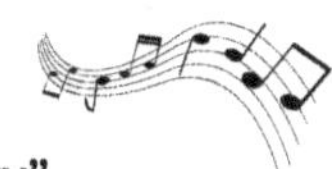

**"Nasty"**
Written by Janet Jackson, Jimmy Jam, and Terry Lewis
Performed by Janet Jackson

**"Runaround Sue"**
Written by Dion DiMucci and Ernie Maresca
Performed by Dion DiMucci

**"C'est la Vie"**
Written by Robbie Nevil, Duncan Pain, and Mark Holding
Performed by Robbie Nevil

**"Since I Fell for You"**
Written by Buddy Johnson
Performed by Bob James and David Sanborn
featuring vocals from Al Jarreau

**"Stormy Weather"**
Written by Harold Arlen & Ted Koehler
*(Replaced with new music on Hulu streaming)*

**"Danger Ahead"**
Theme song of Dragnet
(Radio series, 1949-1957),
(TV Show, 1951-1959, original / 1967-1970, revival)
Written by Walter Schumann
*(Replaced with new music on Hulu streaming)*

# S03 E12
# Sam and Dave

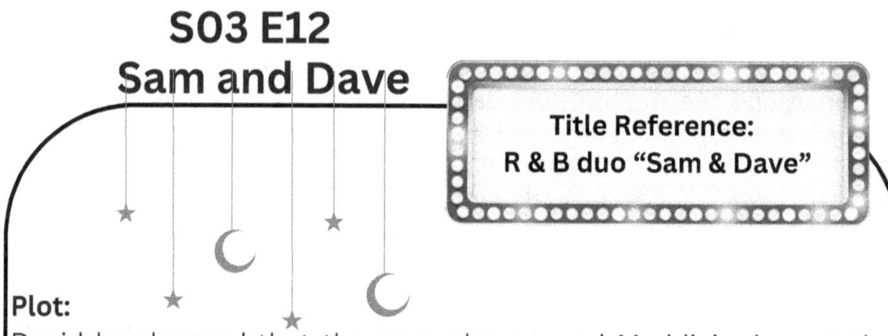



**Plot:**

David has learned that the man who opened Maddie's door at the end of the previous episode is Maddie's former boyfriend Sam from many years ago. Not only is he well educated, but he is also an astronaut. This is a huge blow for David.

Maddie and David are hired by a woman with a strange request. She wants to know if her lover is falling back in love with his wife. David organizes a stakeout that night, but Maddie has a date with Sam and refuses to cancel it.

Later on in the evening, David decides to interrupt their dinner at a lavish restaurant. He has plans to tell her how he feels while Sam is away from the table but is unable to get the words out. Then, just as he is about to, Sam returns to the table.

After dinner, David is quite inebriated and is making a fool of himself in front of the diners. Sam takes David and then goes home and sleeps with Maddie.

**Air Date:** February 10, 1987

**Teleplay by:**
Charles H. Eglee
Roger Director

**Story by:**
Karen Hall
Ron Osborn
Jeff Reno

**Director:** Sam Weisman

**CAST CREDITS**

**Mark Harmon** ... **Sam Crawford** (recurring guest star)
**Jeff Jarvis** (uncredited)
**Bill Washington** ... Maître D'
**Randall "Tex" Cobbs** ... Guy at Gas Station
**Julia Jennings** ... Rita McClafferty
**Howard Mann** ... Gas Station Cashier
**Caitlin Clarke** ... Elaine Johnson (uncredited)
**Gary Cole** ... Alan McClafferty (uncredited)

### Agnes Rhyme:

Blue Moon Detective Agency, has your dog jumped the fence, did Fido get lost, put us on his scent, at our low dog-finder cost, we'll hit the ground running, get to the pound fast, and retrieve your loved one, before he gets ga...

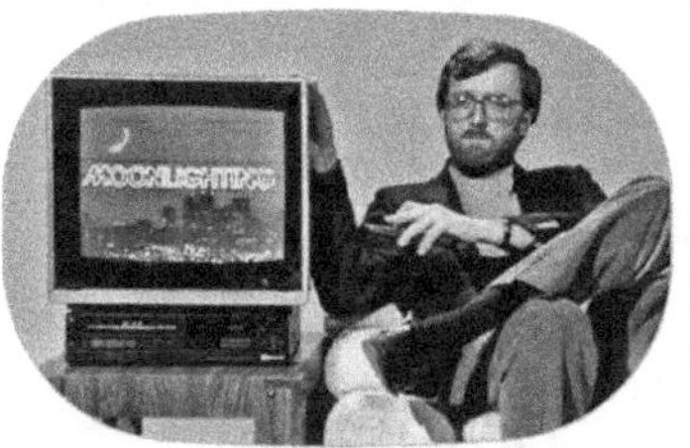

*TV critic Jeff Jarvis begins this episode recapping s03e11, "Blonde on Blonde," assuming viewers might not have tuned in thinking there "was another rerun" (which was common).*

### FUN FACT #1:

Mark Harmon was named *People Magazine*'s "Sexiest Man Alive" in 1986.



### STATS:

*Door Slams: 2*
*Feet out of Elevator: 1*
(Agnes's feet)
*Maddie's Outfit Changes: 3*
*Agnes Rhymes: 1*

### GREAT LINES:

**Maddie:** *The store was having a sale. I just needed a dinner dress.*

**David:** *Did you need to get one that was cut down to South America?*

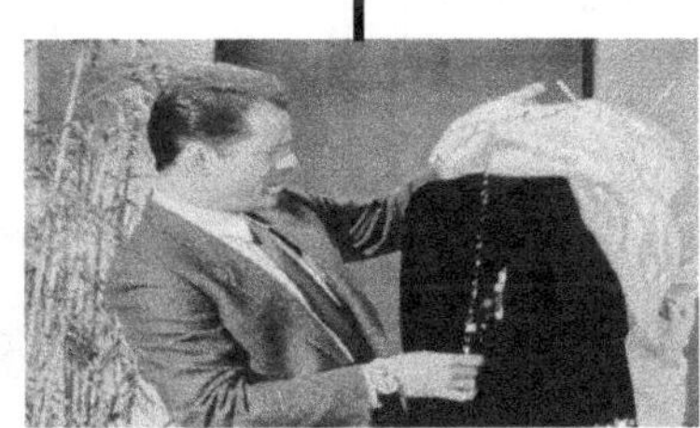

*David opens a "Turturice" garment bag*

*There was a huge curiosity around the show and about "Is it going to be on this week?" even!*

*~ Executive Producer Jay Daniel*
*Moonlighting the Podcast*

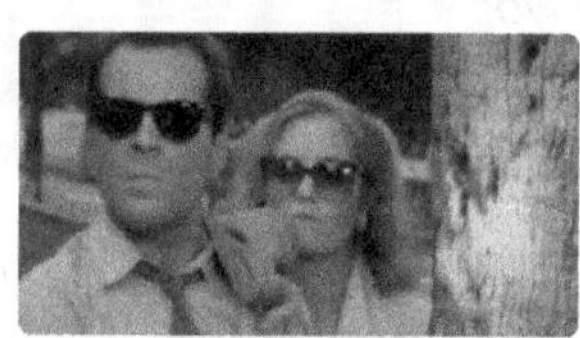

## Partners or Associates?

Throughout the series, Maddie and David's relationship is often called into question. But it's not *that* relationship we're talking about; it's the other one: partners or associates? Most of the time, Maddie introduces David as her "associate," while David gives himself the "partner" title—definitely one of the many power struggles these two have. The matter seems to be settled in s05e05, "Shirts and Skins," when Maddie offers to make David a "full partner," but by the time we get to s05e07 "I See England, I See France, I See Maddie's Netherworld," Maddie reverts back to introducing David as her "associate." So which is it: partners or associates?

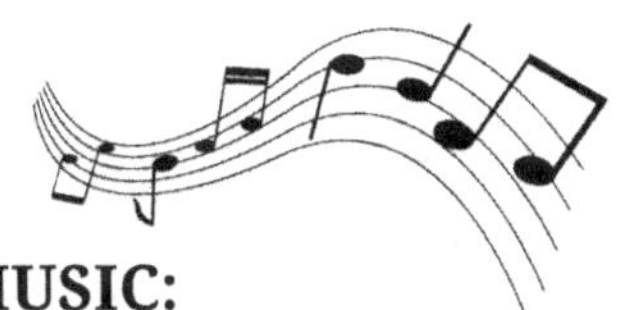

# ORIGINAL MUSIC:

**"Oh, What A Beautiful Mornin'"**
Music by Richard Rodgers
Lyrics by Oscar Hammerstein II
Performed by Allyce Beasley

**"Moon River"**
Music by Henry Mancini
*(Replaced with new music on Hulu streaming)*

**"All the Way"**
Music by Jimmy Van Heusen
Lyrics by Sammy Cahn
Performed by Frank Sinatra

**"It Was a Very Good Year"**
Written by Ervin Drake
*(Replaced with new music on Hulu streaming)*

**"Since I Fell for You"**
Written by Buddy Johnson
Performed by Bob James and David Sanborn
*(Replaced with new music on Hulu streaming)*

**"The Way We Were"**
Written by Alan Bergman, Marilyn Bergman and Marvin Hamlisch
*(Replaced with new music on Hulu streaming)*

**"Misty"**
Composed by Erroll Garner
*(Replaced with new music on Hulu streaming)*

---

### *Trouble on the set?*

In response to rumors of infighting between Bruce and Cybill on the set of *Moonlighting* being the cause of episode delays, Bruce answered the media question "Is there trouble on the set?" by embracing Cybill and planting a passionate kiss on her backstage at the 1987 Golden Globe Awards while the press cheered them on. The pair were all smiles as Bruce proclaimed, "There is no trouble on the set"—do we believe them?

# S03 E13
# Maddie's Turn to Cry

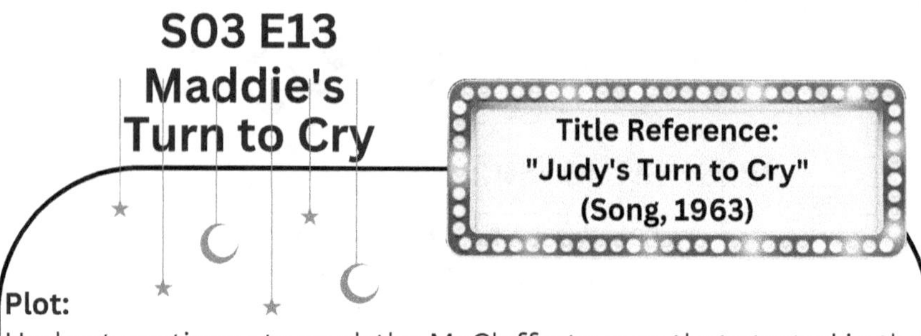



**Plot:**

Herbert continues to work the McClafferty case that started in the previous episode. The case involves uncovering whether their client's lover is betraying her by falling back in love with his wife. Maddie and David work a stakeout and witness McClafferty's wife's suicide.

Maddie gets home late from the case. Sam is up waiting for her and surprises her with a wedding proposal.

Maddie and David continue to investigate the case when they realize that the wife was murdered.

Meanwhile, Maddie is exploring her feelings between David and Sam. She leaves Sam in the middle of the night and drives to David's home to find out what he wanted to tell her so urgently the other night when he interrupted her dinner.

While they are talking, she has a realization and believes that she has solved the case. They approach the killer, which begins a *Moonlighting*-style car chase involving a milk truck and a bowling alley. After the killer is captured, a touching scene unfolds between Maddie and David as they talk about how much fun they have had that evening. Then Maddie suddenly remembers that Sam is waiting for her at home.

**Air Date:** March 3, 1987

**Teleplay by:**
Roger Director
Ron Osborn
Jeff Reno

**Story by:**
Charles H. Eglee
Karen Hall

**Director:** Allan Arkush

### CAST CREDITS

**Mark Harmon** ... Sam Crawford (recurring guest star)
**Caitlin Clarke** ... Elaine Johnson
**Gary Cole** ... Alan McClafferty
**Julia Jennings** ... Rita McClafferty
**Biff Wiff** ... Milkman

> **Bert Rhyme:**
> *(Answers for Agnes)*
> Blue Moon Detective Agency, if you want a rhyme, call another time.

## OUTFIT ROLE CALL:
- Maddie wore the white raincoat previously  in s03e05, "All Creatures Great and . . . Not So Great," and again in s03e14, "I Am Curious... Maddie."

## LOOK FOR #1:
Bruce Willis "going commando" while wearing the gray sweatpants in the last part of the episode.

## LOOK FOR #2:
Bruce Willis catching a whiff of Elaine Johnson's cigarette smoke and coughing, then gesturing to cut the scene.

## FUN FACT:
This isn't the only episode in which Maddie tells David he "smells awful." He smells awful in s02e09, "Atlas Belched," and s02e15, "Witness for the Execution."

## BREAKING THE FOURTH WALL:
**David:** "My, my, my, my, my, imagine that: somebody coming out of the closet on our show. . . . Where's the *National Enquirer* when you need 'em?" *(in response to tabloid fodder at the time).*

## STATS:

*Door Slams: 1*
*Feet out of Elevator: 0*
*Maddie's Outfit Changes: 3*
*Agnes Rhymes: 1*

## GREAT LINES:

> **Maddie:** *I hate you, David Addison.*
> **David:** *I hate you too, Maddie Hayes. I've always hated you.*

## F-BOMB PAST THE CENSORS:
During the stakeout, while Maddie and David sit in the van, David attempts to entertain Maddie with a reenactment of the game show *The Dating Game* and drops the f-bomb while laughing at the end.

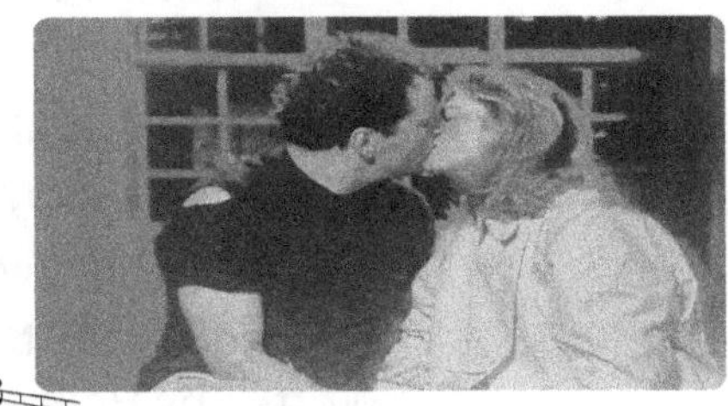

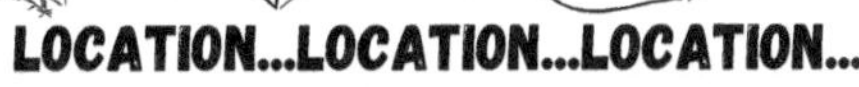

## LOCATION...LOCATION...LOCATION...
~ **Corbin Bowl (Bowling Alley)** – 19616 Ventura Boulevard, Tarzana, California, USA

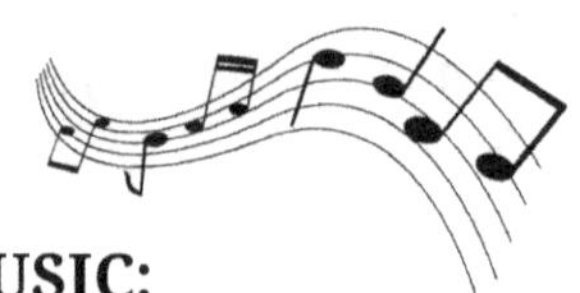

# ORIGINAL MUSIC:

**"Moon River"**
Music by Henry Mancini
Lyrics by Johnny Mercer
*(Replaced with new music on Hulu streaming)*

**"All the Way"**
Music by Jimmy Van Heusen
Lyrics by Sammy Cahn
Performed by Frank Sinatra
*(Replaced with new music on Hulu streaming)*

**"Someone to Watch Over Me"**
Written by George Gershwin
Performed by Linda Ronstadt

**"Nowhere to Run"**
Written by Holland-Dozier-Holland
Performed by Martha & the Vandellas
*(Replaced with new music on Hulu streaming)*

**"It Was a Very Good Year"**
Written by Ervin Drake
*(Replaced with new music on Hulu streaming)*

**"Misty"**
Composed by Erroll Garner
*(Replaced with new music on Hulu streaming)*

**"Stop in the Name of Love"**
Written by Holland-Dozier-Holland
Performed by the Supremes
*(Replaced with new music on Hulu streaming)*

# S03 E14
# I Am Curious ... Maddie



**Plot:**

Maddie arrives home in the morning after a night on the case with David. While Maddie is asleep, Sam pays a visit to David asking him to back off from his relationship with Maddie.

When Maddie gets to Blue Moon later, she finds David sitting in her office—he's upset she didn't tell him Sam proposed to her, even though they were out all night together.

Sam is upset that Maddie is noncommittal with her answer to his proposal, especially when her mother calls and Maddie tells her there is nothing to report. Agnes and Bert go to David in his office to tell him that Sam has come to Blue Moon to take Maddie to dinner and urge him to go talk to her. David rushes down to confront them in the garage and ends up having a fistfight with Sam, known as "the barrage in the garage."

Maddie ultimately decides that she is not ready for marriage but wants to give Sam "one for the road." However, she is shocked to find that it is David, not Sam, in her bed. A fight ensues between Maddie and David over what's just happened, and they end up making love.

**Air Date:** March 31, 1987

**Teleplay by:**

Glenn Gordon Caron (as Glenn Caron)
and Jeff Reno

**Story by:**

Ron Osborn
Karen Hall
Roger Director
Charles H. Eglee

**Director:** Allan Arkush

## The Working Title
### "The Big Bang"

## CAST CREDITS

**Mark Harmon** ... Sam Crawford (recurring guest star)
**Caitlin Clarke** ... Elaine Johnson
**Gary Cole** ... Alan McClafferty
**Jack Goode Jr.** ... Bartender

## STATS:

*Door Slams: 4*
*Feet out of Elevator: 1*
*Maddie's Outfit Changes: 3*
*Agnes Rhymes: 0*

## CONTINUITY #1:

When Agnes and Maddie are at the bar, the bartender sets Maddie's drink down twice.

## OUTFIT ROLE CALL:

- Maddie wears the white raincoat at the end of s03e05, "All Creatures Great and . . . Not So Great" and s03e13, "Maddie's Turn to Cry."

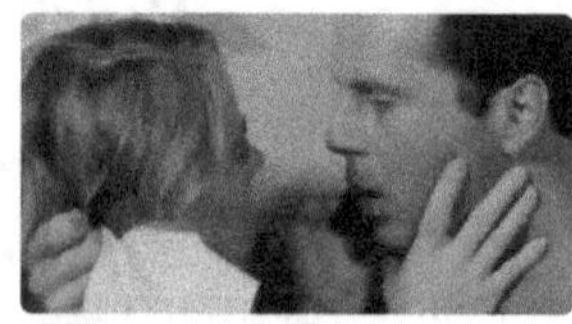

## CONTINUITY #2:

During the fight, it's David's right shoulder that hits the wall, but later he rubs his left shoulder when talking about taking pain pills. (Bruce actually had a broken collarbone from a skiing injury; look for bruising on his chest and arm.)

## GREAT LINES:

> **David:** *...and the rest, as they say, is kismet.*

## CULTURAL REFERENCES:

~ **Oprah** - Daytime talk show host
~ **Vanna White** - Co-host of *Wheel of Fortune* (Game Show, 1975-present)
~ **Divorce Court** - (TV Show, 1984-1993)
~ **Buck Rogers** - Sci-fi character

## FUN FACT #2:

Viewers were promised a new episode, but "I Am Curious . . . Maddie" was delayed a week so it would coincide with the premiere of ABC's new show *Max Headroom* (TV Series, 1987-1988).

## FUN FACT #3:

#77 on *TV Guide's* 100 Most Memorable moments in TV History list (1996).

## PUBLIC SERVICE ANNOUNCEMENT:

*Let's keep this short and to the point: No, Moonlighting did not end, become unpopular, or lose ratings because Maddie and David slept together.*

**That is all. Thank you.**

## TRICK PHOTOGRAPHY

While the cast and creative team were filming the "barrage in the garage" here in "I Am Curious . . . Maddie," there was a little problem getting all the actors on set at once during filming. One part of that was Cybill's pregnancy and the other was a little mishap Bruce Willis had on a ski slope. Jay Daniel explained further when he was on *Moonlighting the Podcast.* Jay said, "We were shooting in an underground garage scene, and once again I'm driving to work and I hear on the radio that David Addison, uh, Bruce Willis . . . has had a little skiing accident, broken his collarbone, and I'm on the way to shoot a scene with him. So it ended it up that I had his double there, and so I just shot the scene with the double . . . you know, over his shoulder to who David's talking to and a wide shot where you can't really see David's face, etc. . . . and then, a few days later, actually it'd been more like a week later, I went back with Bruce and shot the scene again, and I think I had one of the actors that was there. I never had Cybill and Bruce together." And that, folks, is the magic of television.

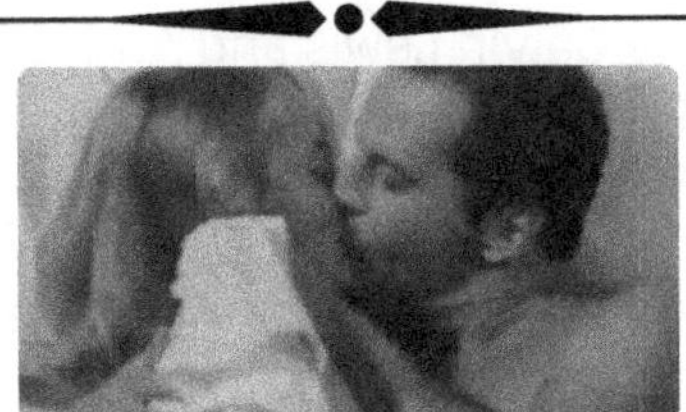

## LET'S GET . . . VERTICAL?

David always wanted to get "horizontal," but that's not exactly how they did it on *Moonlighting.* As the story goes, when Maddie and David *finally* sleep together for the first time, the bed scene was filmed with the mattress propped *vertically* against a wall with the actors leaning against it—you may notice that Maddie's hair falls straight around her face instead of back, as it normally would if they were lying down. The reason they couldn't "get horizontal" is that Bruce had a broken collarbone from a skiing accident and Cybill was pregnant with her twins at the time. You might also notice that doubles for both of them are used in the "rolling around on the downstairs floor" scene, as they were both in too fragile a state for that kind of action at the time. Other changes include Maddie slapping David with her left hand instead of her right hand as she normally would, due to the fact Bruce's injury was on the left side of his body. One other moment to look for during this historic television event: many viewers at the time were upset that David did not tell Maddie he loved her before they, well, "big banged," but in fact, David does say "I love you" to Maddie once they've moved up to her bedroom, which you can see if you're a good lip reader. The powers that be just chose to play music over it.

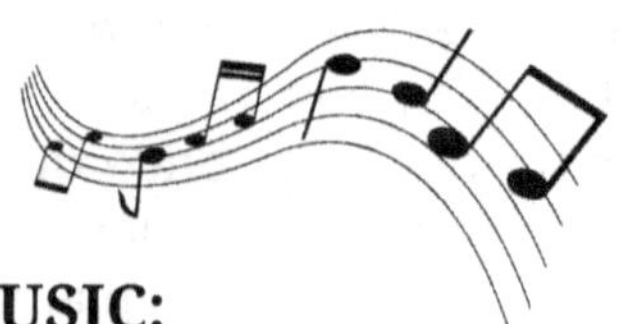

# ORIGINAL MUSIC:

### "La Bamba"
Written by Ritchie Valens
Performed by Ritchie Valens
*(Alternate version of song used on Hulu streaming)*

### "All the Way"
Music by Jimmy Van Heusen
Lyrics by Sammy Cahn
Performed by Frank Sinatra

### "When a Man Loves a Woman"
Written by Calvin Lewis and Andrew Wright
Performed by Percy Sledge
*(Replaced with new music on Hulu streaming)*

### "Someone to Watch Over Me"
Written by George Gershwin
Performed by Linda Ronstadt
*(Replaced with new music on Hulu streaming)*

### "Stormy Weather"
Written by Harold Arlen and Ted Koehler
*(Replaced with new music on Hulu streaming)*

### "Singin' in the Rain"
Music by Nacio Herb Brown
Lyrics by Arthur Freed
Performed by Bruce Willis

### "Be My Baby"
Written by Jeff Barry, Ellie Greenwich and Phil Spector
Performed by the Ronettes

### "Watch Out"
Written and performed by Patrice Rushen
*(Replaced with new music on Hulu streaming)*

# S03 E15
# To
# Heiress Human

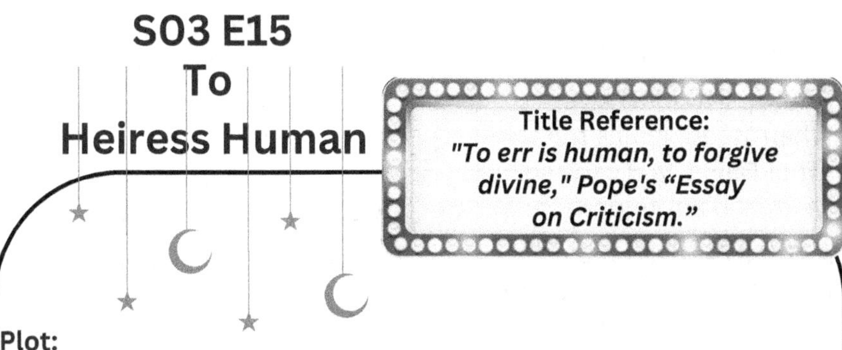

**Title Reference:**
*"To err is human, to forgive divine," Pope's "Essay on Criticism."*

**Plot:**

It's now the morning after Maddie and David have slept together, and each has a different perspective on the evening. While David is in a wonderful mood thinking that he's finally got Maddie in his grasp, she wants to pretend that "last night never happened." Maddie suggests they make "a pact" that their sleeping together not only did "not happen," but also will not happen again. David refuses her "pact," and is hurt. Ultimately, they end up making love again . . . and again throughout the episode.

Meanwhile, a wealthy heiress, Margaret Kendall, approaches Blue Moon to prove that her boyfriend loves her and is not after her money. Margaret's father disapproves of the relationship and is willing to do whatever it takes to stop it going any further to protect his assets. She wants to prove her father wrong.

Subsequently, her father is (seemingly) killed in a house fire and both his daughter and the boyfriend confess to the crime, both attempting to save the other from prosecution.

**Air Date:** May 5, 1987

**Written by:** Kerry Ehrin

**Director:** Sam Weisman

### CAST CREDIT

**Ann Hearn** ... Margaret Kendall

**William Hickey** ... Mr. Kendall

**Scott Paulin** ... Robert Murphy

**Bill Marcus** ... Desk Sergeant

**FUN FACT:**
The plot of the episode is similar to *The Heiress* (Movie, 1946) starring Olivia de Havilland.

**REVEALING MISTAKE:**
When Maddie pulls the sheet off of David, you can see he's wearing black underwear.

**ART IMITATING LIFE:**
Robert tells David, *"You're a good listener, man. You oughta be a bartender"* - Bruce worked as a bartender in NYC during the 1980s.

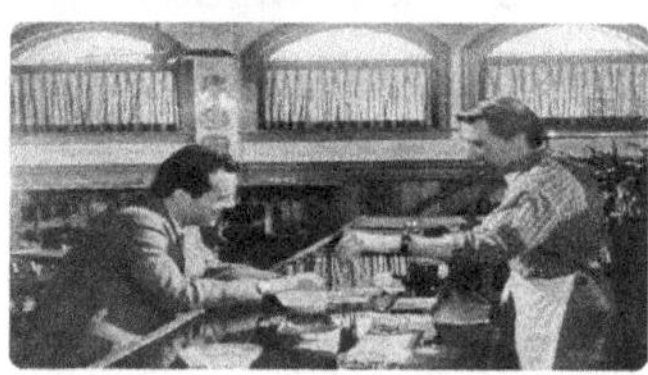

**STATS:**

*Door Slams: 1*
*Feet out of Elevator: 0*
*Maddie's Outfit Changes: 4*
*Agnes Rhymes: 0*

**GREAT LINES:**

" 
*David: She done doed it.*
*Maddie: She did? Doed? Damn.*
"

**BREAKING THE FOURTH WALL:**

**David:** "You hear that, Maddie? 'Quite dead,' and people say we don't have good plots."

***NOT* SO FUN FACT:**
This is the only episode in which we see Maddie and David spar, flirt, have deep talks, and sleep together, all while solving entertaining mysteries. A taste of what could have been.

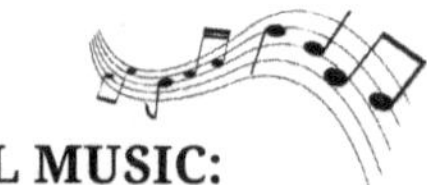

**ORIGINAL MUSIC:**

**"Double Shot of My Baby's Love"**
Written by Cyril E. Vetter and Don Smith
Performed by Bruce Willis

**"Jericho"**
Written by Mick Hucknall
Performed by Simply Red
*(Replaced with new music on Hulu streaming)*

---

### PACT CRAP
As attracted to each other as Maddie and David are, they're great deniers. We saw this with the kiss in s02e15, "Witness for The Execution." They both agreed "it didn't happen." Before that, in s02e04, "The Dream Sequence Always Rings Twice," neither could quite fess up to the sexy dreams they'd had about each other the night before. There are even some intimate moments in s03e08, "It's a Wonderful Job," and s03e09, "The Straight Poop," that are never mentioned again. Here, Maddie wants to make a pact (multiple pacts, in fact) that what happened the night before (and keeps happening) didn't. Pact schmacht, it happened—and we *all* like that it did.

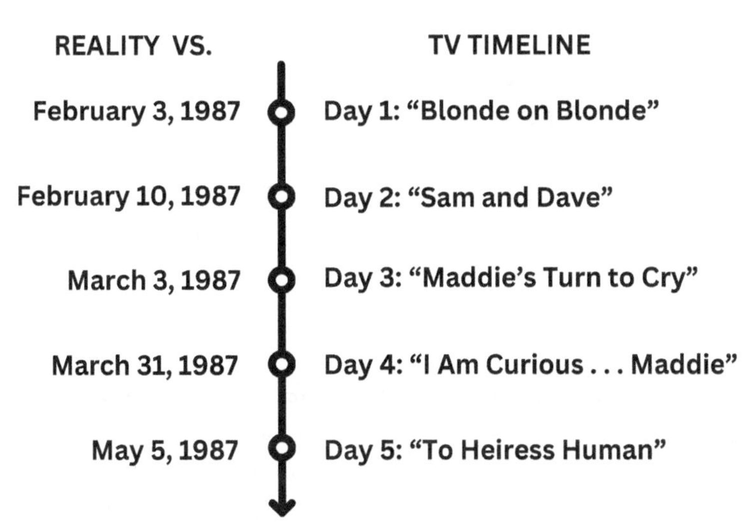



### PICTURE THIS:

It's 1987, and finally, it's happening: Maddie and David are getting together. We're to the good stuff . . . the stuff all the prior stuff has been leading up to . . . only it takes so long to get to the good stuff that the network has to keep reminding us of all the stuff that led up to the good stuff! In the land of Blue Moon, it's only five days from s03e11, "Blonde on Blonde" (Maddie's urges), to s03e15, "To Heiress Human" (the morning after), but the five shows aired over a three-month time period (February 3 to May 5), which is why Cybill isn't noticeably pregnant in "Blonde on Blonde" but is noticeably pregnant in "To Heiress Human"—crazy stuff!

## The Spontaneity of *Moonlighting*

On *Moonlighting the Podcast,* executive producer Jay Daniel talked about Glenn Gordon Caron's writing process on *Moonlighting.* Jay said, "His perfectionism, it had to be right, and this particular scene that he just wrote, he wouldn't hesitate to rip it up and throw it away and start again. So we ended up behind a lot, but I think his way of working created kind of a spontaneity, 'cause it really was kind of the first time [the actors] ever heard themselves say those lines. It was coming at the moment in this way. So it added spontaneity. It made it real."

# S04 E01
# A Trip
# to the Moon

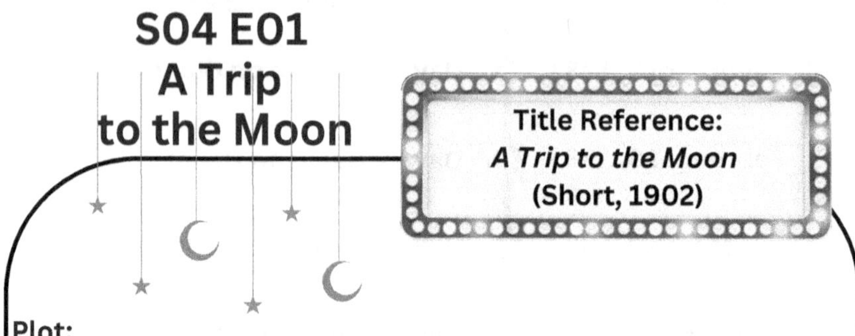


**Plot:**

So many questions are going through Maddie's mind. She has now been with David for a month, and she is wondering where their relationship is going. From her perspective, they don't have a relationship, because all they do is sleep together. David tries to resolve the situation by taking her out on a proper date. They get a late start on the evening and end up at a laundromat, where they discuss their relationship, dance to the Muzak, and express their love for each other, but she still doesn't know what she wants. Maddie leaves David in the laundromat saying she needs to be alone and think. She goes home, and the next thing you know, she's on a plane, flying off into the sunset.

There are three fantasy sequences in this episode. Maddie receives relationship advice from Dr. Joyce Brothers. David receives relationship advice from none other than Ray Charles while he sings and plays the piano in David's living room. And the third is an homage to *The Honeymooners* filmed in black and white, in which Cybill, Bruce, Allyce, and Charles Rocket play the leads from the classic Jackie Gleason series.

**Air Date:**
September 29, 1987

**Written by:**
Glenn Gordon Caron

**Director:** Allan Arkush

### CAST CREDIT
**Charles Rocket**
... Richard Addison playing Ed Norton
**Dr. Joyce Brothers**
**Ray Charles and the Raelettes**
**Harold J. Surratt** ... Cab Driver
**Stephanie Shroyer** ... Airline Employee

## Agnes Rhyme:

> Blue Moon Detective Agency, we've been here three years, taking care of your woes, finding lost persons, telling unfaithful bows, in honor of our birthday, we're offering a deal, let us solve your murder, we buy you a meal, a night on the town, just a little gift from us, when there's murder in your life, give us your business.

**LOOK FOR:** 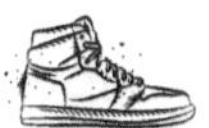
Bruce takes a page out of Cybill's book and is wearing white high-top sneakers when he runs to block the door so that Maddie will not leave the office.

**FUN FACT #1:**
The line "Go to a foreign [European] country and hide under a bed" is used by Paul McCain in s01e04, "The Next Murder You Hear."

**FUN FACT #2:**
This same laundromat was used in the Oscar-winning picture *Everything, Everywhere All at Once* (Movie, 2022).

**FUN FACT #3:**
This episode was filmed in April '86, but aired in September '86 due to Cybill's pregnancy.

**OUTFIT ROLE CALL:**
- Maddie wears the white dressing gown again in s05e10, "When Girls Collide."

### STATS:

*Door Slams: 1*
*Feet out of Elevator: 0*
*Maddie's Outfit Changes: 5*
*Agnes Rhymes: 1*

### GREAT LINES:
— 66 ——————

***David:*** *You can't deny it, Maddie, you got a bad case of me. And I got a bad case of you . . . and I never have had a bad case of anyone before.*

—————— 99 —

### FUN FACT #4:

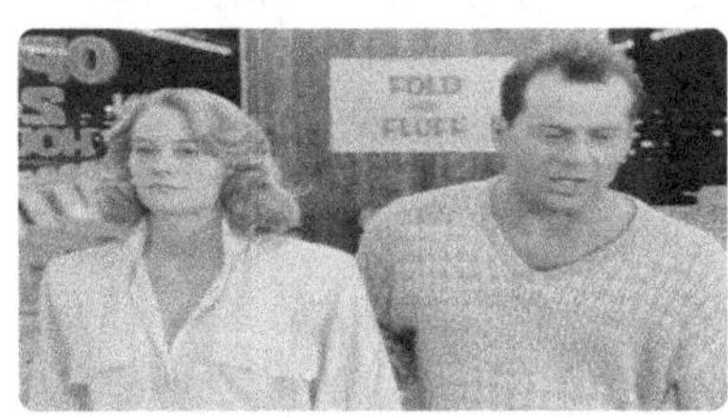


The (original) songs Maddie and David dance to in the laundromat are:
- **"Breaking Up Is Hard to Do"**
- **"Shall We Dance?"**
- **"Lara's Theme"**
- **"Hello, Dolly!"**

## LOCATION...LOCATION...LOCATION...

~ **San Fernando Majers Coin Laundry (laundromat interior)** - 260 South Meyer Street, San Fernando, California, USA

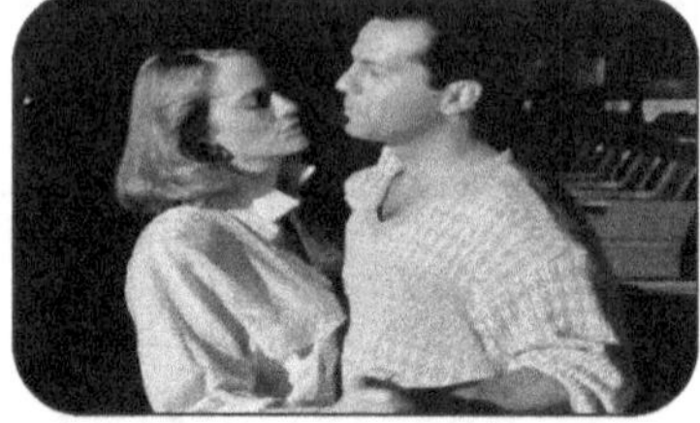


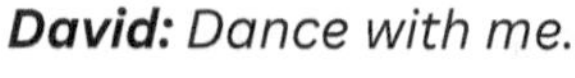

> **David:** *Dance with me.*
>
> **Maddie:** *You've used that line on me before, David. It's not going to work.*
>
> **David:** *It always works. It has to work.*

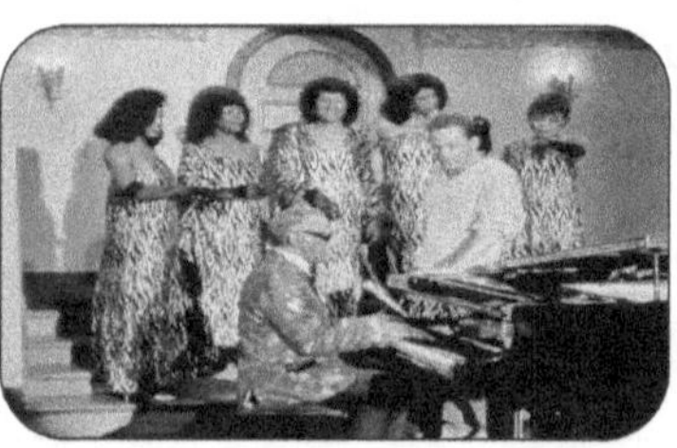

Ray and the Raelettes entertained cast and crew inbetween takes

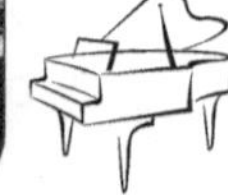

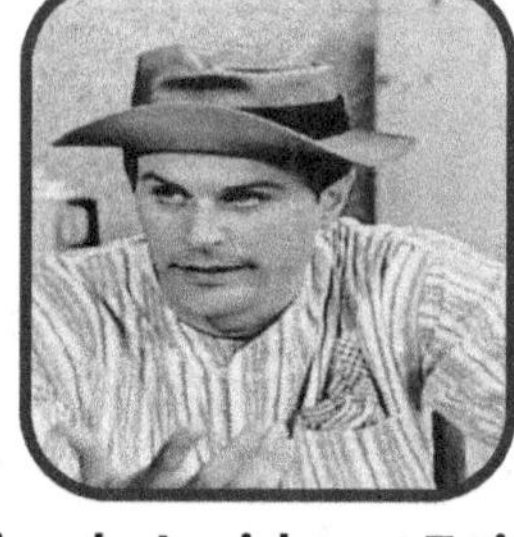

## LIGHTING DETAIL:

Look for the shadow of the Blue Moon logo from the office widow behind Agnes during her rhyme.

## An Episode Inside an Episode

Charles Rocket plays Ed Norton, Ralph Kramden's neighbor from *The Honeymooners* (TV Series, 1955-1956), in this spoof inside the episode called *The Bluemooners*.

---

### RAY CHARLES AND THE RAELETTES

We've heard cast and creators alike exclaim many times, "Everybody was on *Moonlighting*!"—and it's really true! The show was so popular at the time that all Glenn had to do was pick up the phone and invite someone on. If they weren't calling him first, that is. It's such a classic moment to have Ray Charles and the Raelettes serenading David and chastising him about his relationship with Maddie. We hear Bruce's memories of this day in the DVD commentary for "A Trip to the Moon"—he says he never left the set that day and Ray played tunes in between takes. What an amazing day on the *Moonlighting* set!

## ORIGINAL MUSIC:

**"Hit the Road Jack (Dave)"**
Written by Percy Mayfield
Performed by Ray Charles and the Raelettes

**"(Tune of) Georgia on My Mind"**
Written by Hoagy Carmichael and Stuart Gorrell
Performed by Ray Charles and the Raelettes with original lyrics

**"What'd I Say"**
Composed and performed by Ray Charles and Raelettes

**"Shall We Dance?"**
Music by Richard Rodgers; Lyrics by Oscar Hammerstein II
Played as Muzak in laundromat
*(Replaced with new music on Hulu streaming)*

**"Hello, Dolly!"**
Written by Jerry Herman
Played as Muzak in laundromat
*(Replaced with new music on Hulu streaming)*

**"Breaking Up Is Hard to Do"**
Written by Neil Sedaka and Howard Greenfield
Played as Muzak in laundromat
*(Replaced with new music on Hulu streaming)*

**"Lara's Theme"**
Music by Maurice Jarre
*Doctor Zhivago* (1965)
Played as Muzak in laundromat
*(Replaced with new music on Hulu streaming)*

— • • • —

## STOP THAT BLONDE!

From day one, Addison took a very *hands-on* approach when attempting to reason with Maddie and get her to see things *his* way. In the Pilot episode, David chases Maddie down the hall, shows up on her date, and insists they dance together to get what he wants. Of course, David's physical way of making Maddie stop, look, and listen became a common occurrence, present in episodes like s02e11, "The Bride of Tupperman," in which he chases, blocks, and elevator hops along with her while very adeptly convincing her to change her plans. In s02e03, "Money Talks, Maddie Walks," David spins her, steps in front of her, and follows her all the way to Buenos Aires to get her to listen. In s02e17, "Funeral for a Door Nail," Maddie has to physically drag David along with her to the door as he pleads his case about attending the wedding in the Windy City. A very physical man indeed . . . do you think Maddie minded?

# S04 E02
# Come Back
# Little Shiksa

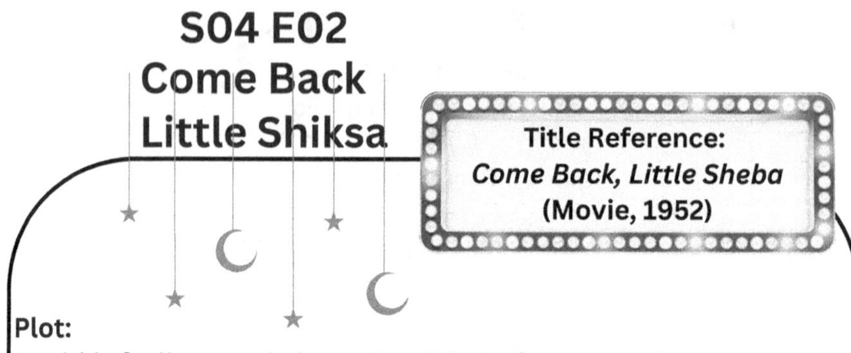


**Plot:**

David is feeling good about the night before in the laundromat and even tells Agnes that he finally has Maddie "in a relationship." He is unaware that Maddie has left Los Angeles and is now at her parents' home in Chicago.

Donald Chase arrives and wants to hire Blue Moon to locate a woman whom he met at a charity event. He doesn't know her name; he only has one of her valuable earrings and reports that she has a beauty mark on her face.

Maddie's parents are immediately suspicious given that she has turned up unannounced at their home and is not being forthcoming about the duration of her stay.

David and Bert begin to investigate the Chase case and track down the woman he's looking for in a department store. Melissa reveals to them that she is on the run from her very dangerous husband and believes that David and Bert are out to kill her.

Because Maddie has disappeared and the case reflects his dilemma, David becomes enraged and smashes Maddie's BMW in the underground garage. This episode includes another fantasy sequence, in which Maddie and David are depicted in Claymation.

**Air Date:**
October 6, 1987

**Written by:**
Jeff Reno and Ron Osborn

**Director:** Allan Arkush

**CAST CREDIT**
**Robert Webber** ... Alexander Hayes
**Eva Marie Saint** ... Virginia Hayes
**John Goodman** ... Donald Chase
**Kay Lenz** ... Melissa
**Frances E. Nealy** ... Roberta

**FUN FACT #1:**
Bruce Willis and John Goodman have been friends since 1979 when Bruce bartended at an NYC bar called Chelsea Central.

**FUN FACT #2:**
Actor C. Thomas Howell makes a cameo appearance as the shop assistant moving the mannequin.

**FUN FACT #3:**
Bruce Willis filmed the first *Die Hard* (Movie, 1988) at the same time he filmed season four of *Moonlighting*.

**FUN FACT #4:**
Cybill Shepherd let producers know in February of 1987 that she was pregnant with twins and was put on bed rest by doctors shortly after. For this reason, most of her side of season four was filmed months before Bruce filmed his part.

**FUN FACT #5:**
The parking garage used in this episode is the same garage used in s03e15, "Witness for the Execution," where they had their first "real" kiss.

**LOOK FOR #1:**
The cut of David using his key to unlock Maddie's door is used again in s04e04, "Tale in Two Cities."

**STATS:**

*Door Slams: 0*
*Feet out of Elevator: 1*
*Maddie's Outfit Changes: 1*
*(Claymation Maddie Outfits: 3)*
*Agnes Rhymes: 0*
*Smashed BMW: 1*

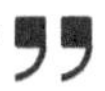

**GREAT LINES:**

**Donald Chase:** *You see, I've fallen in love with a woman, and I think maybe she's fallen in love with me, but I don't know where she is. I need very much to talk to her.*

**David:** *There's a lot of that going around.*

**LOOK FOR #2:**
David's arrival at Maddie's home was filmed in one cut using a crane until he gets to the top of the stairs.

**LOOK FOR #3:**
The BMW wrecked in the episode is not the car they normally drove in the series.

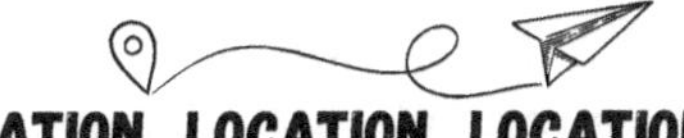

## LOCATION...LOCATION...LOCATION...

**~ Alex and Virginia's fictional home address** - 88 East Park Drive, Lake Shore, Chicago, Illinios, USA

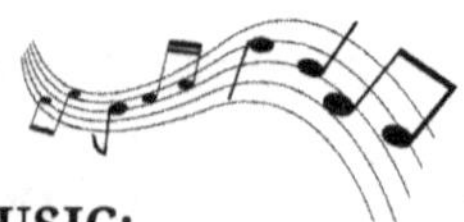



**ORIGINAL MUSIC:**

**"Think!"**
Theme song of game show Jeopardy!
(1964-1975; 1978-1979; 1984-present)
Composed by Merv Griffin
*(Replaced with new music on Hulu streaming)*

**"Manic Depression"**
Written and performed by Jimi Hendrix
*(Replaced with new music on Hulu streaming)*

**"Rama Lama Ding Dong"**
Written by George Jones
Performed by the Edsels
*(Replaced with new music on Hulu streaming)*

**"Da Ya Think I'm Sexy?"**
Written by Rod Stewart, Carmine Appice,
and Duane Hitchings
Performed by Rod Stewart

**"Where You Lead"**
Written by Carole King and Toni Stern
*(Replaced with new music on Hulu streaming)*

⟶ • ⟵

## IS THIS SEAT TAKEN?

Here in "Come Back Little Shiksa" we see a forlorn David slide into Maddie's eerily empty office, sit in her desk chair and plead with her . . . well, Claymation her, to come back . . . or at least let him come there. There are only a few instances throughout the series where we find David . . . or rather Maddie finds David sitting in her desk chair, and anytime he is . . . you can bet he's got something important on his mind. In s02e06, "Knowing Her," Maddie finds David in her seat oozing intensity, hoping she will "visit the worm" for him, as his desire to protect his old flame Gillian grows. In s03e05, "All Creature Great and . . . Not So Great," Maddie is surprised to find David in her office, feet up, morals out, wrestling with the idea of helping a priest find a married woman he's in love with. In s03e14, "I Am Curious . . . Maddie," David lies in wait for Maddie in her chair after receiving a morning visit from Sam and learning that Maddie . . . hasn't exactly told him the whole story about what's going on between them. Talk about being in the hot seat!

# /ˈkeməstrē/

What do you do on a show where the main reason the audience tunes in every Tuesday night is to see the two leads detecting, bantering, and slamming doors—but it's not physically possible to have those two people in the same room together? Claymation! Glenn talked about this choice on *Moonlighting the Podcast:* "They weren't physically able to be together. As extraordinary a power as I am, even I, and God knows I tried, I mean, I got Will Vinton to make a Claymation Cybill, for God's sake. Shows you how desperate I was." Glenn also mentioned he does not subscribe to the *"Moonlighting* Curse" (the show losing its appeal after the leads sleep together) and would not have gotten the characters together if he didn't think it could work, but, alas, we'll never know. Today we may have had an "AI Maddie " or a "hologram David." Hmmm . . . not a bad idea for season six!?

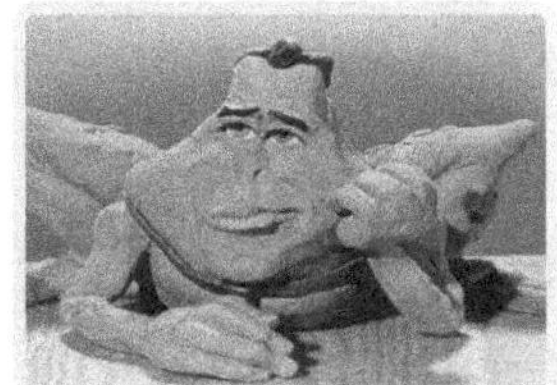

*"Alright, I'm impressed. She turned me into a horny toad."*

## CLAYMATION—VINTON STUDIOS

For the visual to be as realistic as possible, the Claymation figures were created by using Bruce and Cybill as templates. Cybill recorded her side of the dialogue several months earlier. Both Cybill and Bruce were filmed acting out the dialogue so that Vinton Studios could use the footage as a reference to ensure the Claymation reflected the actors' expressions and body movements. Production took photographs of Maddie's office, and then Vinton put together an identical miniature set. So when you see "Claymation Maddie," she is actually set against a photo of her office in the background, not the actual office.

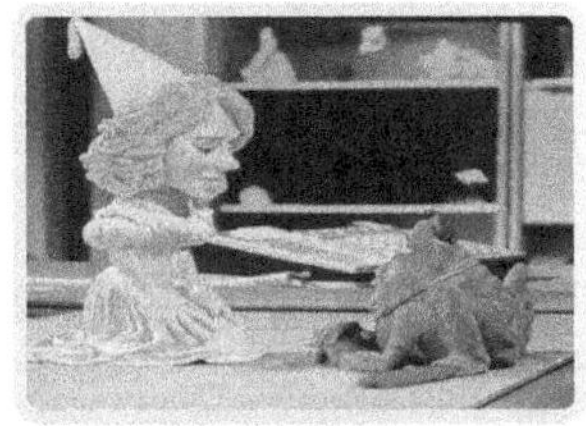

# S04 E03
# Take a Left
# at the Altar



**Plot:**

David is saddened that he hasn't heard from Maddie, as it has been a week since she left. Maddie's parents are worried about her, believing she is hiding something due to her mysterious behavior.

In the meantime, Blue Moon is hired by a man to find a groom who went missing on his wedding day. The man is the bride's brother and wants David to find him and for the groom to go through with the wedding. So David and Bert get on the case. While they are on this man's trail, David and Bert find out that the groom is already married. Subsequently, the groom is found dead, and they believe that the client is the chief suspect.

**Air Date:**
October 13, 1987

**Written by**: Karen Hall

**Director:** Sam Weisman

**CAST CREDITS**
**Robert Webber** ... Alexander Hayes
**Eva Marie Saint** ... Virginia Hayes
**Terry O'Quinn** ... Bryant Wilbourne
**Jane Daly** ... Mrs. Gerardi
**Amanda Plummer** ... Jackie Wilbourne
**Maggie Egan** ... Airport Clerk
**David Q. Combs** ... Cleaning Man
**Tony Pierce** ... Police Detective
**Ted Rogers** ... Craig Gerardi

**FUN FACT #1:**
Bruce Willis and guest star Amanda Plummer both appear in *Pulp Fiction* (Movie, 1994).

**FUN FACT #2:**
The woman with the short blonde hair sitting behind Bruce in the scene at the airport is his cousin.

**FUN FACT #3:**
Originally, part of the theme from *North by Northwest* (Movie, 1959) can be heard during the chase. Eva Marie Saint, who costarred in that film, plays Maddie's mother.

**FUN FACT #4:**
The "beepers" scene was hard to get through because Bruce was laughing so hard every time Curtis entered his office saying "I've brought beepers."

**OUTFIT ROLL CALL:**

- Maddie wears the blue housedress in s04e04, "Tale in Two Cities."

**STATS:**

*Door Slams: 0*
*Feet out of Elevator: 1 (David's)*
*Maddie's Outfit Changes: 3*
*Agnes Rhymes: 0*

**GREAT LINES:**

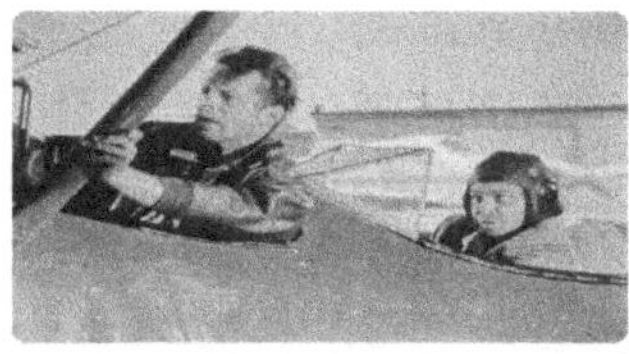
*This is all a bunch of crap. I'm miserable, and I want you to come home.*
**~David**

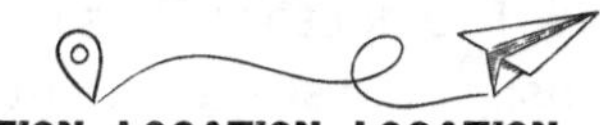

**LOCATION...LOCATION...LOCATION...**
**~ Van Nuys Airport** - 7120 Hayvenhurst Avenue, Van Nuys, California, USA

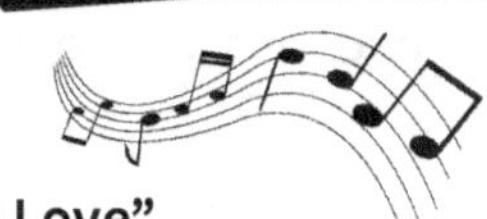

**ORIGINAL MUSIC:**

**"There is Love"**
Composed by Noel "Paul" Stookey
**"The Flight of the Bumblebee"**
Theme song of the US Air Force
Composed by Nikolai Rimsky-Korsakov
Performed by Robert Crawford
*(Replaced with new music on Hulu streaming)*
**"Limbo Rock"**
Written by Kal Mann and Billy Strange
Performed by Chubby Checker and Bruce Willis
*(Replaced with new music on Hulu streaming)*
**"North by Northwest"**
Theme song of *North by Northwest* (1959)
Composed by Bernard Herrman
*(Replaced with new music on Hulu streaming)*

# S04 E04
# Tale in Two Cities



**Plot:**

Alexander and Virginia Hayes are still concerned about their daughter. Maddie evades any questions and won't explain why she is avoiding going back to Los Angeles.

They attempt to cheer her up by throwing a party at their home, which only makes her more agitated. At the party, she meets the doctor from across the street. As an excuse to leave the party, she asks the doctor if he wants to go for a drive because she hasn't been out of the house in a week. During this drive, she informs him that she's been feeling off-kilter of late. She sleeps all the time, yet she is still tired. The doctor offers to give her a checkup, as he has to stop in at the hospital to see a patient anyway.

Back in Los Angeles, David continues to brood. Bert and McGillicudy fight for Agnes's affections, and Bert is enraged as feels he has lost Agnes for good.

Maddie finds out she is pregnant and decides to call Agnes and let her know. Agnes isn't home, so Maddie leaves a message on her answering machine but emphatically states that she is not to tell David.

**Air Date:** November 3, 1987

**Written by:**
Roger Director
and Charles H. Eglee

**Director:** Allan Arkush

### CAST CREDITS

**Robert Webber** ... Alexander Hayes
**Eva Marie Saint** ... Virginia Hayes
**Jack Blessing** ... MacGillicudy
**Cleavant Derricks** ... Leonard Haven
**R. H. Thomson** ... Dr. Steve Hill
**Walter Olkewicz** ... Leon Summers
**Will Nye** ... Blue Moon Staff
**Lisa Mende** ... Eleanor Summers
**April Dawn** ... Opal Summers
**Jean Speegle Howard** ... Mrs. Cousins
**Pamela Bowen** ... Rita Corley
**Romy Walthall** ... Genevieve
**Stan Yale** ... Homeless Man

### Agnes Rhyme:

> *(answering machine)*
> You've reached the machine of Agnes Dipesto, please wait for the beep, and state your manifesto.

### *MOONLIGHTING* MENTION:
*This Is Us* - s03e14, "The Graduates"
(TV Episode, 2019)
**Rebecca is watching this episode of *Moonlighting* on television.**

### FUN FACT:
The three movies Maddie flips through on the TV:
1. **Philadelphia Story** (1940)
2. **Double Indemnity** (1944)
3. **The Thin Man** (1934)

### LOOK FOR:
The cut of David using his key to unlock Maddie's door was taken from s04e02, "Come Back Little Shiksa."

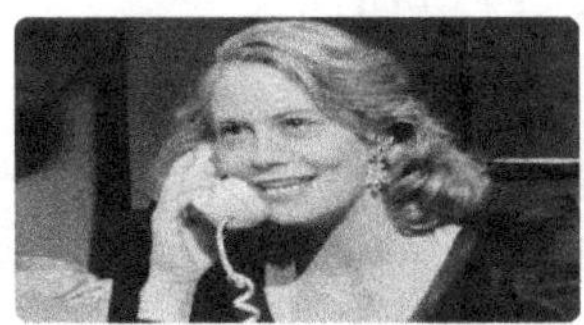

### OUTFIT ROLL CALL:
- Maddie wore the blue housedress in s04e03, "Take a Left at the Altar."
- She wears the same pajamas in s04e07, "Father Knows Last."

### STATS:

*Door Slams: 1*
*Feet out of Elevator: 0*
*Maddie's Outfit Changes: 3*
*Agnes Rhymes: 1*

### GREAT LINES:

> *David: Any day now, you're gonna come up here, peek through this window, and there she'll blow. Hollering, slamming doors, just like she never left.*
>
> *Agnes: You really think so?*
>
> *David (hand over heart): By my mother's pot roast.*

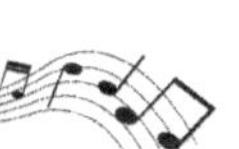

### ORIGINAL MUSIC:

**"Leader of the Pack"**
Written by Shadow Morton, Jeff Barry and Ellie Greenwich
Performed by the Shangri-Las
**"I'm a Man"**
Written by Jimmy Miller and Steve Winwood
Performed by the Spencer Davis Group
**"Cherry Pink and Apple Blossom White"**
By Louis Gugielmi
*(Replaced with new music on Hulu streaming)*
**"Fly Me to the Moon"**
By Bart Howard
*(Replaced with new music on Hulu streaming)*
**"Something about You"**
By Michael Jonzun
*(Replaced with new music on Hulu streaming)*
**"Desafinado"**
By Antonio Carlos Jobim
*(Replaced with new music on Hulu streaming)*
**"Look Sharp"**
By Joe Jackson
*(Replaced with new music on Hulu streaming)*

# S04 E05
# Cool Hand Dave (Part 1)



**Plot:**

Agnes is so excited when she hears the message that Maddie left her on her answering machine about being pregnant. She arrives at work covering her mouth to ensure she doesn't spill the beans. Unfortunately, she can't keep it to herself for long, as Bert knows that she is keeping something from him. She tells him but states in uncertain terms that he is not to tell David.

Despite promising Agnes that he will not tell David, Bert can't help himself and goes straight into David's office to inform him of the news. Upon hearing Maddie is pregnant, David races to the airport intent on booking a flight to Chicago. However, in the airport lounge, he is tricked by convict Scott "Mad Dog" Hundley, on his way to prison, and they switch places. The guards refuse to believe that David is not the prisoner, and he ends up going to jail in Hundley's place.

Agnes is giving herself a facial with avocado when she realizes Bert is below her window with his Uncle Phil's band, serenading her with the song "Sexual Healing." She lets him into her apartment and tells him that she is worried because Miss Hayes said that Mr. Addison never showed up in Chicago. They end up making love. David is escorted to solitary confinement.
To be continued . . .

**Air Date:**
November 17, 1987

**Written by:**
Roger Director
and Charles H. Eglee

**Director:** Allan Arkush

### CAST CREDITS
**Tony Bill** ... Scott "Mad Dog" Hundley
**Tracey Walter** ... Arnie Stegler
**Rocky Giordani** ... Derek
**Ronald G. Joseph** ... Schank
**Cheryl Carter** ... Airline Employee
**Fred Ottaviano** ... Prison Guard
**Darwyn Swalve** ... Darwyn
**Tom O'Brien** ... Inmate
**Jack Murdock** ... Pops
**Al White** ... Prisoner Escort
**Cletus Young** ... Parole Officer
**David Clover** ... Prisoner Escort

## BREAKING THE FOURTH WALL:

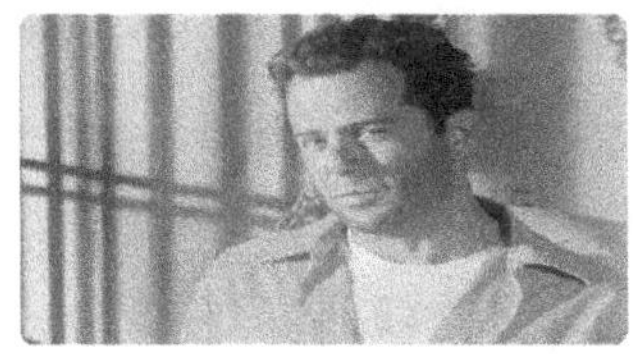

When a prisoner asks him to shine his shoes, David looks at the camera says, *"This better be a dream episode."*

## LOOK FOR:
Agnes and Bert's cold open, which was left off the DVD release, is restored on Hulu.

## FUN FACT #1:
Bruce's and Cybill's respective sides of the phone call were actually filmed months apart, as she was put on bedrest earlier in the year due to her twin pregnancy.

## FUN FACT #2:
Allyce missed going to the Emmys because she and Curtis had to shoot the "Sexual Healing" scene that day.

## STATS:

*Door Slams: 1*
*Feet out of Elevator: 0*
*Maddie's Outfit Changes: 1*
*Agnes Rhymes: 0*

## GREAT LINES:

> **David:** *Whadda ya talking about? I haven't knocked anybody up.*
>
> **Bert:** *Not just anybody, sir. You knocked up the boss.*
>
> **David:** *What?*

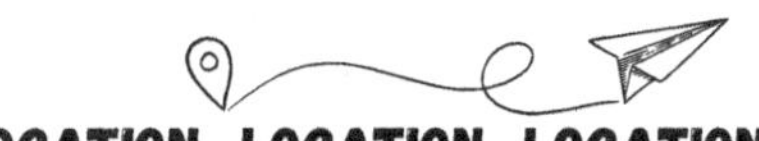

## LOCATION...LOCATION...LOCATION...
**~ Lincoln Heights Jail -**
421 N Ave 19, Los Angeles, CA 90031, USA

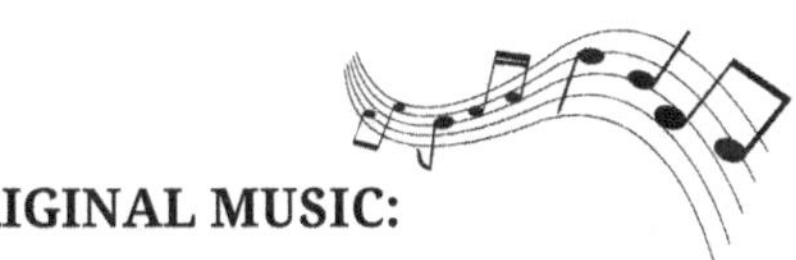

## ORIGINAL MUSIC:

**"When the Red, Red Robin (Comes Bob, Bob, Bobbin' Along)"**
Written by Harry M. Woods

**"Sexual Healing"**
Written by Marvin Gaye, Odell Brown, and David Ritz
Performed by Curtis Armstrong

**"Love Is a Many-Splendored Thing"**
Written by Sammy Fain and Paul Francis Webster
*(Replaced with new music on Hulu streaming)*

# S04 E06
# Cool Hand Dave (Part 2)

**Title Reference:**
*Cool Hand Luke*
(Movie, 1967)

**Plot:**

The lines often get blurred in *Moonlighting*, and this is one example. David is still in prison, and nobody knows where he is. It's not only his friends who are wondering where he is; it's also network executives. They seek the services of a fortune teller, who uses a crystal ball in an attempt to locate David, but all she sees are bars. Following this, they begin auditioning to find a replacement. We begin to see the auditions, with men in line all dressed up in various outfits that David wore in previous episodes. David is released from solitary confinement and placed in a work gang, where his fellow convicts advise him to marry Maddie.

 Bert is using his new, temporary title of Blue Moon supervisor, awarded to him by David, to put the employees in line.

 David witnesses illegal activities by a prison guard, who is about to kill him, but fortunately, a riot starts, allowing David to escape unnoticed.

Agnes and Bert decide to start investigating the whereabouts of "Mr. Addison." The episode features a lengthy musical number performed by the prisoners in the style of "When I Was a Lad" from Gilbert and Sullivan's *H.M.S. Pinafore.*

**Air Date:** December 1, 1987

**Written by:**

Roger Director and Charles H. Eglee

**Director:** Allan Arkush

**FUN FACT #1:**
Listen for the prison guard whistling the *Moonlighting* theme.

**FUN FACT #2:**
"Cool Hand Dave" is the only two-part episode in all five seasons.

**FUN FACT #3:**
Scott Huntley is wearing David's sweater from s04e01, "A Trip to the Moon."

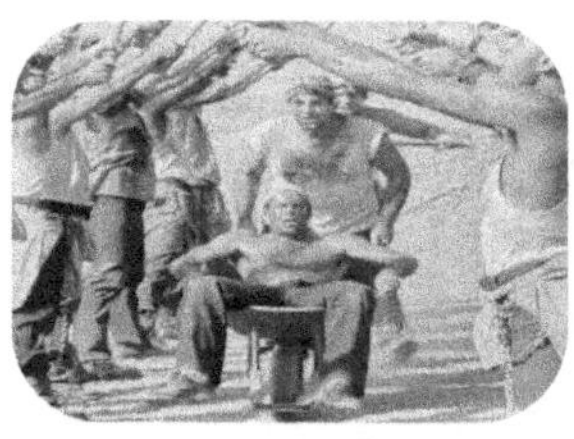

## CULTURAL REFERENCES:

~ **Amenhoteph** - Ancient Egyptian

~ **Julius Caesar** - Roman General and Statesman

~ **Superman** - American Comic Book Hero, DC Comics

~ *Max Headroom* - Cyber Personality (TV Show, 1987-1988)

~ *Escape from Alcatraz* - (Movie, 1979)

~ *Hogan's Heroes* - (TV Show, 1965-1971)

~ *The Great Escape* - (Movie, 1963)

~ **Space Mountain** - Roller Coaster at Disneyland.

**STATS:**

*Door Slams: 0*
*Feet out of Elevator: 0*
*Maddie's Outfit Changes: 0*
*Agnes Rhymes: 0*

## GREAT LINES:

*In this dump, I learned what is essential in life, and this woman is essential.*
*~David*

## Kamikaze Anyone?

- Bruce Willis used to work at the **Kamikaze Club** in the '80s in NYC.
- David orders Maddie a **kamikaze** in the pilot.
- In s04e06, "Cool Hand Dave (Part 2)," the code word to start auditions is "it's **kamikaze** time."
- Agnes orders a double **kamikaze** in s03e14, "I Am Curious . . . Maddie."

**BREAKING THE FOURTH WALL:**
"Have you stopped to consider the consequences of murdering a major television personality?"

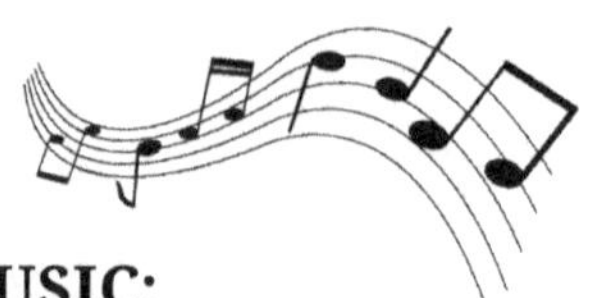

# ORIGINAL MUSIC:

**"Do Wah Diddy Diddy"**
Written by Jeff Barry and Ellie Greenwich
Performed by Manfred Mann

**"Limbo Rock"**
Written by Kal Mann and Billy Strange
Performed by Chubby Checker
*(Replaced with new music on Hulu streaming)*

**"Call Collect Chicago"**
Written by Chic Eglee
Performed by the Chain Gang

**"What's Your Name"**
Written by Claude Johnson
Performed by Bruce Willis

**"The Raiders March"**
Theme song of *Indiana Jones
and the Raiders of the Lost Ark* (Movie, 1981)
Written by John Williams
*(Replaced with new music on Hulu streaming)*

**"Three Blind Mice"**
Composed by Thomas Ravenscroft
Whistled by Bruce Willis

**"Danger Ahead"**
Theme song of *Dragnet*
(Radio series, 1949-1957)
(TV Show, 1951-1959, original / 1967-1970, revival)
Written by Walter Schumann
*(Replaced with new music on Hulu streaming)*

**"Puffin Billy"**
Composed by Edward White
*(Replaced with new music on Hulu streaming)*

**"When I Was a Lad (The Lass That Loved a Sailor)"**
Composed by Gilbert and Sullivan
*H.M.S. Pinafore*

# CAST CREDITS:

**Ronald G. Joseph** ... Captain Schank
**Tracey Walter** ... Arnie Steckler
**Tony Bill** ... Scott Hundley
**Dick Miller** ...Pick up Guy
**Leo V. Gordon** ... Warden Cosgrove
**Charles Parks** ... Inmate
**Penny Santon** ... Madame Palmer
**Anthony DeLongis** ... Chain Gang Soloist
**Nicholas Worth** ... Inmate
**Julius J. Carry III** ... Inmate
**Rocky Giordani Sr.** ... Derek
**Ken Foree** ... Inmate
**Jack Murdock** ... Pops
**Jack Blessing** ... McGillicuddy
**Darwyn Swalve** ... Darwyn
**Fred Ottaviano** ... Prison Guard
**Tom Reese** ... Grogan
**Raymond Ma** ... David Addison Wannabe
**Matt McKenzie** ... Inmate
**Toni Sawyer** ... ABC Executive
**Wren Brown** ... ABC Executive
**Etan Boritzer** ... Inmate
**R. J. Arterburn** ... Inmate
**Steven Brian Smith** ... Inmate
**John Paul Gamoke** ... Inmate
**Howard Schechter** ... Inmate
**Michael Novack** ... Inmate
**Joseph Romeo** ... Inmate
**Gerard T. Doyle** ... David Addison Wannabe
**Frank Rosch** ... Inmate

# S04 E07
# Father Knows Last

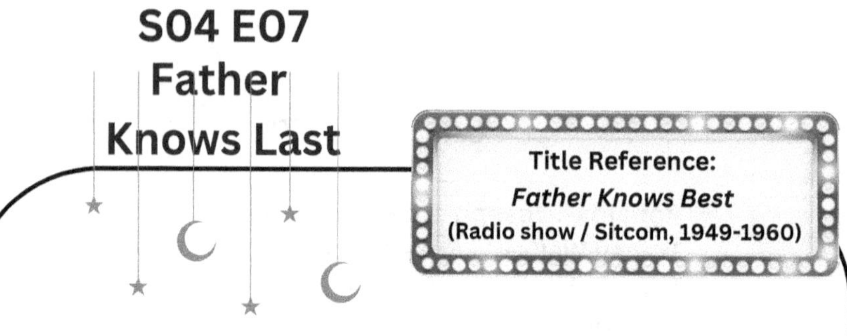


**Plot:**

Maddie's mother has guessed that Maddie's pregnant due to her constant morning sickness. Meanwhile, back at Blue Moon, the furniture is being repossessed, as the bills haven't been paid in David's absence and the employees begin to rebel. Herbert's dictatorial leadership skills are not helping the situation so the employees demand, "No work and pay!"—and walk out. David returns to Blue Moon to find Agnes and Bert in an empty office.

Maddie's father turns up to speak to David. He's found out about the pregnancy and wants David to "do the right thing." David has a fight with Agnes back at Blue Moon, which makes him realize he needs to fully explain the situation to Mr. Hayes. He rushes to the airport and boards the same plane as Mr. Hayes to explain his relationship with Maddie in real detail and to tell him how much he loves her. They resolve their differences on the plane. Mr. Hayes apologizes and gives David a check to restore Blue Moon's financial situation. The next morning, David arrives at Blue Moon being rolled in on Maddie's desk by men replacing the furniture. He makes a speech about how the business is now back operating as normal. The episode ends with David reading a book on fatherhood.

**Air Date:** December 15, 1987

**Written by:** Kerry Ehrin

**Director:** Allan Arkush

### CAST CREDITS

**Robert Webber** ... Alexander Hayes
**Eva Marie Saint** ... Virginia Hayes
**Jack Blessing** ... MacGillicudy
**Cleavant Derricks** ... Leonard Haven
**R. H. Thomson** ... Dr. Steve Hill
**Pamela Bowen** ... Rita Corley
**Harry Morgan Moses** ... Ticket Clerk
**Tom Lacy** ... Plane Passenger
**Beverly Hart** ... Stewardess

## CONTINUITY #1:

In the restaurant, David's Bloody Mary appears, then disappears, then appears with a celery stalk, and then reappears without the celery.

## CONTINUITY #2:

From s01e02, "Gunfight at the So-So Corral," it's clear Blue Moon is on floor twenty (office number 2016), but David tells Leonard, "This is the twenty-third floor."

### WHO KNOWS LAST?

The title has a duality to it where it could mean Mr. Hayes is the last to know what's been happening. It could also refer to David being the last to know everything, since Maddie isn't communicating with him.

## STATS:

*Door Slams: 2*
*Feet out of Elevator: 0*
*Maddie's Outfit Changes: 2*
*Agnes Rhymes: 1*

### GREAT LINES:

*No work and pay!*
*~Blue Moon Wobblies*

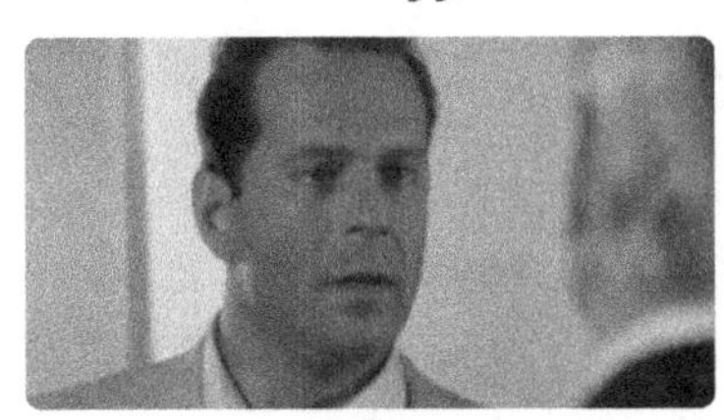

### OUTFIT ROLL CALL:

- Maddie wears the same pajamas in s04e04, "Tale in Two Cities."

## HEAVY LIFTING

With Cybill pregnant and on bed rest during the fourth season, Bruce Willis had the weight of the moon on his shoulders. He had to solve the cases, (mis)manage Blue Moon, and try like hell to hide the misery he felt with Maddie gone, all while filming a little movie called *Die Hard* (Movie, 1988) on his off-hours. Say what you will about what Bruce's career became after *Moonlighting*, we would put any of his subsequent work up against the acting he did in season four of this show. Case in point: the monologue David delivers to Maddie's dad (Robert Webber) on the airplane in this episode, which is probably one of the best dramatic monologues ever delivered on TV. Thank you, Bruce, for all you put into this show. We love you!

# S04 E08
# Los Dos Dipestos



**Plot:**

When Agnes's mother, Clara Dipesto, arrives in Los Angeles for a visit, she has just come from a holiday in Mexico. While she was there, she was given a complimentary souvenir on a tour, which she brings as a gift for Agnes. Unbeknownst to Clara, stolen jewels have been planted in the statue to be smuggled into America.

Agnes approaches Mr. Addison for a raise, as she wants to look after her mom for the duration of her visit. On their way back from brunch, Agnes and her mother are followed, and hence a *Moonlighting* car chase begins. Agnes avoids the car that was chasing them but returns to her home to find that it has been ransacked. Agnes leaves her mother at Blue Moon to keep her safe while she and Bert begin investigating the case.

Several unsavory characters are on the trail to retrieve the statue and are willing to do anything to get it back. A funny hallway sequence ensues to the music of the *William Tell Overture*. Agnes and Bert save the day and capture the thieves in a very unusual and creative way.

Cybill Shepherd does not appear, and Bruce Willis appears only at the beginning and end of this episode.

**Air Date:**
January 5, 1988

**Written by:**
Douglas Steinberg

**Director:**
Gerald Perry Finnerman

**CAST CREDITS**
**Imogene Coca** ... Clara Dipesto
**Reni Santoni** ... Arredondo
**Ron Troncatty** ... Paul Burden
**Ellen Albertina Dow** ... Mrs. Baer
**Gary Epper** ... Man in Cantina
**Gonzalez Gonzalez** ... Mexican Singer
**Robin Welch** ... Ballerina
**Tom Ashworth** ... Shaving Man
**Katherine James** ... Housewife

## STATS:

Door Slams: 1
Feet out of Elevator: 0
Maddie's Outfit Changes: 0
Agnes Rhymes: 1

## GREAT LINES:

**Carla Dipesto:** *Who's that with Mr. Violin?*

**Bert:** *Mr. Viola*

**Carla Dipesto:** *Mr. Viola's with Mr. Violin?*

## FAMILY TIES:

In this episode, we meet Agnes's mother, played by the wonderful comedic actress Imogene Coca.

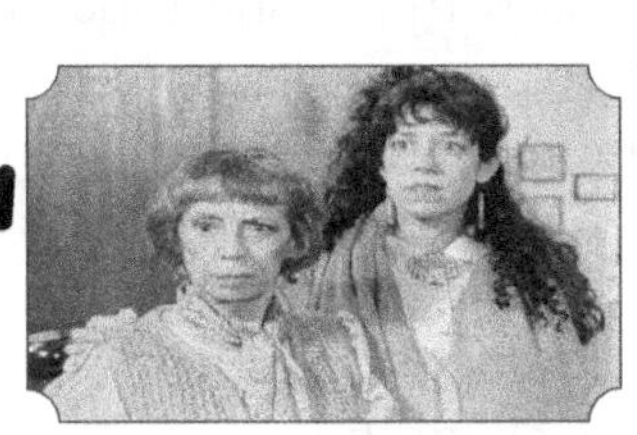

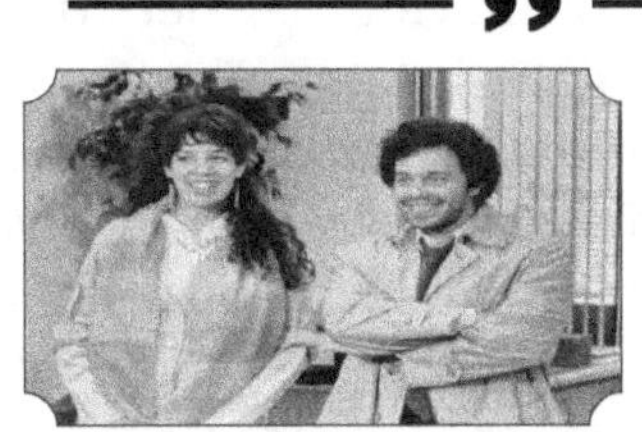

**BREAKING THE FOURTH WALL:**
**Agnes's Mother:** "What about your Miss Hayes and Mr. Addison?"
**Agnes:** "They're not in tonight's episode."

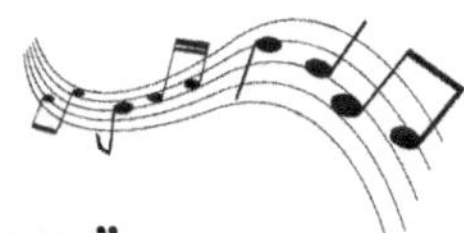

## ORIGINAL MUSIC:

**"Oklahoma"**
Theme song of *Oklahoma* (Play, 1943)
Music by Richard Rodgers
Lyrics by Oscar Hammerstein II
Performed by Allyce Beasley and Imogene Coca

**"Anything You Can Do, I Can Do Better"**
Written by Irving Berlin

**"William Tell Overture"**
Written by Gioachino Rossini

# S04 E09
# Fetal Attraction

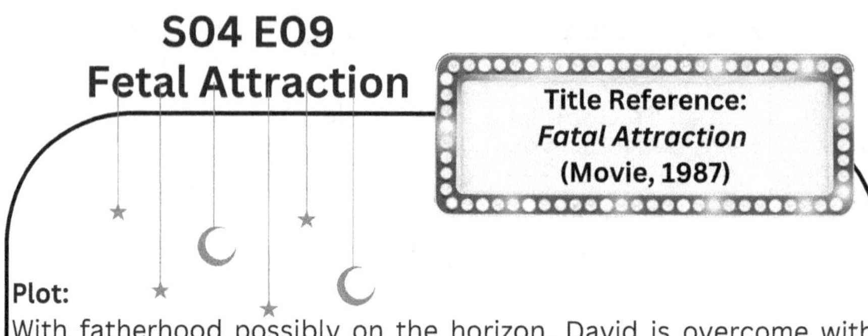


**Plot:**

With fatherhood possibly on the horizon, David is overcome with emotions and all that he has to learn and begins to research as much as he can, even using Bert as a guinea pig. He even asks Agnes about motherly instincts.

He decides to enroll in a Lamaze class, but unfortunately, the instructor says he is unable to attend as he has no partner to work with. But then an unwed pregnant woman named Terri shows up at Blue Moon asking for help. The Lamaze instructor told her that David didn't have a partner to practice with, so she thought they might be a good match. They agree to be partners in the class.

The relationship becomes a little complicated when Terry develops feelings for David. Maddie receives a package in Chicago from Blue Moon full of childbirth books. She calls Agnes and finds out it was David who sent them. Agnes updates Maddie on what David has been up to with his research into having children.

As Maddie is packing in her room, her mom walks in surprised to see that she is leaving. Maddie explains that she needs to return to Los Angeles to attempt to work things out.

**Air Date:** January 19, 1988

**Teleplay by:**
Charles H. Eglee
Roger Director

**Story by:**
Ron Osborn
Jeff Reno
Kerry Ehrin

**Director:**
Allan Arkush

### CAST CREDITS

**Brooke Adams** ... Terri Knowles
**Eva Marie Saint** ... Virginia Hayes
**Robert Webber** ... Alexander Hayes
**Janet Maclachlan** ... Angela Bridges, R.N.
**Sandra Bogan** ... Mrs. Jacobson
**Mimi Cozzens** ... Saleslady
**Jason Ross** ... Delivery Man
**Gwen Van Dam** ... Waitress
**Anna Garduno** ... Nurse
**Clinton Allmon** ... Mr. Purdy

## Agnes Rhyme:

Blue Moon Detective Agency, your clerk's been embezzling, your favorite cat's left, hubby's been seeing some blond or brunette, mysteriously left out of granny's estate, laid down a bad bet, stood up by a date, your tiara's missing, no one to trust, come to Blue Moon, we promise a bust.

### LOOK FOR #1:
David plays "Maddie's Theme" on Terri's cello in her apartment.

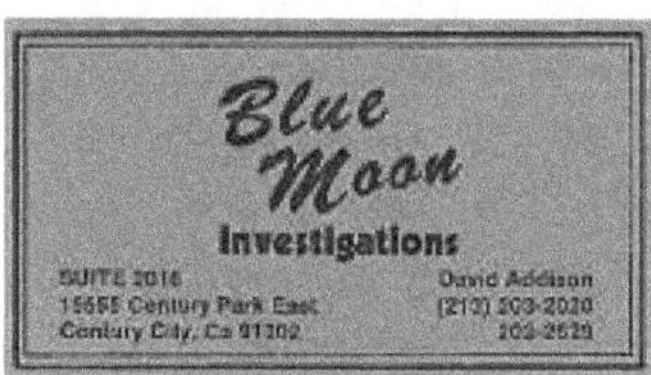


### CONTINUITY:
When Terri is standing in David's bedroom doorway, her sweater alternates between being open and closed.

## STATS:

*Door Slams: 1*
*Feet out of Elevator: 0*
*Maddie's Outfit Changes: 2*
*Agnes Rhymes: 1*

### GREAT LINES:

— 66 ————

*Terri: Some wine?*
*David: No . . . I want to stay bright-eyed and bushy-tailed.*
*Terri: I don't think that anyone's gonna ask you to operate heavy machinery. No cracks about my weight.*

———— 99 —

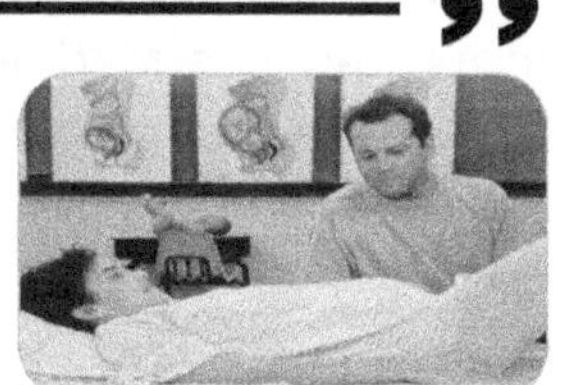

### LOOK FOR #2:
The cold open, omitted from the DVD release, has been restored on Hulu treaming.

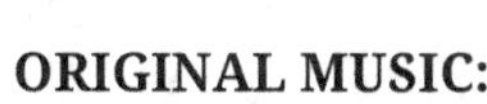

### ORIGINAL MUSIC:
**"I Got Rhythm"**
Composed by George Gershwin; Lyrics by Ira Gershwin
**"You Must Have Been a Beautiful Baby"**
Music by Harry Warren
**"Baby Face"**
Written by Harry Akst; Lyrics by Benny Davis
*(All replaced with new music on Hulu streaming)*

# S04 E10
# Tracks of My Tears

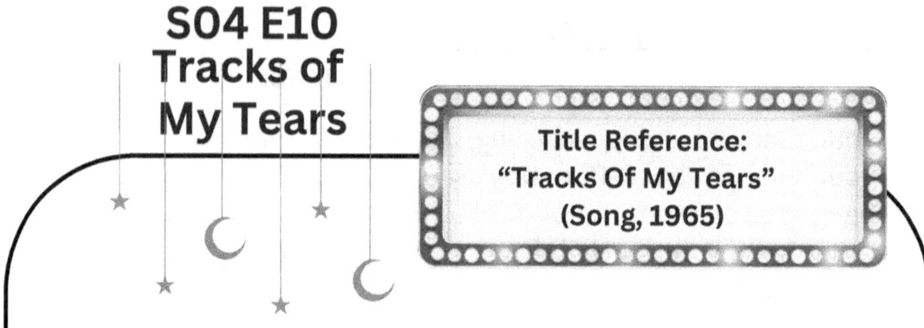



**Plot:**

This episode begins with several dream sequences that include guest star Pat Boone as the future David. After these dreams (and nightmares), Maddie wakes up and she is on the train traveling back to Los Angeles. She is still unsure whether or not she and David should resume their relationship.

Maddie then meets a man on the train named Walter Bishop, and they tell each other about their lives, even though Maddie does blur the truth a little.

You finally see Maddie walking down the hallway to Blue Moon. She's apprehensive, not knowing what sort of welcome awaits her there.

As soon as they see Maddie, the employees roll out the red carpet; they're so excited to see her back at work.

David is so happy that she has finally returned but they get into an argument when she says she needs more time. David has had it with waiting; he has been waiting for four and half months. They both apologize and say that they have missed each other. David thinks things are now going well until Maddie drops the biggest bombshell ever to be imposed on *Moonlighting* fans.

**Air Date:** February 2, 1988

**Teleplay by:**
Judith Kahan

**Story by:**
Debra Frank
Kerry Ehrin

**Director:** Paul Krasny

## CAST CREDITS

**Dennis Dugan** ... Walter Bishop
**Pat Boone** ... The New David
**Henry G. Sanders** ... Conductor
**Geoffrey Lardner** ... Cecil
**Ivy Jones** ... Passenger #1
**Mark Voland** ... Passenger #2
**Dave Nicolson** ... Passenger #3

## Agnes Rhyme:

> Blue Moon Detective Agency, you could be a man who just stabbed his wife, or even the woman at the other end of the knife, I hate to sound heartless, or rude or cold, but we're really busy, I'll have to put you on hold.

## FUN FACT #1:

This episode marks the first time Maddie and David have been in the same room since s04e01, "A Trip to the Moon!"

## FUN FACT #2:

The scene in which David appears outside Maddie's French doors and then smashes the glass and embraces her recreates the scene from *Body Heat* (Movie, 1981) with William Hurt and Kathleen Turner, whose character's name is 'Matty' in the film.

## LOOK FOR #1:

David Addison is a chocolate milk man, but the Pat Boone version of David drinks plain milk.

## LOOK FOR #2:

Cybill wearing New Balance shoes with her nightgown as she walks into the living room during the *Body Heat* scene.

## STATS:

*Door Slams: 3*
*Feet out of Elevator: 2*
*Maddie's Outfit Changes: 6*
*Agnes Rhymes: 1*

## GREAT LINES:

— " —

***New David:*** *Does a bear have fur? Does water turn to ice when you freeze it?*

— " —

## OUTFIT ROLE CALL:

- Maddie wears the peach dress again in s04e14, "And the Flesh Was Made Word," and s05e01, "A Womb with a View"

## REVEALING MISTAKE:

Maddie comes into Blue Moon at 3:18, but a few minutes later, when she and David hug in her office, her watch says 2:10 and his says 9:30.

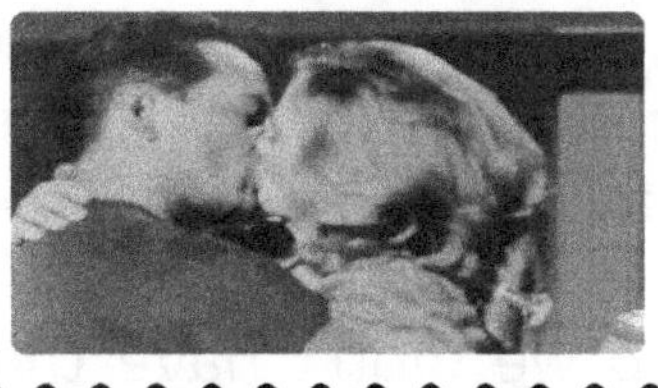

## BREAKING THE FOURTH WALL:

**Maddie:** How are you all doing? What's happened?

**Agnes:** Well, we've been busy: five of our clients killed their spouses for the insurance money. Eight were part of love triangles where one member was killed by the other two. And Bert and I did episodes of our own.

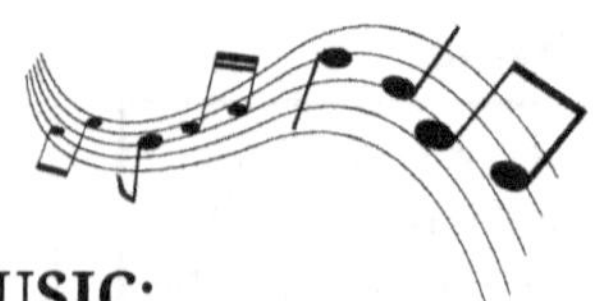

## ORIGINAL MUSIC:

**"Tutti Frutti"**
Written by Dorothy La Bostrie and Little Richard
Performed by Pat Boone

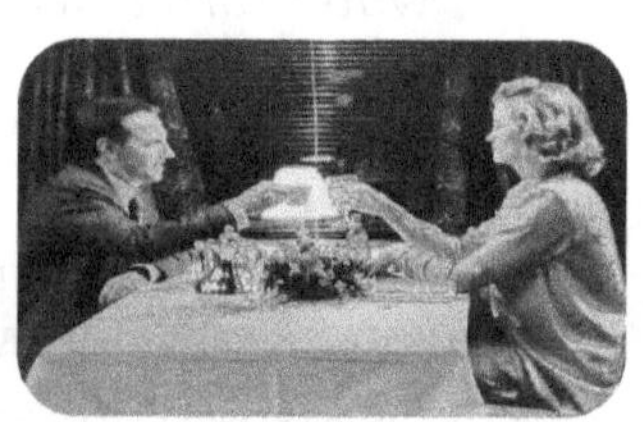

*"Let's gamble!"*

## CHECKMATE: Adding Walter Bishop

When Glenn Caron visited *Moonlighting the Podcast*, he talked about the choice to add Walter Bishop as Cybill's love interest. Glenn said, "I was certainly involved in the Walter Bishop choice. In fact, I thought, *Oh! we'll get Dennis*. I mean, I needed a male for her to play with, and my recollection is we needed to shoot somebody, she wasn't available, so we shot Bruce. Now Bruce had to go make the movie they'd been delaying, so we had Cybill back. So we didn't have those two people, which is of course what everybody wanted. So we dreamt up this Walter Bishop thing, and to me, what I was imagining was he was that guy who's in all those forties movies who you look at and go, 'Why Is she with him? He's boring; she should be with Cary Grant' or this one or that one, but they always have that guy. The fan reaction was so strong and so swift, and of course, it was before the internet, so people picked up their phones or wrote a letter, and I remember going to Dennis and saying "Okay, my bad, this isn't going to work."

# S04 E11
# Eek! A Spouse!



**Plot:**

The news of Maddie's marriage to Walter affects the office, but David is seemingly happy with the news. David then reveals that he is not upset because he doesn't believe she actually married Walter. He tests her to prove her love for Walter.

Maddie gets upset when David calls her Mrs. Bishop in front of a client. David believes that Maddie got married to spite him. Agnes confides in Miss Hayes that she feels let down and disappointed. She never thought that she would marry someone other than David.

David says to Terri, "It's almost showtime, kiddo," as delivery is imminent. Herbert offers to find out more about Maddie's husband because nothing makes sense.

Blue Moon is hired by a woman to pay her husband's mistress to leave town. The husband is subsequently shot dead by his wife, supposedly in self-defense. Herbert smells a rat; the case seems too easy.

Maddie and David get on the case when there is a new clue. They approach the killers, but they get away. Of course, this is followed by the usual *Moonlighting*-style car chase which includes a Mercedes convertible, Maddie's BMW, and a post office van.

**Air Date:** February 9, 1988

**Teleplay by:**
Ron Osborn
Charles H. Eglee

**Story by:**
Roger Director
Kerry Ehrin
Jeff Reno

**Director:** Artie Mandelberg

### CAST CREDITS

**Dennis Dugan** ... Walter Bishop

**Cristine Rose** ... Lauren Baxter

**Gerald Anthony** ... Anthony Baxter

**Kathleen Layman** ... Bridget Graves

**John C. Anders** ... Policeman

**James F. Dean** ... Mailman

**Patricia Lee Willson** ... Onlooker

Blue Moon Detective Agency, your best gal Friday's got her hand in the till, that faithful bookkeeper's been giving you swill, call Blue Moon pronto, we'll sniff out that cheat, and get your business back on its feet, our fee ain't cheap, but we'll bust our chops, 'cause our team is back together and everything's . . . sort of okay.

## CULTURAL REFERENCES:

~ *Magnum, P.I.* (TV Series, 1980–1988)

~ *Jake and the Fatman* (TV Series, 1987–1992)

~ Angela Lansbury, *Murder, She Wrote* (TV Series, 1984–1996)

~ Giant cockroach reference to Kafka's *Metamorphosis* (Novella, 1915)

~ *The Exorcist* (Movie, 1973)

**REVEALING MISTAKE:**
Walter (Dennis Dugan) clearly has blue eyes, but he tells Maddie his eyes are brown.

**LOOK FOR #1:** 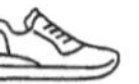
Cybill's heels change to sneakers when they run outside and get in the car to chase the women but change back to heels at the bus stop.

**LOOK FOR #2:**
The Baxters' "stormy marriage" and Anthony's affair with someone opposite from him reflect Maddie and David's current situation.

## STATS:

*Door Slams: 0*
*Feet out of Elevator: 0*
*Maddie's Outfit Changes: 3*
*Agnes Rhymes: 1*

## GREAT LINES:
**David**: *You, me, the bed, nice way to end an episode.*

**CONTINUITY:**
Maddie and David fight and slam down their phones; then, a minute later, David calls her back and asks if he woke her up.

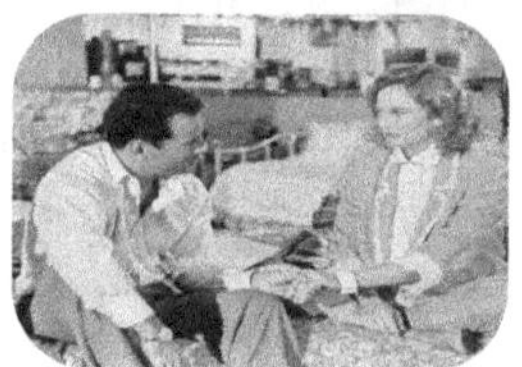

**BREAKING THE FOURTH WALL:**
**David** (to camera): That's alright; you know I'll be there with her (at the chase).

## Comments on *Morning...*

- **"You got that right."** s02e10, "'Twas the Episode Before Christmas"
- **"Morning, come on; morning, begins the day; proceeds the afternoon; becomes Electra."** s02e10, "'Twas the Episode Before Christmas"
- **"Morning . . . it is 'til twelve, then it becomes afternoon."** s03e13, "Maddie's Turn to Cry"
- **"Morning . . . that's why the sun's up."** s04e11, "Eek! A Spouse"
- **"Right you are."** s03e02, "The Man Who Cried Wife."

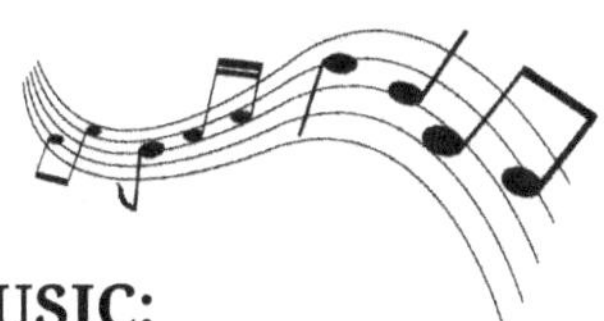

## ORIGINAL MUSIC:

**"Lightnin' Strikes"**
Written by Lou Christie and Twyla Herbert
Performed by Bruce Willis

**"The Sabre Dance"**
Written by Aram Khachaturyan

**"Rock-a-Bye Baby"**
Composed by Effie I. Canning

**"I Didn't Mean to Turn You On"**
Written by Jimmy Jam and Terry Lewis
Performed by Robert Palmer
*(Replaced with new music on Hulu streaming)*

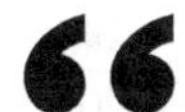

## FUN FACT:

**Moonlighting the Podcast:**
Did you call Walter Bishop
Walter as an homage to Bruce
'cause that's his real name?

**Glenn Gordon Caron:**
I think it might have come from
there, yeah.

# S04 E12
# Maddie Hayes
# Got Married

Title Reference:
*Peggy Sue Got Married*
(Movie, 1986)

## Plot:

David arrives at the office to find the Blue Moon workers all abuzz, dusting and polishing the place down, as they are expecting a special guest. Herbert, however, is not so excited at the prospect of meeting Walter, as he believes that he is *"the human goiter on the neck of life*." Walter arrives and David introduces himself while playing down his relationship with Maddie, contrary to what Walter has been told. During another of their usual fast-paced fights, Maddie says that she wishes that she had a big, fancy wedding so she could prove how much she loves Walter. David has a brainwave and decides to throw a wedding for Maddie. Herbert and McGillicuddy decide it would be a great idea if they throw Walter a bachelor party.  What follows is another of the many hilarious and memorable scenes in *Moonlighting*, in which the stripper calls in sick and Herbert has to dress up as the stripper for the bachelor party. He proceeds to pop out of the oversized cake and do the stripper's routine, unbeknownst to his audience, including McGillicuddy. David attends the wedding with his Lamaze class partner, Terri. Maddie walks down the aisle wondering who this strange woman is that is sitting with David. During the ceremony, Terri goes into labor, which begins a crazy series of events at the hospital. A huge debate ensues during a chaotic hospital scene, with Maddie and David fighting. They both believe they hate each other until Terri (while she is in labor) exclaims that they love each other and *"for God's sake would you two kiss already!"*  *Moonlighting* fans get another passionate kiss!  In the meantime, Walter has delivered the baby. We are now blessed with a new member of the *Moonlighting* family, Walter Hayes Addison Knowles. The episode ends with a touching scene between Maddie and David.

**Air Date:** March 1, 1988

**Written by:** Charles H. Eglee
and Roger Director

**Director:** Paul Krasny

### CAST CREDITS
**Brooke Adams ...** Terri Knowles
**Dennis Dugan ...** Walter Bishop
**Charles Rocket ...** Richie Addison
**Jack Blessing ...** MacGillicudy
**Bruce French ...** Rev. Hackley
**Nancy Parsons ...** Admissions Nurse
**Allan Kolman ...** Limo Driver
**Melanie Vincz ...** Nurse #1
**Katherine Huston ...** Nurse #2

## ART IMITATING LIFE #1:

When David talks about the "guy in the cooler commercials," Bruce Willis was doing *Seagrams Golden Wine Cooler* commercials at the time.

### CULTURAL REFERENCES:
~ *I Love Lucy* (TV Series, 1951-1957)
~ *Play Misty for Me* (Movie, 1971)
~ **Kaiser Wilhelm** - Former German Emperor

## ART IMITATING LIFE #2:

In the DVD commentary for this episode, Cybill stated that there was a lot of truth behind the words that Maddie says to David in the end—alluding to behind-the-scenes trouble over the previous year or two.

## FUN FACT:

Maddie and Walter's limo driver (Allan Kolman) also had a part in s03e03, "Symphony in Knocked Flat."

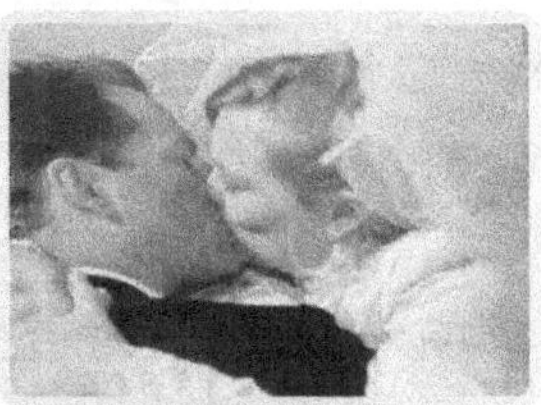

## STATS:

*Door Slams: 1*
*Feet out of Elevator: 0*
*Maddie's Outfit Changes: 3*
*Agnes Rhymes: 0*

## GREAT LINES:

*Maddie: Boy, when it rains, it pours—two men leaving one woman on her wedding day?*

*David: You want me to feel sorry for you?*

*Maddie: No, it was a joke. How could I expect you to feel sorry for me? But you know, David, I didn't do any of it to hurt you, none of it . . . but it did and I'm really sorry. I'm really sorry.*

## BREAKING THE FOURTH WALL:

**Maddie**: "I didn't say I wanted a big church wedding!"

**David**: "Oh yes, you did. You want the network to roll the tape back?"

## LOOK FOR #1:

There was a scene cut from a previous script in which David gives Maddie a necklace with a moon pendant—part of it remains in the episode. Maddie is looking at the necklace and holding it close just before Walter joins her in the room in his oversized tux.

## LOOK FOR #2:

Cybill's wedding shoes change to sneakers when she chases David and Terri outside the church.

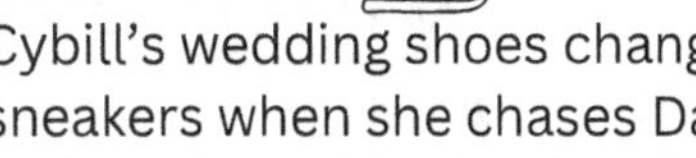

**LOCATION...LOCATION...LOCATION...**

~ **First United Methodist Church of North Hollywood** - 4832 Tujunga Avenue, Los Angeles, California, USA.

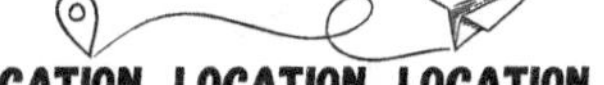

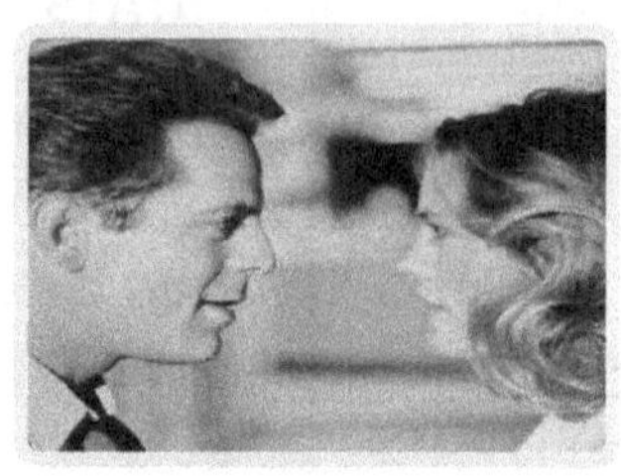

## *"Jealous, Jealous, Jealous!"*

It was way back in s02e06, "Knowing Her," that David accuses Maddie of being jealous of Gillian and calls her a "green-eyed snake." On that occasion, Maddie denied it—"Jealous of what? Of who?"—but seeing how she reacts to Terri in this episode, there's no denying. Maddie is so distracted by David's attractive, *pregnant* companion that she is unable to concentrate on her vows for a single second. That aforementioned green-eyed snake rears its ugly head again! But this isn't the only time in the series we've seen this, and Maddie's not the only one who has been jealous. David's jealousy over Maddie's infatuation with Paul McCain in s01e04, "The Next Murder You Hear," prompts him to make an "indecent proposal" to Maddie — and receive a sore foot in return. Maddie was jealous enough in s03e06, "Big Man on Mulberry Street," after she found out David had been married, to fly across the country. Not long after "Big Man," in s03e13, "Maddie's Turn to Cry," David is accused of being "jealous, jealous, jealous" (and now we get his denial: "Of who? Of what?") when Maddie and Sam quickly become an "us," and the list goes on. Despite their best efforts to hide it — they must have been "in care" from the very beginning.

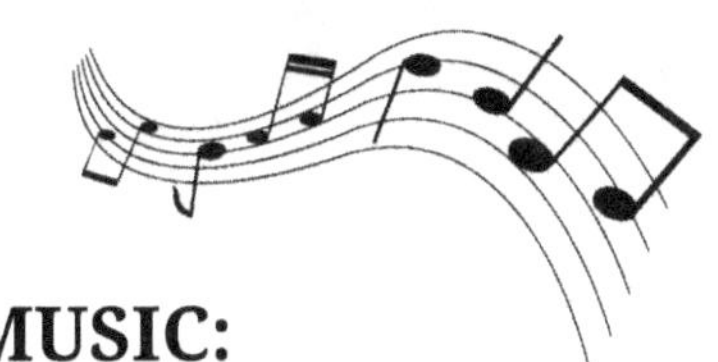

## ORIGINAL MUSIC:

**"Oh, Pretty Woman"**
Written by Roy Orbison and Bill Dees
Performed by Roy Orbison

**"The Lady Is a Tramp"**
Music by Richard Rodgers
Lyrics by Lorenz Hart
Performed by Curtis Armstrong

**"Wedding March"**
Written by Felix Mendelssohn

**"The Syncopated Clock"**
Composed by Leroy Anderson
*(Replaced with new music on Hulu streaming)*

**"Jungle Love"**
Written by Morris Day and Jesse Johnson
Performed by Morris Day and The Time
*(Replaced with new music on Hulu streaming)*

**"The Bugs Bunny Overture (This Is It!)"**
Written by Jerry Livingston and Mack David
*(Replaced with new music on Hulu streaming)*

# S04 E13
# Here's Living with You, Kid



**Plot:**

For several weeks now, Herbert has been put in charge of guarding an experimental species of grapefruit, but Agnes is all he can think about. He finally gets up the courage to ask Agnes to move in with him but is deflated to find out that she feels she isn't ready to make that commitment.

While he is sitting on his couch, Herbert begins to see his life with Agnes in the movies he is watching. His disappointment begins a series of parodies of Rudolph Valentino movies and the movie *Casablanca*, in which he plays Rick. However, in both of these movies, Agnes rejects his advances. In the end, Agnes agrees that she loves Herbert and would love to move in with him.

**Air Date:** March 15, 1988

**Teleplay by:**
Jeff Reno
Ron Osborn

**Story by:**
Roger Director
Charles H. Eglee
Kerry Ehrin

**Director:** Artie Mandelberg

**CAST CREDITS**

**Ben Piazza** ... Captain Renault
**Johnny Brown** ... Sam
**Jack Blessing** ... Victor Laszlo
**Eric Sinclair** ... Customer #1
**Don Draper** ... Customer #2
**Shelly Desai** ... Customer #3
**Marcelo Tubert** ... Bartender
**Harold Cannon-Lopez** ... Maître D'
**John David Conti** ... Technician

**FUN FACT#1:**
This is the only episode in which neither Cybill Shepherd nor Bruce Willis appears.

**FUN FACT#2:**
The original lampshades from the movie *Casablanca* were used for this episode.

**FUN FACT #3:**
Christine Kauffman, one of the Blue Moon employees, has two lines in this episode. The employees were not normally given speaking lines, to keep costs down.

### STATS:

*Door Slams: 0*
*Feet out of Elevator: 0*
*Maddie's Outfit Changes: 0*
*Agnes Rhymes: 0*

### GREAT LINES:

> **Sam:** *Of all the gin joints in all the towns in all the world, she walks into yours.*
> **Bert:** *Hey! I'm supposed to say that!*
> **Sam:** *Oh, sorry!*
> **Bert:** *It's only the best line in the script!*

**LOOK FOR:**
The Blue Moon door in this episode has no office number.

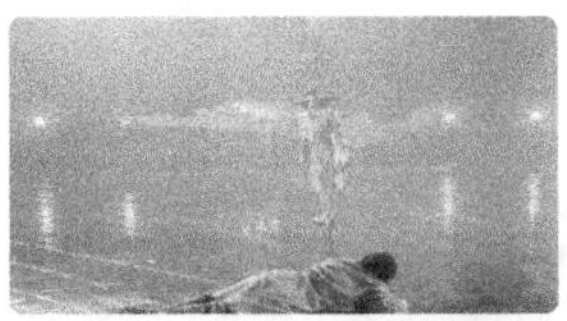

The plane used in the background in the final scene is actually a miniature but appears normal size thanks to the use of "forced perspective" photography.

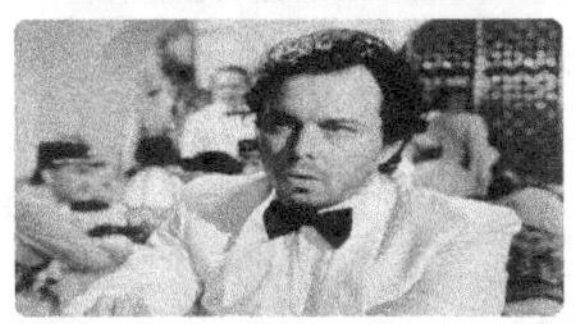

This was a dream role for Curtis Armstrong, who had always loved the movie *Casablanca* and was so happy when the opportunity to play Rick (Bert) presented itself.

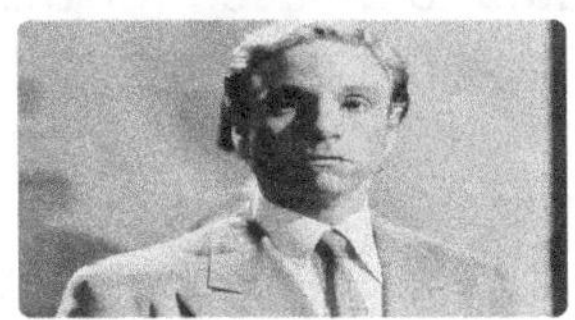

Jack Blessing (McGillicuddy), was the perfect choice to play the role of Victor Laszlo (played by Paul Henreid in the original); his looks, the accent, the attitude—he had it all.

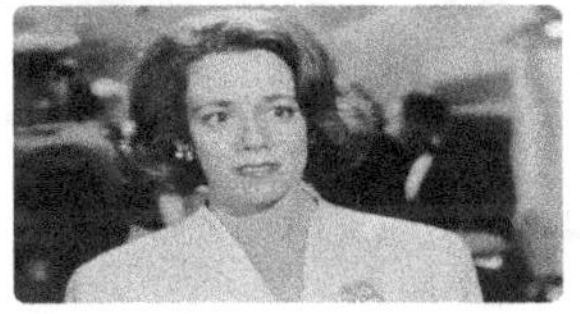

Allyce Beasley originally wanted to portray her role like Ingrid Bergman, with an accent; however, she was told that she had to retain her role as Agnes Dipesto in this episode.

# THE BEGINNING OF A BEAUTIFUL FRIENDSHIP

In the DVD commentary for this episode, Allyce and Curtis talk about how they enjoyed making this episode even though the hours were grueling. They remember some thirty-six-hour days on set, and all while Allyce had a seven-month-old son. Curtis shared that *Casablanca* (Movie, 1942), was a movie he adored so much that it's "rooted in his soul." It was nice to hear that Curtis and Allyce not only loved doing the *Casablanca* scenes together but also enjoyed the "Sheik" scenes, a parody of Rudolph Valentino movies. Curtis mentioned he still has some of the title cards from this part of the episode. The *Moonlighting* crew went to extremes to ensure the authenticity of the set so that it was a flawless tribute to *Casablanca*—this included searching for original props from the movie.

Curtis also remembered that there was a dispute in the writers' room, as some felt that *Casablanca* had been spoofed before so many times and that therefore this would not be a successful episode. But Charles Eglee and Roger Director's decision prevailed, and they began shooting. Apparently, Ben Piazza, who played the role of Captain Renault, had a 105-degree fever during filming.

An interesting tidbit: when word got out that *Moonlighting* was shooting a parody of *Casablanca*, the *LA Times* jumped the gun and released an article assuming that Cybill and Bruce were going to play Ilsa and Rick, when in fact it was Allyce and Curtis. Allyce also remembered that the wig she wore in the *Casablanca* scenes was so tight that she almost fainted. Also, the car you see in the final scene was previously owned by actor George Raft.

Another interesting piece of trivia: The scenes in which the plane leaves the airport were actually shot during the filming of *Casablanca* but were not used in the final cut of the film; therefore, permission was granted for the cuts to be used for this episode.

Just as *Casablanca* was the beginning of a beautiful friendship for Rick and Louis, *Moonlighting* was the same for Allyce and Curtis, who have remained the best of friends after all these years. They had their own style of on-screen chemistry, a love story that for *Moonlighting* fans will never be forgotten. To Allyce and Curtis: "Here's looking at you, kids." Thanks for the memories.

## ORIGINAL MUSIC:

**"La Marseillaise"**
National Anthem of France
Written by Claude Joseph Rouget de Lisle

**"Chopsticks"**
Written by Euphemia Allen

**"It Had to Be You"**
Composed by Isham Jones
*(Replaced with new music on Hulu streaming)*

**"Star Eyes"**
Composed by Gene de Paul and Don Raye
*(Replaced with new music on Hulu streaming)*

---

**CULTURAL REFERENCES:**
~ **M** - Chief of the Secret Intelligence Service in *James Bond* films.
~ **Miss Moneypenny** - Character in James Bond films.

---

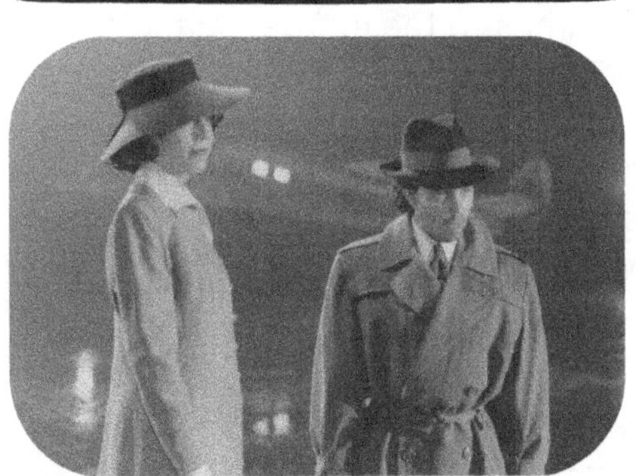

*On the set of "Here's Living with You, Kid."*
*Photo courtesy of Curtis Armstrong*

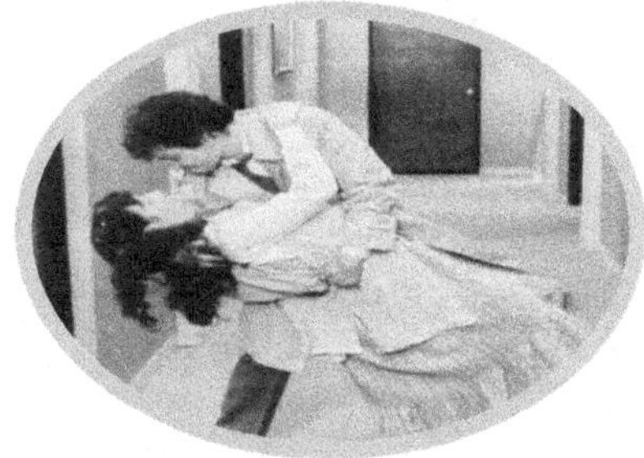

*And so it goes: it was happily ever after for Agnes and Bert when she agrees to move in with him.*

# S04 E14
# And the Flesh Was Made Word



**Plot:**

Maddie and David are approached by a client, Brian Gates, to find a mystery woman whom his business partner, John Wicklow, is infatuated with. Gates feels that Wicklow is so distracted, unreliable, and unstable that his company will be forced into bankruptcy. Unfortunately, after some investigation by Maddie and David, the woman Wicklow is infatuated with turns out to be Gates's wife. The marriage of Maddie and Walter is finally annulled which in turn leads to a joyous celebration with the "Wobblies."

David takes Terri home from the hospital and tells her he feels he has to work things out with Maddie. When the client turns up dead and his partner admits to the murder, Maddie has this feeling that the wife is somehow involved. When they approach Mrs. Gates, it leads to classic *Moonlighting* chase scene, except this time, it's on foot! David attempts to start over with Maddie. They agree to schedule dinner, a Lamaze class, and a "talk" every Tuesday night at 9:00 p.m. (which is also when *Moonlighting* aired in the States). There was a writers' strike during filming; therefore this episode was several minutes short, so being the good trooper that he is, Herbert summons up the courage to sing "Woolly Bully" in Egyptian attire as the cast and crew look on.

**Air Date:** March 22, 1988

**Written by:** Kerry Ehrin

**Director:** Paul Krasny

### CAST CREDITS

**Brooke Adams** ... Terri Knowles
**Ana Alicia** ... Mary Erin-Gates
**Dennis Dugan** ... Walter Bishop
**Stan Ivar** ... Brian Gates
**Mark Arnott** ... John Wicklow
**Raymond Forchion** ... Crime Scene Cop
**Curly Howard** ... (Archive Footage)
**Roger Director** ... Writer on Strike
**Charles H. Eglee** ... Writer on Strike
**Kerry Ehrin** ... Writer on Strike

## FUN FACT #1:
Kerry Ehrin wrote this episode and the character's name is Mary Erin. Coincidence?

## FUN FACT #2:
Because of the 1988 writers' strike, which started during the filming of this episode, the show fell short on pages to shoot, which it why they filled the time singing "Wooly Bully."

## FUN FACT #3:
Walter Bishop turns to the camera and says "Okay, you happy now?" because the show received so many calls and letters from fans upset that Maddie was with a guy other than David, which is why his role on the show ended abruptly.

## OUTFIT ROLE CALL:
- Maddie wore the peach dress in s04e10, "Tracks of My Tears," and wears it again in s05e01, "A Womb with a View"

## STATS:

*Door Slams: 1*
*Feet out of Elevator: 0*
*Maddie's Outfit Changes: 4*
*Agnes Rhymes: 0*

## GREAT LINES:

**Walter:** *Being married to you was the greatest two weeks of my life.*

## BREAKING THE FOURTH WALL:
**David:** "I'm going to close my eyes, and whoever stole the soundtrack, put it back."

## CONTINUITY:
Terri's baby is completely bald when she's holding him, but when she sets him in the crib, he has a wild head of hair.

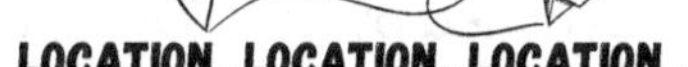

### LOCATION...LOCATION...LOCATION...
~ **Marie Callendar's Restaurant** - 5773 Wilshire Boulevard, Los Angeles, California USA

### SO LONG, FAREWELL
When Glenn Gordon Caron joined Grace and Shawna on *Moonlighting the Podcast*, he discussed his feelings about making episodes of *Moonlighting*. Caron said, "My whole thing was 'Let's make it so good; let's try and pack it with so much entertainment that you can watch it more than once.' ABC was always very upset because I would spend a lot of money, frankly. I would continue to make the episode until I felt it was good enough to show on television." "And the Flesh Was Made Word," s04e14, is the last episode of *Moonlighting* on which Glenn served as executive producer.

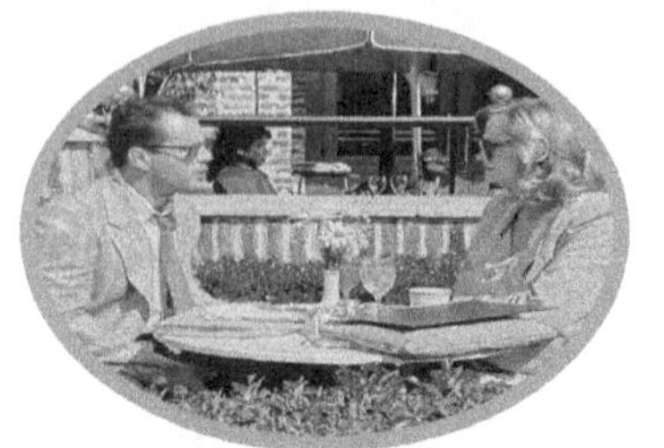



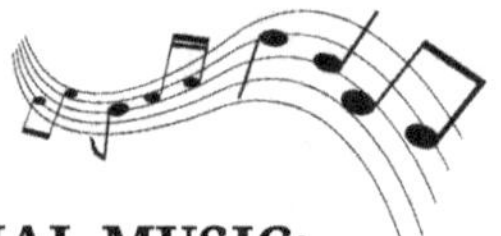

## ORIGINAL MUSIC:

**"Happy Days Are Here Again"**
Written by Milton Ager and Jack Yellen
*(Replaced with new music on Hulu streaming)*

**"Carmen Overture"**
Score to *Carmen* (Opera, 1975)
Composed by Georges Bizet

**"Wooly Bully"**
Written by Domingo Samudio
Performed by Sam the Sham and the Pharaohs
Lip Synched by Curtis Armstrong

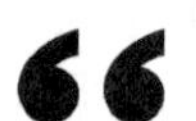

— 66 —

**There were so many amazing moments and we had such a great time. I still remember Bruce singing "Good Lovin'" when we shot that, I mean that was just like a joy machine.**

*~Glenn Gordon Caron*
*on his memories of making* Moonlighting
**Moonlighting the Podcast**

— 99 —

# S05 E01
# A Womb with a View

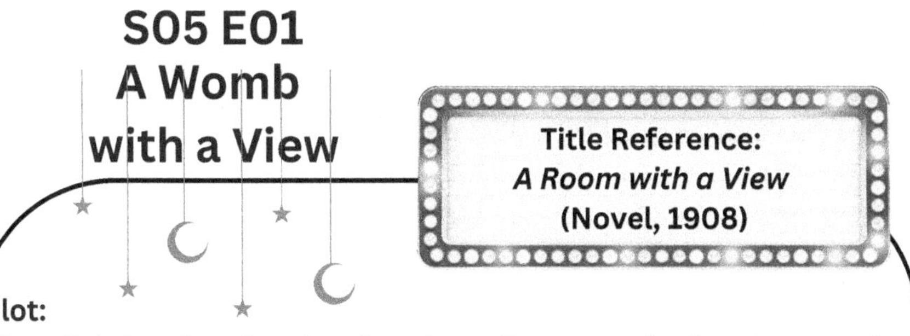

**Title Reference:**
*A Room with a View*
**(Novel, 1908)**

**Plot:**

*Moonlighting* breaks the fourth wall yet again in the opening sequence, which includes a dance number with cast and crew to welcome viewers back for another season. We see a pregnant Maddie heading to work in the morning, and then the camera pushes in to the baby inside.

Bruce Willis plays Maddie's unborn baby, Baby Hayes, who is given an introduction to his future life in utero. After he has been shown all the visions of the world and also the world of Maddie and David, he decides he is not happy with their constant arguing. The angel, Jerome, who has arrived to prepare the baby for his birth, assures Baby Hayes that Maddie and David love each other and that their arguing is "chemistry."

During her baby shower, as Maddie dances with David; she begins to feel ill. She is rushed to the hospital, where she tragically has a miscarriage. Jerome receives notification that Maddie and David are no longer destined to be Baby Hayes's parents, but that he will be born to another family. Adding a little humor and also references to other shows at the time, he informs Baby Hayes that it may be the family of *Growing Pains* or possibly *The Cosby Show*. The episode ends with the baby and the angel walking up a huge staircase in front of a beautiful moon singing the song "On the Sunny Side of the Street."

**Air Date:** December 6, 1988

**Written by:**
Glenn Gordon Caron
and Charles H. Eglee

**Director:** Jay Daniel

**CAST CREDITS**

**Joseph Maher** ... Jerome
**Sagan Lewis** ... Dr. Weed

**FUN FACT #1:**
The role of Baby Hayes is similar to Bruce Willis's later role as the voice of "Mikey" in *Look Who's Talking* (Movie, 1989).

**FUN FACT #2:**
During the five-month writers' strike in 1988, production was put on hold for this episode. It would normally have been shot in August, but began shooting in October instead. Production used this extra time to make the necessary script changes and put the episode together. This included rehearsing the dance sequence, creating the womb, and building the book, a huge prop that had "blue screens" on the pages so images could be added later in post-production.

**FUN FACT #3:**
Baby Hayes's womb, designed by James Agazzi, had to be kept inflated with a giant fan while Bruce was being filmed inside it. The noise the fan made was removed later in post-production. This portion of the episode was shot on Stage 6 at Fox Studios.

**FUN FACT: #4:**
This episode was shot in eleven days. Normally an episode would be shot in about eight days.



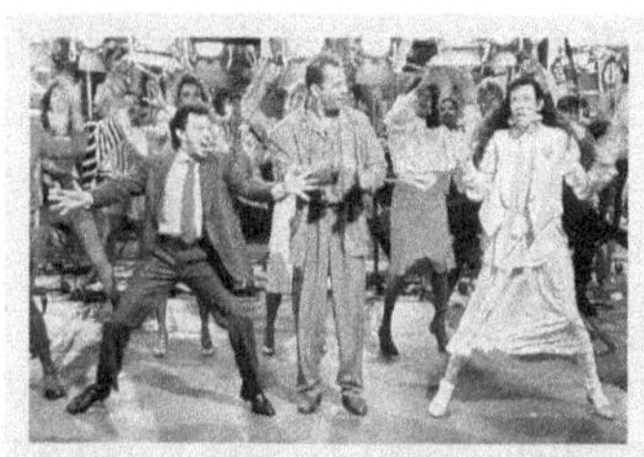

**GREAT LINES:**

— 66 —

**Baby Hayes:** *Why are they talking at the same time?*

**Jerome:** *It's called chemistry.*

— 99 —

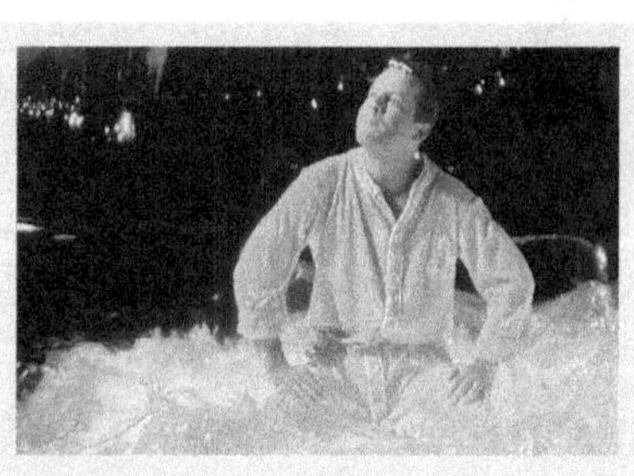

**OUTFIT ROLE CALL:**
- Maddie wore the peach dress in s04e10, "Tracks of My Tears," and s04e14, "And the Flesh Was Made Word."

**RELATIONSHIP STATUS:**
At this point in the series, it's hard to tell if Maddie and David are a couple or not. At the end of s04e14, "And the Flesh Was Made Word," David agreed to help Maddie with the baby and be there for her but wasn't sure if he could forgive her. Here David is ogling au pairs one minute and lovingly feeling Maddie's belly—hand over hand—and dancing happily . . . as happily as we've ever seen them. So . . . what's the status?

◆

**AGNES RHYME:**
Blue Moon Detective Agency, some lowdown no-good Nick made off with your dough, we can't solve your case 'cause we don't have a show, we went off the air at the end of last season, 'cause management wouldn't listen to reason, Blue Moon's still here, though there's one thing we're sans, our millions of loyal intelligent fans, but hang in there mister, it'll just be a bit, when you won't have to deal with this rerun sh . . . ut my mouth, oh my goodness, gotta go.

◆

**POSTPRODUCTION:**
The images and films that Jerome is showing Baby Hayes to educate him about the world had to be located and approved before the release of the episode. This was quite a hefty task, especially back then. The editorial and postproduction team did a great job in collating all the imagery, getting it cleared, and creating the montages in time for the air date.

**AWARD:**

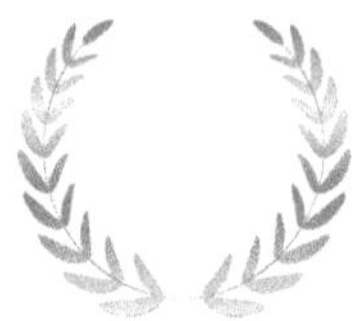

**James J. Agazzi** (production designer) and Bill Harp (set decorator) won an Emmy Award for Outstanding Art Direction for a Series for this episode.

---

## ORIGINAL MUSIC:

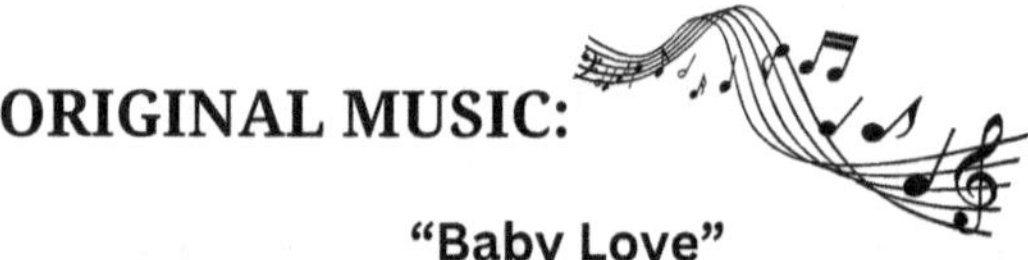

**"Baby Love"**
Written by Brian Holland, Lamont Dozier, and Eddie Holland
Performed by the Supremes

**"Mickey's Monkey"**
Written by Brian Holland, Lamont Dozier, and Eddie Holland
Performed by the Miracles

**"What a Wonderful World"**
Written by Bob Thiele and George David Weiss
Performed by Louis Armstrong

**"The Girl from Ipanema"**
Music by Antônio Carlos Jobim
Lyrics by Norman Gimbel
Performed by Bruce Willis

**"The Good, the Bad and the Ugly"**
Theme song of *The Good, the Bad and the Ugly* (Movie, 1966)
Composed by Ennio Morricone

**"On the Sunny Side of the Street"**
Written by Jimmy McHugh and Dorothy Fields
Performed by Bruce Willis and Joseph Maher

---

**"**

[*Moonlighting*] wouldn't have
existed without Jay Daniel.

*~Glenn Gordon Caron*
*Moonlighting the Podcast*

**"**

# S05 E02
# Between a Yuk and a Hard Place



**Plot:**

Maddie avoids facing her feelings about her miscarriage and throws herself into her work. She has been avoiding David and David has been avoiding work, but Agnes, in her usual, caring way, decides to intervene in a very creative way and recruits McGillicuddy to help. David has planned a trip out of town, and they need to stop that from happening. Herbert and McGillicuddy continue their rivalry in the office, while Maddie and David feel uncomfortable around each other.

 A woman wants to hire Maddie and David to find a mystery woman in her husband's past. She thinks that her husband may be concealing that he has been married before, and she thinks he may still be in love with his previous wife. The client subsequently dies in an accident. It is later discovered that the man's previous wife died also and that he was tried for her murder. The man was acquitted but later confessed to the crime. He also confesses to the murder of his current wife , though Maddie is not sure and takes steps to prove his innocence. Agnes's scheme works: Maddie and David get stuck in the elevator overnight and have no choice but to face their feelings about the miscarriage.

**Air Date:** December 13, 1988

**Written by:** Kerry Ehrin

**Director:** Dennis Dugan

### CAST CREDITS

**Cristina Raines-Crowe** ... Joan Spring

**Nicholas Cascone** ... Harold Swinburn

**Rod McCary** ... Dennis Spring

**Teresa Willis** ... Nice Blonde Girl

**Paul Marin** ... Bald Man

**Kate Murtagh** ... Elderly Woman

**Agnes Rhyme:**

> Blue Moon Detective Agency, good morning to you, it's a wonderful day, everything's great, we're happy to say, the world's full of cheer, there's reason for glee, thanks to quick work by MacGilicuddy and me.

**FUN FACT #1:**
Cristina Raines, who played Joan Spring, said in a 2014 interview that Bruce and Cybill got along, and he was "very protectiveof her."

## MUZAK:

**The songs playing in the elevator are . . .**

- **"Downtown"**
- **"Mack the Knife"**
- **"Lara's Theme"**
  *(Maddie and David danced to this song in the laundromat in the original series.)*
- **"You Must Have Been a Beautiful Baby"**

**REVEALING MISTAKE:**
David walks up to the elevator whistling the song "You Must Have Been a Beautiful Baby," so why does the song upset him in the elevator (assuming the reason he gets upset is because of the loss of their own baby)?

**FUN FACT #2:**
Bruce Willis's cousin, Teresa, plays the role of a potential client in this episode.

**LOOK FOR #1:**
Maddie and David continue to hold hands after Dennis Spring confesses to killing his wife.

## STATS:

*Door Slams: 0*
*Stuck in the Elevator: 2*
*Maddie's Outfit Changes: 2*
*Agnes Rhymes: 1*

**GREAT LINES:**
— 66 —
**Dennis:** *I killed my wife.*
**David:** *Well, this has been a hoot, but we've got a meatloaf back in the oven at the trailer park.*
— 99 —

**LOOK FOR #2:**
As Joan Spring is asking about Tina's yearbook, Bruce looks as if he's about to say a line, but pulls back as Cybill responds.

**LOOK FOR #3:**
Cybill's heels turn to sneakers in the chase scene.

**BREAKING THE FOURTH WALL:**
"Alright, Harold, tell us everything you know about this episode."

**OUTFIT ROLE CALL:**
- Maddie wears the same pajamas in s05e10, "When Girls Collide," and s05e12, "Eine Kleine Nacht Murder."

**CULTURAL REFERENCES:**
~ **Hitchcock** - music from both *Vertigo* (Movie, 1958) and *North by Northwest* (Movie, 1959) can be heard (plus a man obsessed with birds.)

~ *The Shining* - (Movie, 1980) "Here's David!" David also imitates Jack Nicholson freezing at the end of the movie.

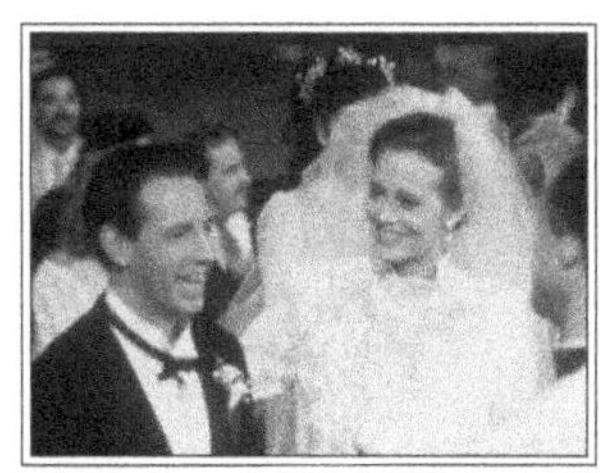

**DENNIS DUGAN**
*aka Walter Bishop,
aka* Moonlighting
*director, aka Cy.*

Did you know that Dennis Dugan was one of the unknown number of men who originally auditioned for the role of David Addison Jr.? As the story goes, he gave a great audition but was just not the type of guy you'd immediately picture being cast as Cybill Shepherd's love interest. As luck would have it, later in the series, Glenn needed another man to pair up with Maddie, and Dennis and his great audition came to mind. Turns out fans weren't too happy with Maddie being with a man other than David, and the entanglement quickly had to be untangled. However, Dennis was interested in directing—and, bonus, he got along great with both Cybill and Bruce (just listen to the DVD commentary for s05e13, "Lunar Eclipse," to hear how much affection he has for them both), so he was quickly moved to a role behind the camera. But the *Moonlighting* multitasker didn't stop there; he later played one more role in the series . . . or Walter Bishop did. Anyway, the rest, as they say is TV history.

---

### INSIDE JOKE? "The Skip Squats"

When Maddie and David knock on Harold Swinburn's door, David introduces himself and Maddie as the Skip Squats (Hank and Sissy). Similarly, in s05e07, "I See England, I See France, I See Maddie's Netherworld," David tells the landlady that he and Maddie are the Skip Squats—and reiterates the name Skip Squat when the landlady asks a second time. Furthermore, during the DVD commentary for s03e07, "Atomic Shakespeare," as Cybill, Bruce, Jay, and Glenn comment on the names in the end credits, they read the name of a crew member, Skip—and Bruce chuckles and says, "The Skip Squats —we're the Skip Squats" [sometimes sounds like Skip *Squads*], just as he did in the show. Perhaps this is one of those "nicknames" Bruce assigned to people (as described in Curtis Armstrong's book "Revenge of the Nerd") and Bruce worked it into the show? The mind reels.

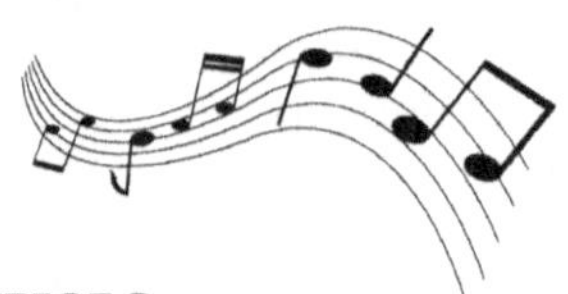

## ORIGINAL MUSIC:

**"Working in the Coal Mine"**
Written by Allen Toussaint
Performed by Lee Dorsey

**"You Must Have Been a Beautiful Baby"**
Music by Harry Warren
Whistled by Bruce Willis
Played as Muzak in elevator

**"Downtown"**
Music by Tony Hatch
Played as Muzak in elevator

**"Mack the Knife"**
Music by Kurt Weill
Played as Muzak in elevator

**"Hello, Dolly!"**
Music by Jerry Herman
Played as Muzak in elevator

**"Lara's Theme"**
Music by Maurice Jarre
*Doctor Zhivago* (Movie, 1965)
Played as Muzak in elevator

**"What a Friend We Have in Jesus"**
Hymn written by Joseph M. Scriven
Music by Charles Crozat Converse
Performed by Cybill Shepherd and Bruce Willis

**"Swing Low, Sweet Chariot"**
Written by Wallis Willis
Performed by Cybill Shepherd and Bruce Willis

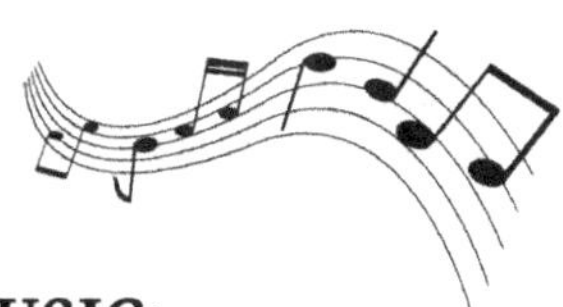

# ORIGINAL MUSIC:

**"Surfin' Bird"**
Written by Al Frazier, Carl White,
John Harris (as Sonny Harris) and Turner Wilson Jr.
Performed by The Trashmen

**"Little Honda"**
Written by Brian Wilson and Mike Love
Performed The Beach Boys and Bruce Willis

**"Up, Up and Away"**
Written by Jimmy Webb
Performed by Engelbert Humperdink

**"Theme from Bonanza"**
Written by Jay Livingston and Ray Evans

**"The Man on the Flying Trapeze"**
**"The Daring Young Man on the Flying Trapeze"**
**"The Flying Trapeze"**
Composed by Gaston Lyle, Alfred Lee
Lyrics by George Leybourne

**"Flight of the Bumblebee"**
Music by Nikolai Rimsky-Korsakov
Song from *The Tale of Tsar Saltan* (1967)

**"The Army Air Corps Song"**
Written by Robert Crawford

**"On the Rocks"**
Written by Bernard Herrmann
Song from *North by Northwest* (1959)

# S05 E03
# The Color
# of Maddie

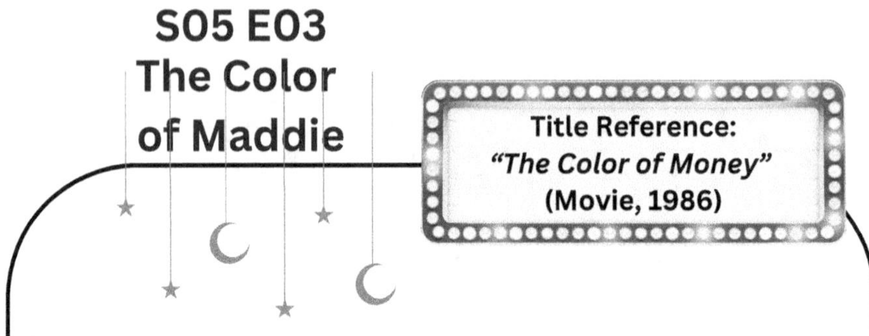


**Plot:**

Herbert and McGillicuddy continue their sparing. David is confused as to why Maddie is accepting him for who he is when he arrives to work late with a hangover and his usual dark glasses. In a strange turn of events, Maddie asks Agnes for relationship advice.

Blue Moon is hired to find out whether the man Nora Cooper is living with is really her husband. Ten years ago she married him, but he disappeared not long after. Cooper got on with her life, dated, and even got serious a few times.

Several months ago, this man claiming to be her husband showed up on her doorstep and explained that he had been in a Mexican jail. He had left her because he knew the authorities were on his tail and he didn't want her involved. While Maddie and David investigate the case, they discuss how familiar they are with each other after all these years. In the Cooper case, the husband appears to have been killed in a car bomb; then Nora Cooper is murdered. Regardless, Maddie and David continue to investigate the case, but it takes an unusual turn when it is revealed that it is all a case of mistaken identity.

**Air Date:** December 20, 1988

**Written by:** Barbara Hall

**Director:** Artie Mandelberg

**CAST CREDITS**

**Karen Landry** ... Nora Cooper
**Graham Beckel** ... Maximillian Petrovsky
**Alan McRae** ... Charlie
**Drew Pillsbury** ... Eddie
**Gene Hartline** ... Biker

## *MOONLIGHTING* MENTION:
*Take Two* - "Death Becomes Him" (TV Episode, 2018)
**Eddie and Sam introduce themselves to the motel manager as "David Addison and Madolyn Hayes."**

## LOOK FOR: 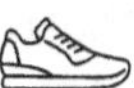
Cybill wears sneakers while they're chasing Richard Cooper / Maximillian Petrovsky.

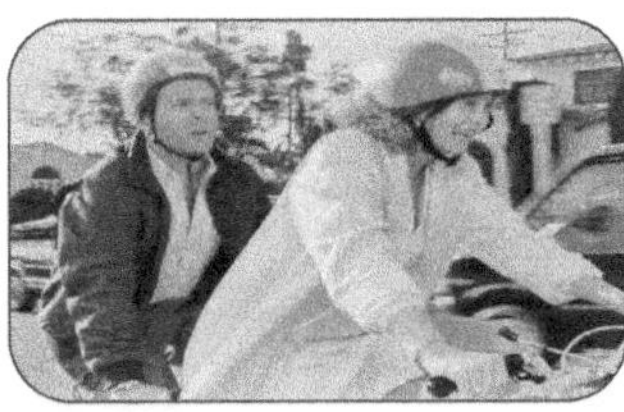

## CONTINUITY:
Charlie's car that blew up was green. But there was a yellow car parked in that spot when Maddie and David first arrive at the pool hall.

## LIGHTING DETAIL:
Look for the shadow of the Blue Moon logo from the office window reflected behind Maddie and David during the "ladder talk."

## STATS:

*Door Slams: 0*
*Feet out of Elevator: 0*
*Maddie's Outfit Changes: 3*
*Agnes Rhymes: .5*

## GREAT LINES:

> *Maddie: Pump harder!*
> *David: I'm pumping as hard as I can.*
> *Maddie: I know for a fact you can pump harder when you want to!*

## BREAKING THE FOURTH WALL:
**David**: "Hold it, hold it, you can't just bump us off right now and leave all these people in suspense?"

**Maddie & Richard Cooper:** "Why not?"

**David**: (looks at script) "Well, because we've got at least seven major plot points here to cover."

## ALL EARS
When Maddie says she's "all ears" during their car talk, David looks her up and down and says "unfortunately, not *all* ears." This phrase is spoken through similar interactions and conversations in and s02e13, "In God We Strongly Suspect." and s02e14, "Every Daughters Father Is a Virgin."

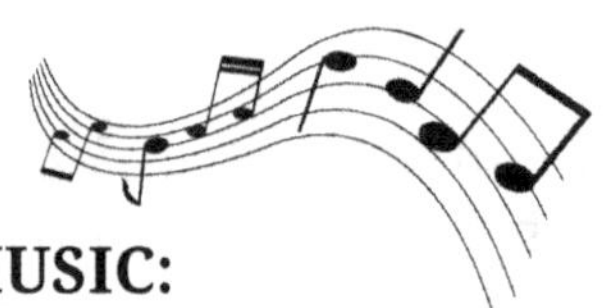

## ORIGINAL MUSIC:

**"Honky Tonk Women"**
Written by Mick Jagger and Keith Richards
Performed by Hank Williams Jr.

**"Daisy Bell (Bicycle Built for Two)"**
Written by Harry Dacre

**"Magic Carpet Ride"**
Written by John Kay and Rushton Moreve
Performed by Grandmaster Flash & The Furious Five

**"The Nutcracker Suite: Dance of the Sugar Plum Fairy"**
Ballet by Pyotr Ilyich Tchaikovsky

**"Ta-ra-ra Boom-de-ay"**
Written by Henry J. Sayers

David mentions the song **In a Gadda-da-Vida by Iron Butterfly (1968)** for the second time. Previously he mentioned it in s02e05, "My Fair David," while discussing the bet.

# REFLECTIONS

Have you ever noticed how, more often than not, the cases that our favorite detectives take on, mirror what's going on in their own relationship? Here in "The Color of Maddie," Nora Cooper isn't sure if she really knows the man she's married to. Likewise, Maddie and David debate how well they really know each other, even after all they've been through. Another example of a case connecting with Maddie and David personally Is s02e05, "My Fair David," where David's maturity is in question while they investigate the kidnapping of Mrs. Greydon's "professional screwup" son. In s02e09, "Atlas Belched," a young executive fears the loss of his job while Maddie sells Blue Moon. When Sam, Maddie's ex, appears in s03e12, "Sam and Dave," the client wonders if her lover is "falling back in love" with his wife. In s03e15, "To Heiress Human," a wealthy woman's father disapproves of her bartender boyfriend just as Maddie ponders if David is the type of man she's supposed to be with. Thank you to all the *Moonlighting* writers who took such care when crafting the plots, which connected the business and personal side of Maddie and David's world in such a wonderful way.

# S05 E04
# Plastic Fantastic Lovers

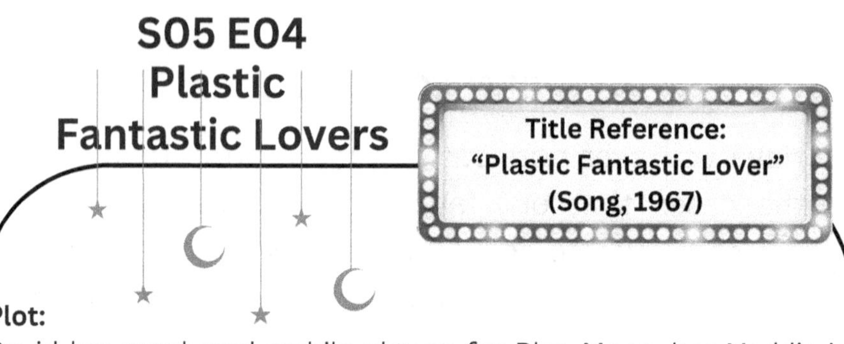


**Plot:**

David has purchased mobile phones for Blue Moon, but Maddie is not comfortable with this new technology and is finding it hard to learn how to use them. Maddie and David are hired by an eccentric millionaire, Hunziger, to get some "dirt" on his plastic surgeon, Dr. Brill. Brill botched an experimental surgery on Hunziger's face, and now the client is a prisoner in his own house. The client wants concrete evidence that the botched surgery was a deliberate act by Brill. In a reversal of roles, David doesn't want to take the case, but Maddie disagrees, so they take it.

Maddie makes an appointment with Dr. Brill to get more information, while David works on the receptionist. They both find that the surgeon usually treats only women and then has affairs with them after he has made them "perfect."

Due to the nature of the case, Maddie and David debate whether their own relationship was ever more than superficial. It is revealed that the client's wife is one of Dr. Brill's patients, and they are having an affair. During a stakeout, Maddie and David follow Hunziger's wife to the surgeon's office, where they find Brill dead. Comical scenes follow as Maddie and David chase through the building to catch the killer. At the end of the episode, they almost kiss once again, but unfortunately for the fans, they stop short.

**Air Date:** January 10, 1989

**Written by:** Jerry Stahl

**Director:** Allan Arkush

### CAST CREDITS

**Michelle Johnson** ... Michelle Hunziger

**Andrew Robinson** ... Leslie Hunziger

**Nicholas Pryor** ... Dr. Simon Brill

**Jennifer Tilly** ... Nurse Saundra

**Monty Bane** ... Butler

**Stanley DeSantis** ... Desk Clerk

## LOOK FOR:

One of the noses up on the wall is labeled "Mark Harmon," who played Sam Crawford, Maddie's love interest in season three.

## FUN FACT #1:

The age of technology is upon us, as this episode is filled with talk of computers, cell phones and video clients. Oh my!

## FUN FACT #2:

Stanley Donen, who directed s03e06, "Big Man on Mulberry Street," cast Michelle Robinson, who plays Leslie Hunziger, in the role of Jennifer Lyons in *Blame It on Rio* (Movie, 1984). She was only two months out of high school.



## GREAT LINES:

> **Maddie**: *When I first walked into your office, what'd you think?*
>
> **David**: *That you were high-strung, overdressed, over-bred, had a hair-do from another century and were probably the most drop-dead gorgeous broad I'd ever seen in my real life!*

## REVEALING MISTAKE:

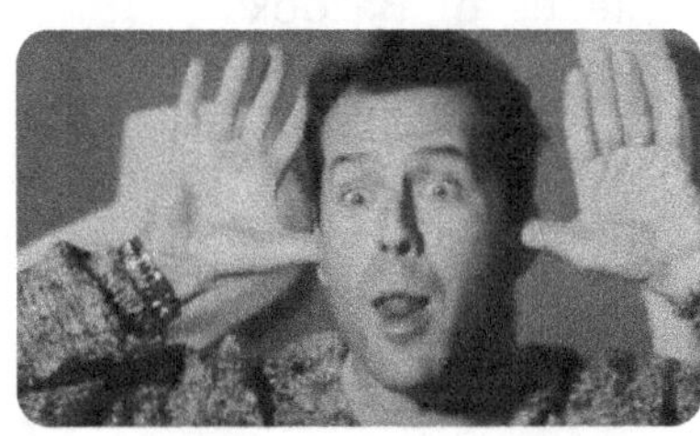

Bruce Willis is wearing his real-life wedding ring (from his marriage to Demi Moore) in the end scene where the body parts are being thrown around.

## BREAKING THE FOUTH WALL:

*"Twenty-two episodes a season is impossible." ~David*

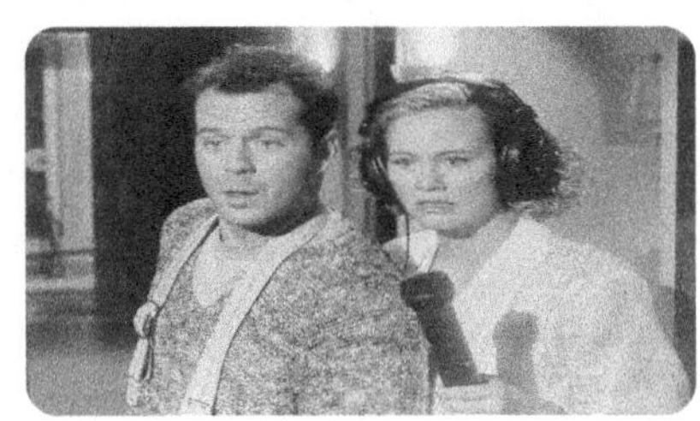

## LOCATION...LOCATION...LOCATION...

~ **JW Marriott** - 900 West Olympic Boulevard., Los Angeles, California, USA

~ **Pink's Hot Dogs (David offers to take Maddie here)** - 709 North La Brea Avenue, Los Angeles, California, USA

## GOOD CLEAN FUN

At the end of this episode, David offers to spot Maddie (and wash her back) in the shower—for safety purposes only, of course! But if you ask us, the man is a bit obsessed with Maddie's shower habits. Back in s01e02, "Gunfight at the So-So Corral," David made sure Maddie's bathroom had a shower massager. And remember how in s03e04, "Yours, Very Deadly," David asks Maddie, "When we start showering together, which side do you want me to scrub first?" David finally gets his wish in s05e07, "I See England, I See France, I See Maddie's Netherworld," only they're tied up and clothed! Leaves us to wonder if David ever made this fantasy a reality during that month they spent together leading up to s04e01, "A Trip to the Moon." Hmmm, one of them needs to come clean!

## CULTURAL REFERENCES:

~ David mentions **Pink's Hot Dogs**, which is a roadside hot dog stand famous for its tasty hot dogs and long lines—it's been a Los Angeles staple since 1946.

~ David mentions **Bazooka Joe,** a comic strip character featured on a small comic strip wrapped around individual pieces of Bazooka bubble gum.

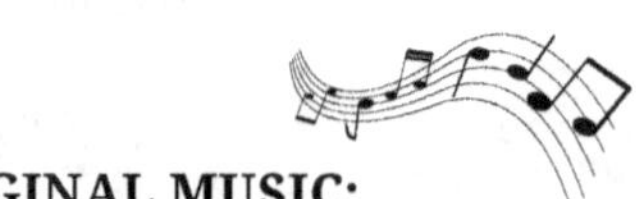

## ORIGINAL MUSIC:

**"Three Blind Mice"**
Written by Thomas Ravenscroft

**"The Tango"**
Composed by Vic Mizzy and Marc Shaiman

**"Listen to the Mockingbird"**
Theme song of *The Three Stooges*
(TV Series, 1922-1970)

**"Plastic Fantastic Lover"**
Written by Marty Balin
Performed by Jefferson Airplane

# S05 E05
# Shirts and Skins

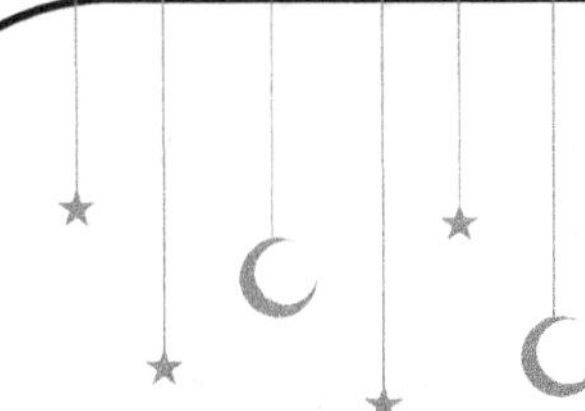



**Plot:**

An advertising agency executive who believed that her boss hired her for her creative mind finds out otherwise when he fires her for not sleeping with him. She proceeds to interrupt his board meeting and ends up shooting him in the leg. Maddie approaches the woman's lawyer to offer her services for free, as she feels this is a case of sexual harassment. Maddie decides to give Agnes a raise, a promotion, profit sharing, and the role of special assistant to the President.

David wants to take the case, but the client is the woman's boss. Maddie and David continue with the cases but on opposite sides. This leads to a division within Blue Moon, the men assisting on David's case while the women assist on Maddie's. They are both very confident that they will win their respective cases. The case takes a turn when a woman shows up in David's office with some interesting information. This episode ends with bloopers from previous episodes.

**Air Date:** January 17, 1989

**Written by:** Roger Director

**Director:** Artie Mandelberg

**CAST CREDITS**
**Jayne Atkinson** ... Robin Fuller
**Joan Pringle** ... Martha Tracy
**Lora Staley** ... Ann Pines
**Jeff Allin** ... Neil Fass
**Tony Abatemarco** ...
Assistant DA ... Bernie Gordon
**Melissa Weber** ... Arlene
**Jerry Hauck** ... Gary Coombs
**Jeff Rochlin** ... Mr. Plusky

**Agnes Rhyme:**

> Blue Moon Investigations, are you the target of somebody's ire, about to be kidnapped, divorced, set on fire? Why wait till your honey's cashed out and fled, the ransom note's read, or maybe you're dead? Our pre-mayhem checkup is perfect for you, for just a few bucks, we'll sniff every clue, we'll pester your friends, dig high, dig low, if your number's up, don't you wanna know?

### FUN FACT:

The plot is an update of the Spencer Tracy/Katharine Hepburn picture *Adam's Rib* (Movie, 1949).

### LOOK FOR #1:

Do you think Maddie's crawl through the air duct was an homage to Bruce's character in *Die Hard,* (Movie, 1988)?

### LOOK FOR #2:

The second of two blooper reels appears during the end credits.

**STATS:**

*Door Slams: 2*
*Feet out of Elevator: 0*
*Maddie's Outfit Changes: 5*
*Agnes Rhymes: 1*

**GREAT LINES:**

— 66 —

**Maddie:** *I want you to be my partner.*
**David:** *Your equal partner.*
**Maddie:** *Equal, partner.*

— 99 —

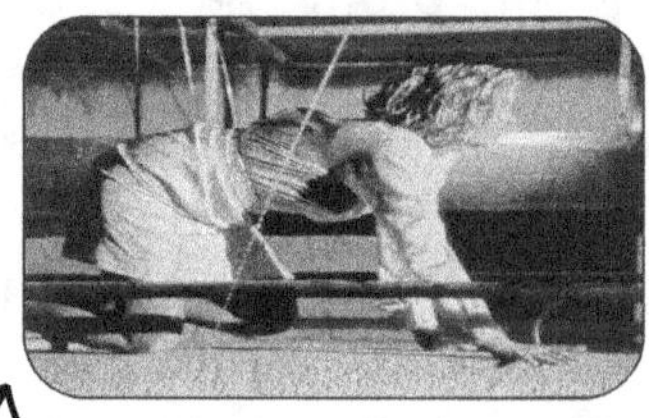

### OUTFIT ROLE CALL:

- Maddie wears the purple and white dress she wore in s03e03, "Symphony in Knocked Flat."

### DENIED!

Even though Maddie and David were playing for different teams here in "Shirts and Skins," David tried to find some neutral ground and offered to take Maddie to dinner, but she had work to do. Earlier in s05e03, "The Color of Maddie," David made dinner reservations and almost had the reluctant Maddie out the door before the phone rang calling them to a case. In s05e04, "Plastic, Fantastic Lovers," it was a double whammy when David first suggested "messing the sheets" in the hotel room and Maddie compared him to the "vile Dr. Brill." Maddie then took a raincheck when David offered to take her for some Pink's hot dogs because it was "beauty night." Finally, when he suggests going out and dancing together more often in s05e10, "When Girls Collide," she simply says, "No thanks." David—you've been denied!

# A CASE OF THE CASES

Considering that Maddie was the owner of a detective agency, there were so few cases that she actually wanted to take. David often had to coax . . . convince . . . coerce her into taking most of the cases, especially in the first three seasons. It all started in s01e04, "The Next Murder You Hear" with the words "Who's the client?" and "We are not taking this case!" these became familiar mantras of Maddie's. David had to work hard to prove to her that there was a case worth taking and show her how it would benefit them. His view was that a win for Blue Moon meant a front-page story in the paper—bringing attention to the agency; she wanted a paying client and a signed contract. Sometimes she would put her foot down (stand her ground, dig her heels in), like in s03e03, "The Man Who Cried Wife," or s02e15, "Witness for the Execution," when she all but forbade David to help Mr. Bower or get involved in Mr. Everett's case—which did not go over well with Addison; he was not a man who responded well to demands. They sparred so much over whether to take a case or who the client might be, David would be stunned when Maddie actually wanted to take a case, such as in s02e13, "In God We Strongly Suspect," when he quipped, "Wait a second, wait a second, wait a second, aren't you gonna tell me we can't take this case?" "Why would I do that?" she asked. He responded, "I don't know; that's what you always do." Some might say this is why they were a good team . . . others might say this is why he was good for her. His "gray area" perspective of the world forced her to see beyond the black-and-white view, which was her default. Maddie and David were often an unstoppable force meeting an immovable object—but seeing who won out in the end made it so much fun to watch.

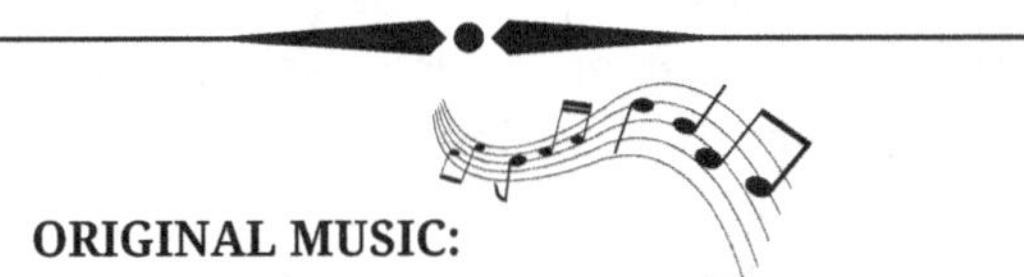

**ORIGINAL MUSIC:**

**"Foggy Mountain Breakdown"**
Written by Lester Flatt and Earl Scruggs
**"The Battle Hymn of the Republic"**
Music by William Steffe
Lyrics by Julia Ward Howe
**"The Pink Panther Theme"**
Composed by Henry Mancini
**"Dueling Banjos"**
By Arthur "Guitar Boogie" Smith
Originally titled, **"Feudin' Banjos"**
on the *Deliverance* (Movie, (1972) soundtrack
**"Yankee Doodle"**
Traditional music of English origin

# S05 E06
# Take My Wife, for Example

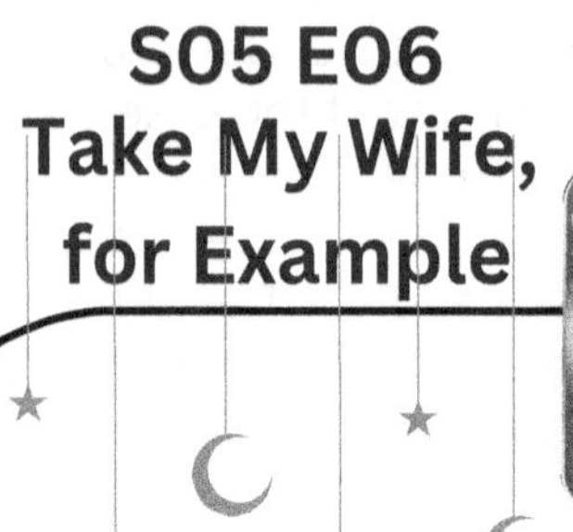



**Plot:**

A divorce lawyer, known as Betty "Barracuda" Russell, and well-known for her fierce tactics, has a heart attack during one of her settlement meetings with her client, Lidia Kraft, her husband, Nathan Kraft, and his divorce lawyer. After her experience in the hospital, Betty came to some realizations about her life and legacy, meaning what she would have left behind had she died. Betty wants to help save the marriage of her client if she can, so she wants to hire Maddie and David to find out whether her client's husband is really in love with his twenty-one-year-old receptionist.
 After a discussion about Maddie's lack of generosity, she decides to buy David a gift—a new car. David, however, is not so happy with the type of car she chose and wants to get rid of it. The plot twists when new information arises regarding Lidia Kraft's recent transgressions. Following this, a murder occurs, and Nathan Kraft is accused of the crime. Yet another chase scene ensues, this one involving David's new car, which, much to his happiness, gets totaled. The episode ends with David gifting Maddie some beautiful pearls that he purchased with the money from his car insurance. Maddie responds by kissing David passionately.

**Air Date:** February 7, 1989

**Written by:** James Kramer

**Director:** Dennis Dugan

## CONTINUITY:

David says here that his birthday is November 27 (same as Jimmy Hendrix), but in s02e13, "In God We Strongly Suspect," David's birthday works out to be right about Bruce Willis's actual birthday, March 19. However, in s04e14, "And the Flesh Was Made Word," his birthday works out to be April 29.

## BARRACUDA, ANYONE?

In s01e03, "Read the Mind... See the Movie," Preston Holt was referred to as a barracuda. In s02e02, "The Lady in the Iron Mask," David referred to "Barbara Wylie" as a barracuda, same as Betty "Barracuda" Russell in this episode—were the writers feeling like a little seafood?

## LOOK FOR #1:

The cold open, omitted from the DVD release, has been restored in Hulu streaming.

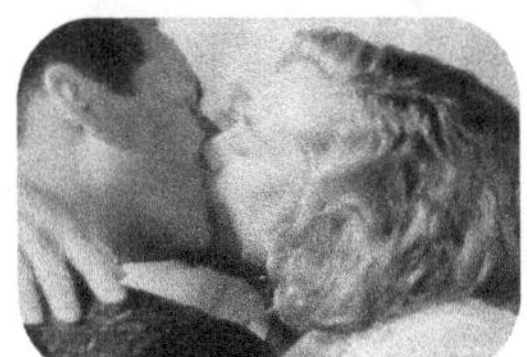

*One more for the road.*

## LOCATION...LOCATION...LOCATION

**~ Beverly Center Shopping Mall -** 8500 Beverly Boulevard, Los Angeles, California, USA

## STATS:

*Door Slams: 1*
*Feet out of Elevator: 1 (David's)*
*Maddie's Outfit Changes:4*
*Agnes Rhymes: 0*

## GREAT LINES:

*Maddie: You're a fantastic lover in just about every category.*

*David: Well, maybe it is my fault, Maddie, but I think six or seven times a night for a man my age is pretty damn good.*

## LOOK FOR #2:

Cybill's heels turn to 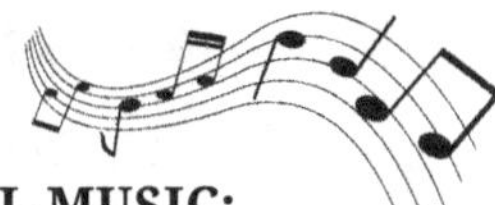 sneakers in the chase scene.

## BREAKING THE FOURTH WALL:

**David:** "Yeah, right, and I don't look half bad in a diaper either."

## ORIGINAL MUSIC:

**"William Tell Overture"**
Written by Gioachino Rossini
**"Just the Way You Are"**
Written by Billy Joel
**"Shop Around"**
Written by Smokey Robinson and Berry Gordy
Performed by the Miracles
**"Comedians' Galop (No. 2)"**
By Dmitry Kabalevsky

## A LITTLE BIT OF TRUTH

Like many plot points that blurred the lines between fact and fiction in *Moonlighting*, the storyline here about David "kissing too hard" is possibly based on a real-life complaint Cybill Shepherd had about how Bruce Willis kissed. In a 2009 interview with Rachael Ray, Shepherd named Willis as both the "best and worst" on-screen kisser. Cybill claimed that Willis used "too much tongue" at the beginning of the show, but she says, that after Bruce married his first wife, Demi Moore, his kissing style was much improved, and Cybill then enjoyed kissing him. Likewise, tabloid stories at the time claimed that Cybill Shepherd "never gave gifts," and here David has a complaint about Maddie's lack of generosity. Could Maddie really never have given David a gift in four years? We wonder what other real-life tidbits are hidden within *Moonlighting* plots?

## CAST CREDITS

**Colleen Dewhurst** ... Betty Russell

**Jane Hallaren** ... Lydia Kraft

**Lawrence Pressman** ... Nathan Kraft

**John C. Moskoff** ... Steven, Nathan's Attorney

**James Staley** ... Priest

**Thomas Murphy** ... Judge

**Samantha Knight** ... Saleslady

**Philip Persons** ... Salesman

**David Kristin** ... Waiter

**Robert Kim** ... Doctor

**Paunita Nichols** ... Nurse

**Steve Jones** ... Bailiff

## S05 E07
## I See England,
## I See France, I See
## Maddie's Netherworld

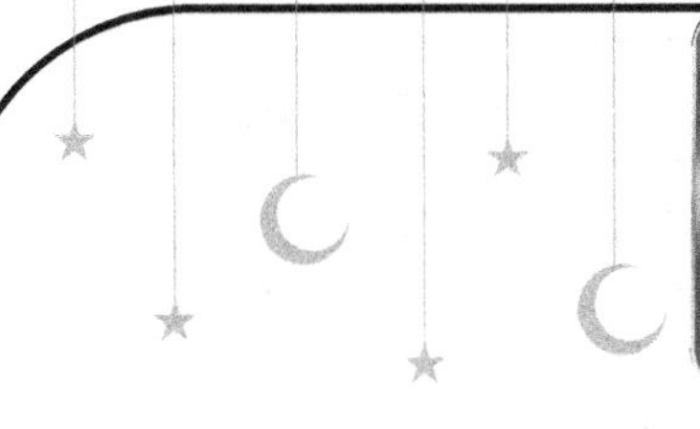



**Plot:**

A man named Harry Soffer arrives at Blue Moon to hire Maddie and David as bodyguards. Agnes shows him into Maddie's office pending Maddie's arrival. Unfortunately, he dies in Maddie's office before she can meet him. Later, a man shows up claiming that he is a friend of Harry's and that they had both won the $12 million lottery. He also explains that to trust each other they cut the ticket in half. He wants to know if Maddie and David found the other half of the ticket on Harry. Maddie and David are now on the case to find the ticket. In a plot twist, it turns out that the case is not about a winning ticket at all. Apparently, Harry stole some highly sophisticated marine designs from a company that he used to work for. They were schematics for a low-noise submarine propeller. Several parties are in pursuit of the plans so that they can sell them to the highest bidder.

 During a tussle with one of the men in seeking the plans, Maddie gets knocked to the ground unconscious, and in a dream, she finds herself in the afterlife, with David as the Grim Reaper. The Kipper Kids make a guest appearance in this scene as gravediggers.

**Air Date:** February 14, 1989

**Written by:** Chris Ruppenthal

**Director:** Paul Krasny

## LOOK FOR #1:
David introduces himself and Maddie as the "Skip Squats" here, just as he did in s05e02, "Between a Yuk and a Hard Place."

## REVEALING MISTAKE:
Harry Soffer just died and he's already buried with an engraved headstone, which would take months to get.

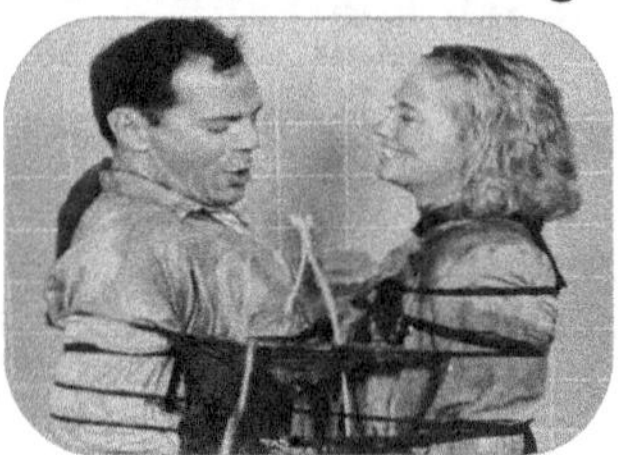

## OUTFIT ROLE CALL:
- Maddie wore the pink dress in s03e09, "The Straight Poop."

## LOOK FOR #2:
Bruce has his hand on Cybill behind during the scene where they stand by Agnes's desk laughing as the men from the coroner's office come in.

## STATS:

*Door Slams: 1*
*Feet out of Elevator: 0*
*Maddie's Outfit Changes: 6*
*Agnes Rhymes: 0*

## GREAT LINES:

> *David: She's a little standoffish at first; you may want to let me frisk her.*

## BREAKING THE FOURTH WALL:

**Maddie:** "The client is dead."
**David:** "Well, Maddie, we can't always get the best actors for these smaller roles."

## LOOK FOR #3: 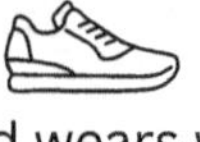
Cybill Shepherd wears white sneakers in her office while she, Agnes and David wait with the body in her office. She is also wearing sneakers in the next scene when her new chair is delivered and again in the garage looking for Soffer's car.

## FUN FACT:
Bruce Willis mentioned in the commentary for s04e01, "A Trip to the Moon," that he thinks this episode is the best of the later seasons. Also, in the commentary for s03e07, "Atomic Shakespeare," he told Cybill they should do the commentary for "the one where we're in the shower scene tied up and we're both laughing" —too bad they never got around to it!

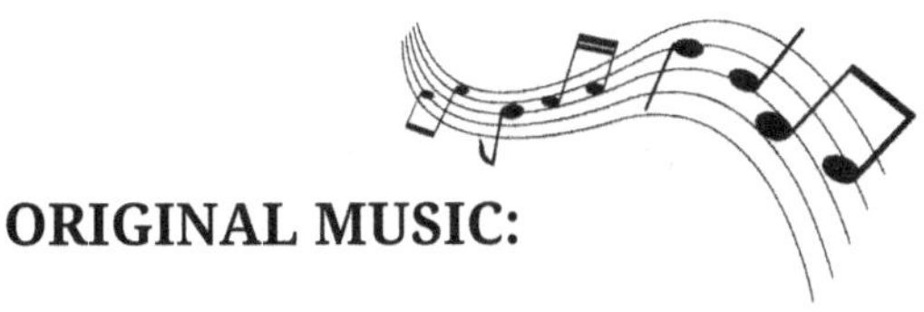

## ORIGINAL MUSIC:

**"Funeral March of a Marionette"**
Theme song of *Alfred Hitchcock Presents* (TV Series, 1955-1962)
Written by Charles Gounod

**"The Anvil Chorus"**
Act 2, scene 1 of *Giuseppe Verdi's Il Trovatore*, (Opera, 1853)

**"The Syncopated Clock"**
Composed by Leroy Anderson

**"The Giant Crab"**
Composed by Bernard Herrmann

**"Cabaret"**
Music by John Kander
Lyrics by Fred Ebb
Performed by Bruce Willis and Cybill Shepherd

**"Shall We Dance?"**
Music by Richard Rodgers
Lyrics by Oscar Hammerstein II

• • •

## LAUGHING OUT OF CHARACTER

*Moonlighting* was such a funny show, and the cast and creative team had such a great time making it (well, most of the time) that even Cybill and Bruce had trouble keeping a straight face sometimes (and staying in character)—as evident in the shower scene here in "I See England, I See France, I See Maddie's Netherworld," in which they really *did* look like they were having fun! A few other episodes to look out for in which it's evident that it's the actor and not the character who is finding humor in the scene are s01e02, "Gunfight at the So-So Corral"; s01e04, "The Next Murder You Hear"; s02e07, "Somewhere Under the Rainbow"; s03e02, "The Man Who Cried Wife"; s03e04, "Yours, Very Deadly"; s03e07, "Atomic Shakespeare"; s03e14, "I Am Curious . . . Maddie"; and s05e02, "Between a Yuk and a Hard Place," where everyone's yukking it up in the scene with all the birds, which you can see in the episode and in the season five bloopers (at the end of s05e05, "Shirts and Skins!").

## CAST CREDITS

**Phil Simms (II)** ... Harry Soffer

**Jon Korkes** ... Winston Guy

**Michael Flynn** ... Icku

**Kipper Kids** ... Graveyard Ghouls
(Martin Von Haselberg & Brian Routh)

**Gloria Cromwell** ... Landlady

**Ron Howard George** ... Bickie

**Fritz Bronner** ... Paramedic #1

**Randy Olea** ... Paramedic #2

**Martin Charles Warner** ... Delivery Man

**Kenneth J. Martinez** ... Doctor

**Stuart Nelson** ... Paramedic #3

**Don Maxwell** ... Man

**Eddie Hailey** ... Orderly

## NICE TIE

In the DVD commentary for s03e07, "Atomic Shakespeare," Cybill reported that she'd changed her tune about being tied up over the years, but while working on *Moonlighting*, she wasn't a fan. It all started in the Pilot episode when she and David were tied up in Maddie's kitchen by the soft-spoken Simon. Then, in s02e08, "Portrait of Maddie," she was tied to a chair while the thief got away but "slithered great" over to David to be set free after solving the mystery. In "Atomic Shakespeare," we see Cybill's real-life anger coming through when she is tied up in the church while Kate awaits being married off to Petruchio against her will. Interestingly, Cybill didn't seem to mind so much being tied up with Bruce here in "I See England, I See France, I See Maddie's Netherworld"; maybe this is where she started to rethink her stance on bondage.

# S05 E08
# Those Lips, Those Lies

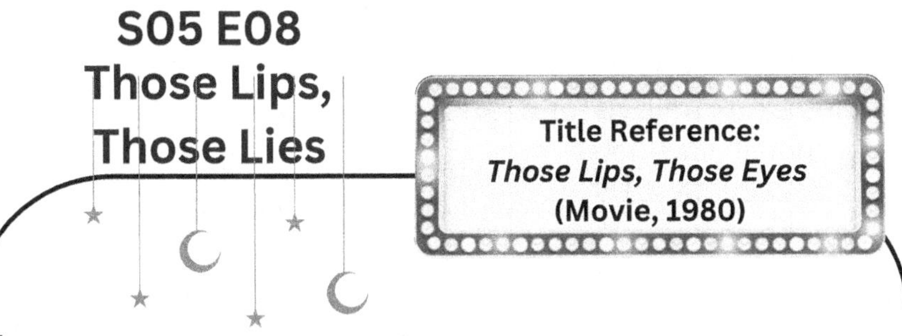


**Plot:**

This episode opens in classic *Moonlighting* "breaking the fourth wall" style. The credits roll, but without Al Jarreau singing the theme song. In 1989, this episode marked the show's move from Tuesday to Sunday nights (during the original run in the States) and Al had apparently not been told about the move so did not "show up" to sing the theme song. David stops the credits from rolling and asks what's going on. Maddie decides to take over the singing, but David is not amused, so he begins to sing the theme song; however, Maddie is not amused and stops him. Agnes comes in and saves the day by convincing Herbert to successfully sing the opening song. David's brother, Richie, arrives in town with his new girlfriend, Carla. He asks Maddie and David for a favor. Rita's business partner, Benny, has embezzled all of her money and she wants them to find the missing money. David is reluctant to take the case, as he knows his brother all too well and that he falls in love easily.

After a visit from a mysterious sexy woman in the middle of the night, David is told that Carla and Benny have been running an escort service. Maddie and David also find out that Carla has been using Richie to get some revenge on Benny for taking all her girls, clients, and money.

**Air Date:** April 2, 1989

**Written by:** James Kramer and Chris Ruppenthal

**Director:** Dennis Dugan

## LOOK FOR #1:

Near the end of the episode, David whispers to Maddie, "Don't wait up for me," although it's unclear if they are a couple at this point in the show.

## LOOK FOR #2:

David's hand is on Maddie's thigh in her office while they talk about Richie.

## FUN FACT:

When *Moonlighting* originally aired in the States, this episode marked the move from its original time slot, Tuesdays/9:00 p.m., to Sundays/8:00 p.m. In subsequent episodes, the office number on the "Blue Moon" door is changed from '2016' to '2022' - which is likely productions way of showing that they have "moved."

## STATS:

*Door Slams: 2*
*Feet out of Elevator: 0*
*Maddie's Outfit Changes: 3*
*Agnes Rhymes: 0*

## GREAT LINES:

*Maddie:* You're awfully quiet.

*David:* Am I?

*Maddie:* Yes, you are.

*David:* Oh.

*Maddie:* I mean, usually when we're driving I can't get a word in edgewise.

*David:* Yeah.

*Maddie:* Maybe we've just run out of things to say . . .

*David:* Hmm.

*Maddie:* . . . like some old married couple.

### CULTURAL REFERENCES:

~ **CBGB's** - New York nightclub
~ **Lakers** - L.A. NBA team
~ **Jack Nicholson** - American Actor

## PET NAMES:

A few of the nicknames David has for Maddie:

- **Sweetheart**
- **Sweetcakes**
- **Baby/babe/honey**
- **Kid**
- **Blondie Blonde**
- **The Big Blonde**
- **Goldilocks**

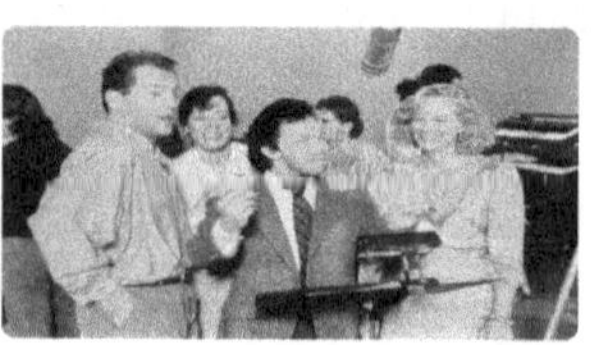

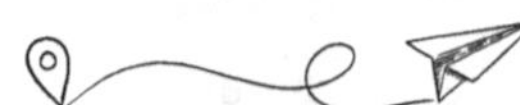

## LOCATION...LOCATION...LOCATION...

~ **El Rey Theater** - 5515 Wilshire Boulevard, Los Angeles, California, USA

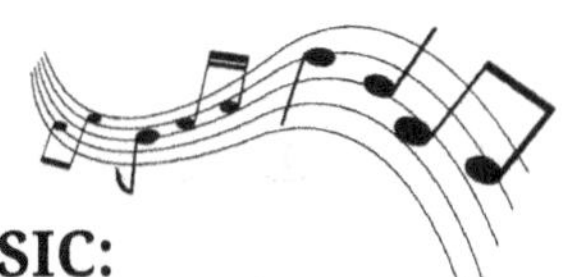

## ORIGINAL MUSIC:

**"Moonlighting"**
Music by Lee Holdridge
Lyrics by Al Jarreau
Performed by Cybill Shepherd, Bruce Willis,
and "Curtis Armstrong" (Al Jarreau)

**"Heat Wave"**
Written by Brian Holland,
Lamont Dozier, and Eddie Holland
Performed by Martha Reeves and the Vandellas

**"Hawaiian Wedding Song"**
**"Ke Kali Nei Au" (Waiting there for thee)**
Written by Al Hoffman, Charles E. King, Dick Manning
Performed by Pacific Island Singers

**"Blue Velvet"**
Written by Bernie Wayne and Lee Morris
Performed by Bruce Willis

**"Girls! Girls! Girls!"**
Written by Jerry Leiber and Mike Stoller
Performed by Elvis Presley

**"Get Up (I Feel Like Being a) Sex Machine"**
Written by James Brown,
Bobby Byrd, and Ron Lenhoff
Performed by James Brown and Bruce Willis

**"I Only Have Eyes for You"**
Music by Harry Warren
Lyrics by Al Dubin
Performed by The Flamingos

**"The Shoop Shoop Song (It's in His Kiss)"**
Written by Rudy Clark
Performed by Betty Everett

**"Love is in the Air"**
Written by Harry Vanda and George Young
**"Lady"**
Written by Lionel Richie

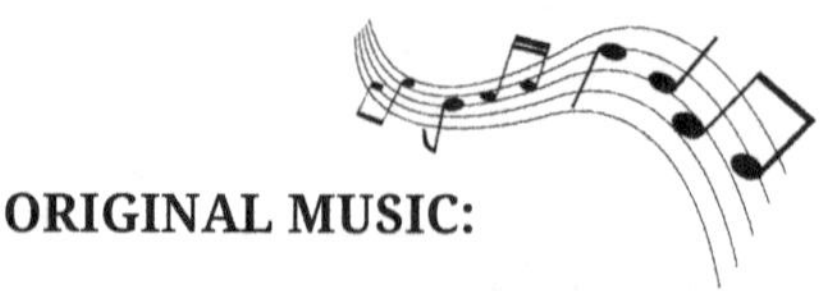

**ORIGINAL MUSIC:**

**"Funky Nassau"**
Written by Tyrone Fitzgerald
and Raphael Munnings
Performed by Bruce Willis and Charles Rocket
**"Chapel of Love"**
Written by Jeff Barry, Ellie Greenwich, and Phil Spector
Performed by Charles Rocket
**"Take Time to Know Her"**
Written by Steven Allen Davis
Performed by Percy Sledge

— • • • —

## LIGHT THIS WAY

The late Gerald "Jerry" P. Finnerman (1931-2011), cinematographer and director extraordinaire, lit fifty-eight episodes of *Moonlighting* and directed two: s04e08, "Los Dos Dipestos," and s05e09, "Perfetc." Camerawork was in his blood, as his father, Perry Finnerman Sr., was also in the biz. Jerry worked on shows such as *Star Trek* (TV Series, 1966-1969), *Mission: Impossible* (TV Series, 1966-1973), and *The Gangster Chronicles* (TV Series, 1980-1981), to name just a few, before *Moonlighting*. We could write a whole *other* book pointing out the many examples that demonstrate the care Jerry took lighting the set of *Moonlighting* and the cast, but in this limited space, we'll just point out a few. Of course, when it comes to lighting *Moonlighting*, we have to start with s02e04, "The Dream Sequence Always Rings Twice," which was the first time Jerry lit black-and-white, and as he explained in his interview with the Archive of American Television in 2002, he "took the lights around so far it scared him," but that's what it took to create shadows and get that look — and what a beautiful look it turned out to be. "Blonde on Blonde," s03e11, is another wonderful example of how the lighting, along with the music choices, was like a supporting character in the show, setting mood and tone. Casting light effects across Cybill's face to highlight her best features and arranging lighting that changes multiple times in a single frame as the actors move through are details Jerry perfected. Look for other lighting moments throughout the series that were subtly created to support a scene or character and think of Jerry Finnerman.

# CAST CREDITS

**Rita Wilson** ... Carla McCabe

**Charles Rocket** ... Richard Addison

**Debra Sandlund** ... Claudette
(aka Debra Stipe)

**Stephanie Dunnam** ... Ginger Largo

**Stephen Burleigh**... Detective Plainer

**Dan Gilvezan** ... Male Model

**Shannon Farnon** ... Woman

**Ed White** ... Man in Restroom

**Michael Speero** ... Benny Largo

**Zack Phifer** ... Waiter #1

**Rafael A. Nazario** ... Waiter #2

**Lisa Stahl** ... Model

# S05 E09
# Perfetc

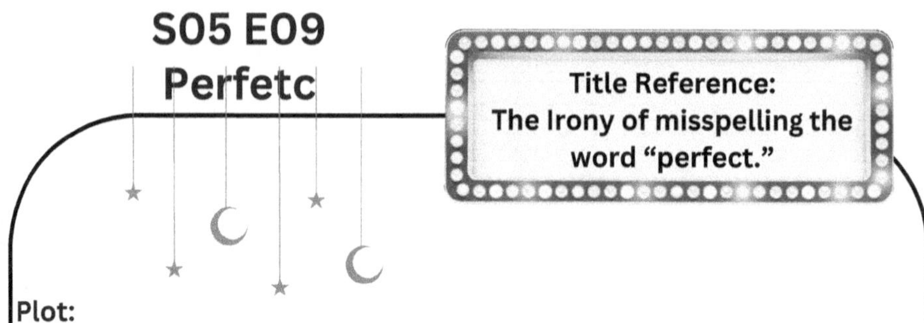


**Plot:**

A dying man wants to hire Blue Moon to prove that he committed the "perfect crime" twenty-five years ago — one that the police, FBI, Interpol, and several large insurance companies haven't been able to solve. The crime was a robbery of priceless artifacts and the dying man wants Maddie and David to find the witness to the crime. The man has done some self-reflection and wants Maddie and David to prove that he is guilty of stealing the artifacts before he dies. David thinks this is the perfect opportunity to provide some great publicity for Blue Moon, but Maddie is not convinced. Maddie and Herbert begin their investigations at the museum with Herbert disguised as a monsignor to distract the Museum curator while Maddie does some investigating.

Just when David has organized the media to come to Blue Moon to announce that the 25-year-old mystery has been solved, the client walks in and says that he wants to cancel the whole thing because he just found out that he's actually *not* dying. In the middle of all this mayhem, the witness is murdered. After further investigation, Maddie and David solve the crime and in the process of doing so, uncover the identity of the killer.

**Air Date:** April 9, 1989

**Teleplay by:**
James Kramer
Chris Ruppenthal
Jerry Stahl

**Story by:**
Jeff Reno
Ron Osborn

**Director:** Gerald Perry Finnerman

### CAST CREDITS
**Tim Thomerson** ... Brock Ash
**Bill Erwin** ... Duncan Kennedy
**Lee Bryant** ... Ms. Van Breegle
**David Ruprecht** ... Police Artist
**Jay Ingram** ... Lt. Fontana
**Leonard R Garner Jr.** ... Reporter #1
**Julie Bennett** ... Woman
**Dore Keller** ... Producer
**Cary-Hiroyuki Tagawa** ... Artist
**Candy Darling** ... Reports #2

### *(Last)* Agnes Rhyme:

Blue Moon Detective Agency, sorry for not answering on the first ring, but we're cleaning and dusting, preparing for spring, getting rid of the old to make room the new, so we give every client his or her due, sorry, operator, we cannot accept an out-of-state call that is collect.

**LOOK FOR #1:** 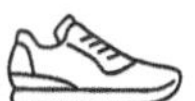

Cybill Shepherd is at it again, clearly wearing sneakers as Maddie and David walk in the room to meet with Dr. Van Breegle and also during the chase scene.

**LOOK FOR #2:**

David gets a glare from Maddie when he pinches her behind just as they meet with Dr. Van Breegle.

**FUN FACT:**

Maddie says she's being "shanghaied" (tricked into doing something) by David in this episode. David says he's been "shanghaied" in s05e02, "Between a Yuk and a Hard Place."

### STATS:

*Door Slams: 1*
*Feet out of Elevator: 0*
*Maddie's Outfit Changes: 4*
*Agnes Rhymes: 1*

### GREAT LINES:

*We are not taking this case!*
**~Madolyn Hayes**

**LOOK FOR #3:**

As Maddie brings boxes into Blue Moon, you can see that the office number on the door has changed from 2016 to 2022.

**OUTFIT ROLL CALL:**

- Maddie wore the pink dress previously in s03e12, "Sam and Dave."

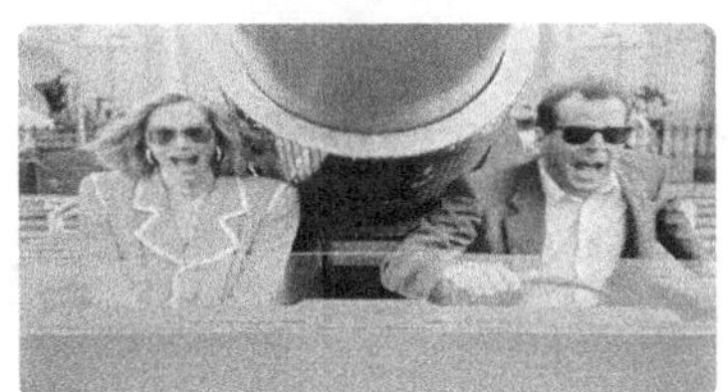

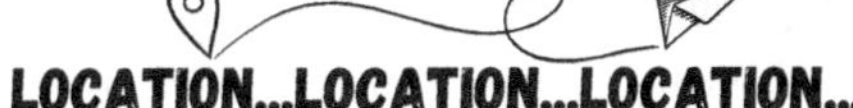

## LOCATION...LOCATION...LOCATION...

**~ Natural History Museum of Los Angeles County -** 900 Exposition Boulevard, Exposition Park, Los Angeles, California, USA
**~ Exposition Park Rose Garden** - 701 State Drive, Los Angeles, California, USA

**CULTURAL REFERENCE:**
David references **Geraldo Rivera**, an American journalist and attorney who was hit in the nose with a chair on *The Geraldo Rivera Show* (TV Series 1987-1998); Bruce Willis dated Geraldo's ex-wife Sherryl Rivera. Sherri was often Bruce's date to award shows during the *Moonlighting* years; he even included her in his 1987 Golden Globes acceptance speech by saying, "And I would like to thank Sherri Rivera for her support, for her guidance, and generally just hanging around with me for the last three and a half years to get me here."

**BREAKING THE FOUTH WALL:**

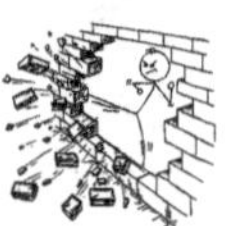

David mentions saving time by not having "six talks in the car, two pairs of shoes, and stunt doubles." He also talks directly to audience multiple times.

**CONTINUITY #1:**
When Dr. Van Breegle hits Maddie and David over the head with the *American Gothic* (Painting, 1930) poster, it is clear that the two faces in the poster have been precut.

**CONTINUITY #2:**
In the last chase scene, the lipstick sculpture collapses. However, in the next shot, lipstick is still pointing upwards.

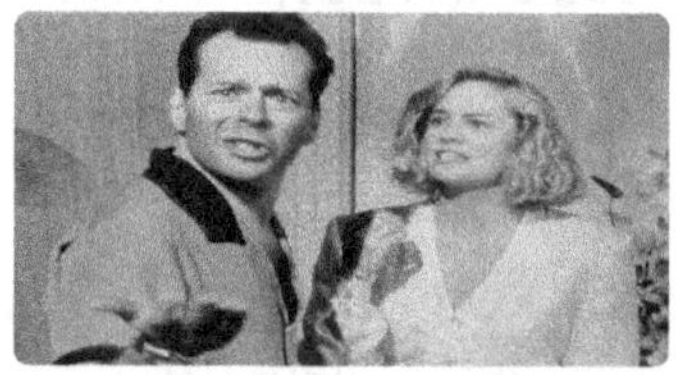

**INSIDE SCOOP?**
The name embroidered on David's bowling shirt is "Twinkle," - possibly a reference to Fred Flintstone, who was known as "Twinkle Toes Flintstone" at the bowling alley.

- - -

## INSIDE JOKE

In this episode, Harem Scarem Carpet Cleaners is the sponsor on back of David's bowling shirt. In the very next episode, s05e10, "When Girls Collide," David announces himself as "Harem Scarem Escorts, David Addison at your service" when he goes to pick up Maddie and Annie. Previously, in s05e04, "Plastic Fantastic Lovers," David tells nurse Saundra he's from Harem Scarem Drapery Cleaning. *Seems* the writers, or maybe Bruce, were keeping themselves amused.

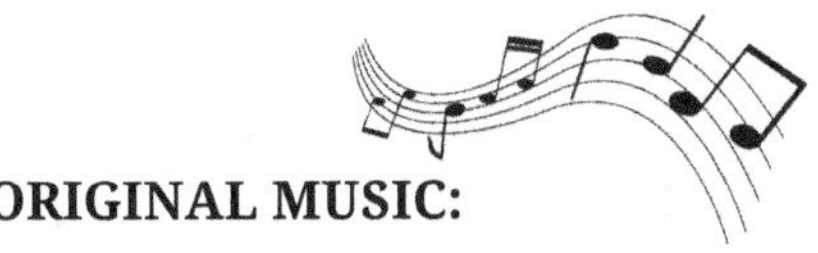

**ORIGINAL MUSIC:**

**"An American in Paris"**
Composed by George Gershwin

**"Mission: Impossible"**
Theme song of *Mission: Impossible* (TV Series 1966–1973)
Written by Lalo Schifrin

**"Danger Ahead"**
Theme song of Dragnet
(Radio series, 1949-1957),
(TV Series 1951-1959, original / 1967-1970, revival)
Written by Walter Schumann

**"Think!"**
Theme song of *Jeopardy!*
(TV Game Show, 1964-1975; 1978-1979; 1984-present)
Composed by Merv Griffin

---

## . . . AND YOUR NAME IS?

There was a long-standing joke in *Moonlighting* dating back to the first season: Maddie or David would call a company or character by the wrong name, sometimes by mistake, but sometimes with great purpose. One example is in s01e06, "The Murder's in the Mail," when Maddie continuously mispronounces Eck Eck as Eek Meek, Yick Yack, and Ick Poo, probably purposely, to annoy David. In s05e08, "Those Lips, Those Lies," Maddie calls Richie's girlfriend Eileen, then Carol; he corrects her twice with the proper name, Carla — and corrects her again when she (correctly) calls Carla, Carla. In s05e09, "Perfetc," Dr. Van Breegle's name is botched a few times as Van *Dreegle*, Dr. Van Breegle corrects the error tirelessly — surely all innocent mistakes. However, when it comes to David calling Gillian Gloria in s02e06, "Knowing Her," and Annie Angie in s05e10, "When Girls Collide," it's surely to give the illusion that he has no interest in these women when that isn't exactly true. But David calling Sam Sid in s03e12, "Sam and Dave," and Walter Bishop Mr. Pawn in s04e10, "Tracks of My Tears" certainly has *snide* written all over it.

# S05 E10
# When
# Girls Collide

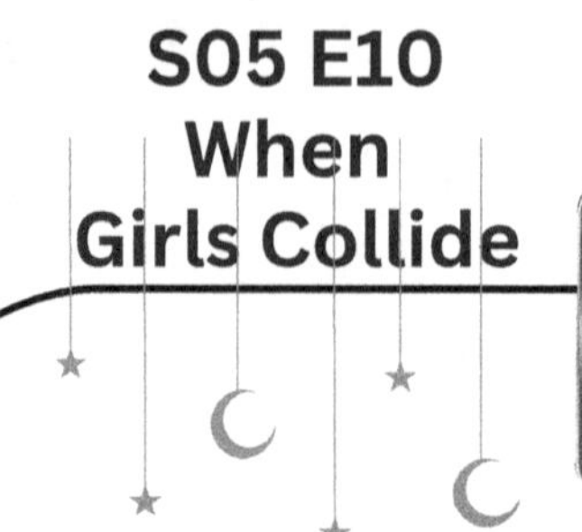



**Plot:**

Maddie's cousin Annie arrives in town to visit Maddie and almost immediately David is smitten by her, and the feelings are reciprocated.

Herbert is obsessed with his latest case and driving Agnes crazy. David takes Maddie and Annie out dancing for the evening. While Maddie and David dance, they discuss their relationship, but neither seems interested in continuing to work on it. When the trio get home, Maddie heads up to bed, but David and Annie stay up talking and then go out on the town. Maddie wakes up the next morning and realizes that Annie is not in her bed and assumes she spent the night with David.

Maddie confronts David back at Blue Moon and informs him that Annie is married. David believes that Maddie is jealous and tells her to mind her own business. Maddie believes that David is only pursuing Annie because he is trying to make her jealous. Things don't end well when Agnes and Maddie show up to bring David and Bert some dinner while on a stakeout.

Bruce Willis's then-wife, Demi Moore, makes a cameo appearance at the beginning of this episode.

**Air Date:** April 16, 1989

**Teleplay by:**
Merrill Markoe (as Leo Tecate)

**Story by:**
Charles H. Eglee
Merrill Markoe (as Leo Tecate)

**Director:** Dennis Dugan

**CAST CREDITS**

**Virginia Madsen** ...
Lorraine Anne Charnock
**Demi Moore** ... Beautiful Woman in Elevator
**Ron Vernan** ...
Seymour Sapperman
**Beverly Sanders** ...
Adelaide Sapperman
**Jay Goldenberg** ... Waiter
**Granville Ames** ... Man in Elevator
**Francis Coady** ...
Man in Restaurant

### FUN FACT #1:

Bruce Willis's real-life wife at the time, actress Demi Moore, is the dark-haired beauty David is infatuated with in the elevator at the beginning of the episode.

### FUN FACT #2:

Virginia Madsen was a friend of Bruce Willis's, and he asked her to come on and play the role of Annie.

### FUN FACT #3:

Virginia Madsen said in a 2014 interview that Cybill and Bruce were "at war" during the filming of these episodes, although things thawed a bit between them during the filming of the final episode, s05e13, "Lunar Eclipse."

### FUN FACT #4:

Merrill Markoe, who wrote the episode, was the head writer for David Letterman in the 80s and was also in a decade long relationship with him.

### OUTFIT ROLL CALL:

- Maddie wears the same pajamas in s05e12, "Eine Kleine Nacht Murder."
- She wore the white dressing gown in s04e01, "A Trip to the Moon."

### STATS:

*Door Slams: 4*
*Feet out of Elevator: 0*
*Maddie's Outfit Changes: 5*
*Agnes Rhymes: 0*

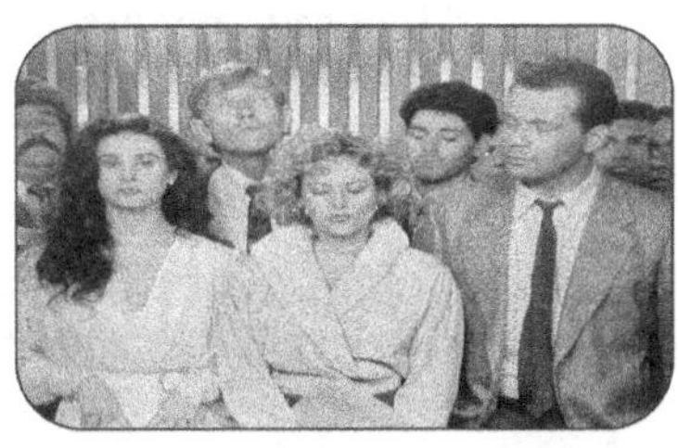

### GREAT LINES:

*Sometimes I'm still intrigued by the relationship between his shoulders and his hips. I'm only human.*
**~Maddie**

### LOOK FOR:

When the clown is making a balloon animal for Annie and David, there is a poster of Bruce Willis's big blockbuster movie "Die Hard' being taken down behind them.

### LOCATION...LOCATION...LOCATION...

~ **Hollywood Walk of Fame** - Hollywood, Los Angeles, California, USA

~ **Grauman's Chinese Theater** - 6925 Hollywood Boulevard, Hollywood, California, USA

~ **C.C. Brown's** - 7001 Hollywood Boulevard, Hollywood, California, USA

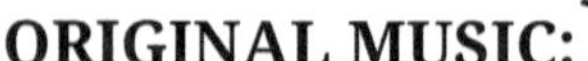

## ORIGINAL MUSIC:

**"Avalon"**
Written by Bryan Ferry
Performed by Roxy Music

**"Silhouette"**
Composed by Kenny G

**"Funeral March of a Marionette"**
Theme song of *Alfred Hitchcock Presents* (1955)
Written by Charles Gounod

**"Just My Imagination (Running Away with Me)"**
Written by Norman Whitfield and Barrett Strong
Performed by the Temptations

**"The Cisco Kid"**
Composed by Harold R. Brown, Charles Miller,
Lee Oskar and Howard E. Scott
Performed by War

**"I Second That Emotion"**
Written by Smokey Robinson and Al Cleveland
Performed by the Miracles

**"Share Your Love with Me"**
Written by Alfred Braggs and Deadric Malone
Performed by Aretha Franklin

---

## WHAT DO YOU THINK?

What better episode is there than this to review the many ways throughout the series David's (and sometimes Maddie's) ability to think is called into question. For example, in s02e11, "The Bride of Tupperman," and s02e10, "'Twas the Episode Before Christmas," David exclaims "I just had a thought!" Maddie responds, "We better get you a doctor" and "There's a first!" In s02e02, "Lady in the Iron Mask," when David says Maddie's not the first to "spring to mind," she responds with a terse "Springs to *what*?" The insults continue in s03e04, "Yours, Very Deadly," when David confesses, "Last night I started thinking," and Maddie quips, "It's about time." In s02e05, "My Fair David," Maddie baits David into throwing an insult back at her when she says, "David, I've been thinking," but alas, he was being *mature*, per their bet, so he resists the urge to mention "seeing smoke rise from her brain" or any jab of that nature. But David's choices in this episode leave us wanting some of the old Maddie Hayes directness from s02e06, "Knowing Her," when she just comes right out and says it, "David Addison, you are an idiot!"

# S05 E11
# In 'n Outlaws



**Plot:**

Herbert is busy planning the Viola family reunion. Agnes is apprehensive about meeting his family. Unfortunately, she misses the party due to being summoned for jury duty. David suggests different ways for her to get out of being selected.

During the deliberation of the jury, Agnes is the only juror unsure of the defendant's innocence, which causes all the jurors to be sequestered until a verdict can be agreed upon. Herbert is devastated that Agnes will miss meeting his family. No one in his family believes Agnes exists, so he decides to leave the party and take on the case and solve it himself so that she can be released. In a hilarious scene, Herbert storms into the courtroom and reveals the real killer while being escorted out of the courtroom by security. This episode includes yet another dream sequence, as Agnes falls asleep while in the jurors' hotel. Herbert finally meets up with his grandmother at the airport and introduces Agnes to her. This is when he finds out that Agnes speaks Italian and is able to translate for him. Herbert resolves his differences with his father. Cybill Shepherd and Bruce Willis appear for only two minutes in this episode but have a very sexy scene.

**Air Date:** April 23, 1989

**Written by:** Marc Abraham

**Director:** Christopher T. Welch

**ART IMITATING LIFE:**
When Agnes finds Kathleen hanging in her office, there's an homage to the orange Reebok high-top sneakers Cybill famously wore on the 1985 Emmy red carpet.

**FUN FACT #1:**
Grace Zabriskie, who plays Rita, played Dotti in Bruce Willis's movie *Armageddon* (Movie, 1998).

**FUN FACT #2:**
The last time we saw Cybill and Bruce kissing in an alternate universe was way back in s03e07, "Atomic Shakespeare"

**OUTFIT ROLE CALL:**
- Maddie wore the gray skirt and striped blouse in s03e01, "The Son Also Rises.

**STATS:**

*Door Slams: 0*
*Feet out of Elevator: 0*
*Maddie's Outfit Changes: 2*
*Agnes Rhymes: 0*

**GREAT LINES:**

— 66 —

*In the throes of passion . . .*
**Maddie (as Kathleen):** *I'll be here when you get back.*
**David (as John):** *Can we start from the same place?*
**Maddie (as Kathleen):** *Better yet, we'll start from the beginning!*

— 99 —

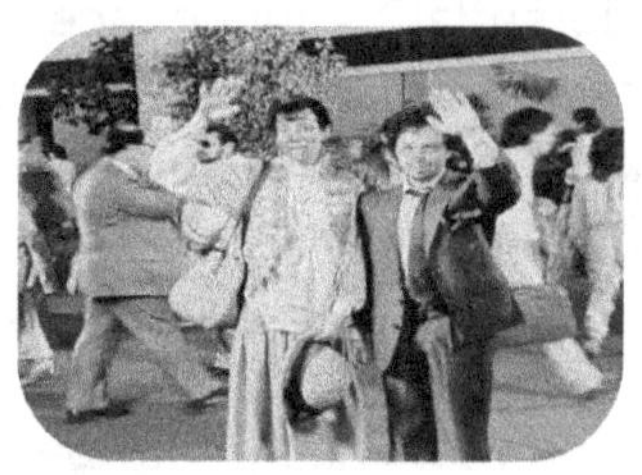

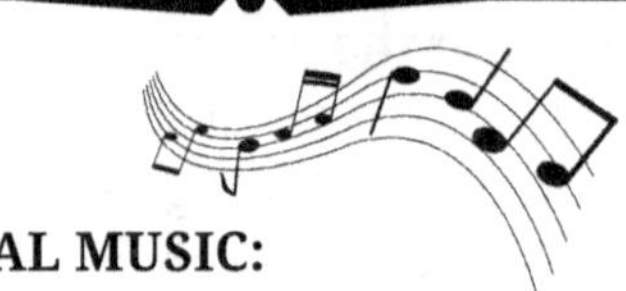

## ORIGINAL MUSIC:

**"Nel blu, dipinto di blu (Volare)"**
Music by Domenico Modugno
Lyrics by Franco Migliacci

**"Lady of Spain"**
Written by Robert Hargreaves,
Tolchard Evans,
Stanley Damerell and
Henry B. Tilsley

**"Jaws"**
Theme song of *Jaws* (Movie, 1975)
Music by John Williams

**"That's Amore"**
Music by Harry Warren
Lyrics by Jack Brooks

**"My Country, 'Tis of Thee"**
also known as **"America"**
Written by Samuel Francis Smith.

## CAST CREDITS

**Val Avery** ... Mr. Viola
**Eddie Mekka** ... Guido Viola
**Susan French** ... Nonni
**Grace Zabriskie** ... Rita (uncredited)
**Patti Deutsch** ... Secretary
**John Capodice** ... Sal Viola
**Ford Rainey** ... Judge
**Victor Bevine** ... District Attorney
**Charles Lanyer** ... Gibson's Lawyer
**Terry L. Beaver** ... John Gibson
**Jonathan Hole** ... Chip
**Fritzi Burr** ... Lenora Viola
**Charlie Holliday** ... Hennessey
**Howard Goodwin** ... Hotel Clerk
**John Lafayette** ... Bailiff
**Victoria Perry** ... Jury Woman #2
**Anne Bellamy** ... Jury Woman #3
**Clinton Allmon** ... Jury Man #1
**Richmond Harrison** ... Jury Man #2
**Dwight Wheaton-Werle** ... Coroner
**Ronald L. Colby** ... Foreman
**Joe Costanza** ... Man in Convertible
**Debra Christofferson** ... Francesca
**Joey D. Vieira** ... Delivery Man
**Pat Crawford Brown** ... Cleaning Lady
**Joel Simon** ... Jury Man #3
**Connie Fredericks** ... Jury Woman #1
**Fritzi Burr** ... Aunt Lenora

# S05 E12
# Eine Kleine
# Nacht Murder

**Title Reference:**
"Eine Kleine Nachtmusik"
(Mozart, 1787)

## Plot:

Maddie decides to take cooking classes. After her class, she goes down to the basement to her car and witnesses a stabbing. The killer then tries to kill her as well. Following this, she is placed under twenty-four-hour police protection. David and Herbert are suspicious of the bodyguard who has been assigned to protect Maddie. They believe he is crooked and that he is planning to kill her himself. Annie moves in with David. Meanwhile, David drops an Anselmo case file at Maddie's house and on the way home sees her bodyguard talking to someone in a limousine, who Herbert later finds out is a major underworld figure.

David returns to Maddie's house to warn her that something is going down at her home tonight and that her bodyguard is a dirty cop. However, David is wrong; the killer shows up as well as other members of his gang to kill Maddie, followed by a SWAT team that damages the ground floor of Maddie's mansion.

**Air Date:** April 30, 1989

**Written by:** Barbara Hall

**Director:** Jay Daniel

## CAST CREDITS

**Joseph Hacker** ... Detective Mick Donegan
**Virginia Madsen** ... Lorraine Anne Charnock
**Ray Wise ...** Murderer
**Barbara Tarbuck** ... Maddie's Classmate
**Richard Camphius** ... Gordon
**Paul Mendoza** ... Desk Sergeant
**Marcia Burrs** ... Cooking Teacher
**Zack Phifer** ... Waiter
**Andrew Reilly** ... Desk Clerk
**William Jack Phillips** ... Delivery Boy
**Kendall McCarthy** ... Cop

## CONTINUITY:

David tells Bert that the license plate number on a silver stretch limousine is J18X812. Later, at the police station, Bert tells a policeman it's a white stretch limousine, license plate 187XB12 (which is actually the correct number as shown earlier in the show).

## FUN FACT #1:

Ray Wise mentioned in Scott Ryan's book, *Moonlighting: An Oral History* (Book, 2021), that he injured his achilles tendon while filming the opening scene. Post-surgery, he wheeled around on a special chair and pretended to be running while chasing Maddie through the parking garage.

## FUN FACT #2:

David says "You dirty rats" to the police officers, in reference to what is widely misremembered as a James Cagney quote. Cagney never actually said "You dirty rats." In *Blonde Crazy* (Movie, 1930), he says: "That dirty, double-crossin' rat!"

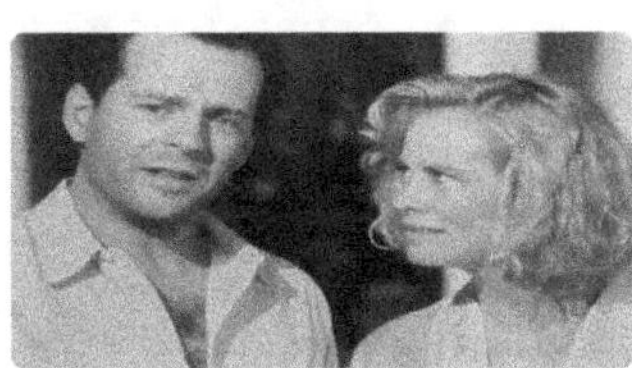

## STATS:

*Door Slams: 0*
*Feet out of Elevator: 0*
*Maddie's Outfit Changes: 6*
*Agnes Rhymes: 0*

## ❝ GREAT LINES:

**Murderer:** *Wait a minute, you expect me to stand here and explain everything to you while I should be making my escape?*
**Maddie:** *Kinda how it works.*
**Murderer:** *You watch too much TV.* ❞

## OUTFIT ROLL CALL:

- Maddie wears the same pajamas in s05e10, "When Girls Collide."

## LOCATION...LOCATION...LOCATION...

~ **David follows Donnigan to a parking lot across from Mar Vista Dry Cleaners** - 3831 Grand View Boulevard, Los Angeles, California, USA
~ **Ambassador Hotel** - 3400 Wilshire Boulevard, Los Angeles, California, USA

## CULTURAL REFERENCES / MUSIC:

~ David mentions - **James Garner**, *The Rockford Files* (TV Series, 1974–1980).
~ **Love Connection** - (TV Game Show, 1983-1994)
~ **Mister Ed** - (TV Series, 1961-1966) / (referencing ***The Godfather*** (Movie, 1972)
~ **"S.W.A.T."** (TV Series, 1975-1976) - Theme song plays over the end scene as Maddie's house is destroyed.
~ **"Casper the Friendly Ghost"** (TV Cartoon Series, 1945) - David sings the TV show theme song, written by Jerry Livingston and Mack David.

# S05 E13
# Lunar Eclipse



## Plot:

The Blue Moon employees are in full celebration mode since they found out that Agnes proposed to Herbert. Herbert and McGillicuddy finally put their differences aside and decide to be friends. Annie's husband, Mark, shows up at Blue Moon to see Annie and Maddie, which throws a spanner in the works. Mark invites David out to lunch and tells him that he has suspicions that Annie is having an affair. He has hired the Lou LaSalle Agency to follow Annie while she is in Los Angeles. The investigator witnesses Herbert taking Annie to Disneyland and reports this back to Mark. Agnes and Herbert go shopping at the mall in preparation for the wedding, and Herbert feels they are being followed. David wants to end his relationship with Annie, so he arranges a situation where Annie finds him in the shower with another woman, (a Blue Moon employee) to prompt her to go back to her husband.

 It's Agnes and Herbert's wedding day and the guests have arrived, but before the ceremony is complete, Herbert notices an investigator taking photos. This is followed by a huge brawl between all the guests, and most of them end up in the pool, including Maddie and Agnes. They all end up in jail, where the priest, who has also been arrested, completes the ceremony for the bride and groom.  David returns to the office to find that all the furniture is gone and that *Moonlighting* has been canceled. The office is now being dismantled by the studio crew. These are the final "breaking of the fourth wall" scenes; Maddie and David leave Studio 20 (where the Blue Moon office is filmed) to approach a powerful producer, Cy, to keep the show running. They are unsuccessful. Outside they see Agnes, who tells them she can't rhyme anymore. Then they run over to a church to ask the priest to marry them, but he refuses. Left alone in the church, Maddie and David begin to reminisce about their relationship since she arrived at Blue Moon. The episode ends with a montage of flashbacks from the show to "We'll Be Together Again," a song by Betty Carter & Ray Charles.

**Air Date:** May 14, 1989

**Written by:** Ron Clark

**Director:** Dennis Dugan

## CAST CREDITS

**James Stephens** ... Mark Charnock
**Virginia Madsen** ... Lorraine Anne Charnock
**Timothy Leary** ... Wynn Deaupayne
**Dennis Dugan, credited** ... Walter Bishop as Cy
**Mark Taylor** ... Walter Whitebread
**George D. Wallace** ... Father
**Joe Grifasi** ... Kapatkin

## FUN FACT #1:

Dennis Dugan, who directed the episode, also plays Cy and is credited as "Walter Bishop" for this role.

## FUN FACT #2:

In the final scene, Maddie and David use the line "Over and out. Six, two and even." This line is also used by David in s02e18, "Camille."

## FUN FACT #3:

Dipesto says she fantasizes about Mark Harmon. Harmon played Maddie's love interest, Sam Crawford, in season three.

## LOOK FOR: 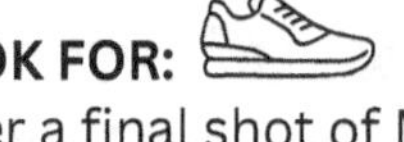

After a final shot of Maddie's feet coming out of the elevator, her pumps turn to sneakers one last time.

## Interview, Glenn Gordon Caron

***Moonlighting The Podcast:*** As the creator, did you ultimately envision them ending up together in the end?

**Glenn Gordon Caron:** It's a great question, I think I did. I think I just assumed they would, why would you present this great romance and have it end any other way?

## STATS:

*Door Slams: 2*
*Feet out of Elevator: 1*
*Maddie's Outfit Changes: 3*
*Agnes Rhymes: 0*

## GREAT LINES:

***Maddie:*** *You know, David, after all these years, all we've been through together. the ups, the downs, the ins, the outs, I just want you to know I can't imagine not seeing you tomorrow.*

**On location: from our personal photo archive**

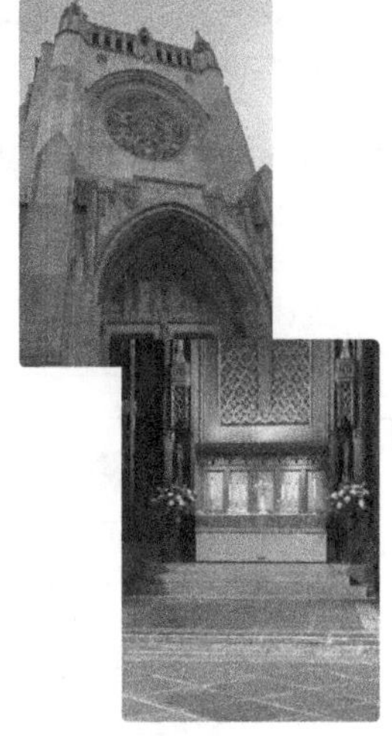

*Church altar from the final scene.*

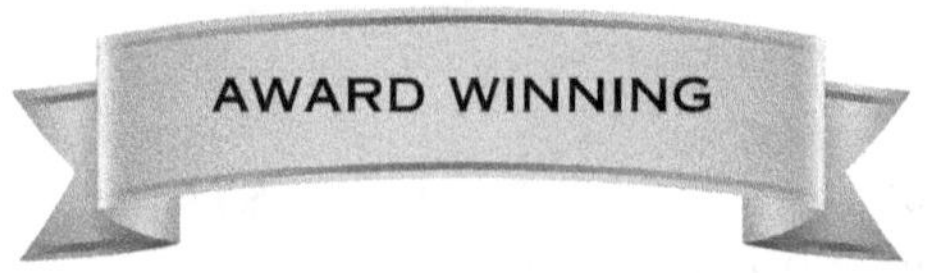


During the run of the series, *Moonlighting* won six Emmy Awards and three Golden Globes. Cybill Shepherd won the Golden Globe for Best Actress in a Television Series Musical or Comedy in 1986, and both she and Bruce won for Best Actress/Actor in a Television Series Musical or Comedy in 1987. From 1986 to 1988, Cybill won the People's Choice Award for Favorite Female TV Performer, with Bruce Willis alongside her as Favorite Male Performer in 1986. Bruce won a Primetime Emmy Award for Outstanding Lead Actor in a Drama Series in 1987.

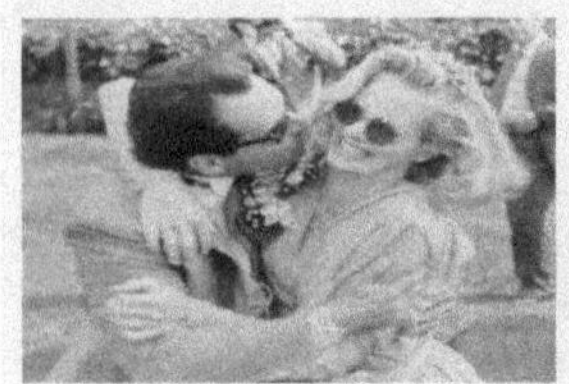 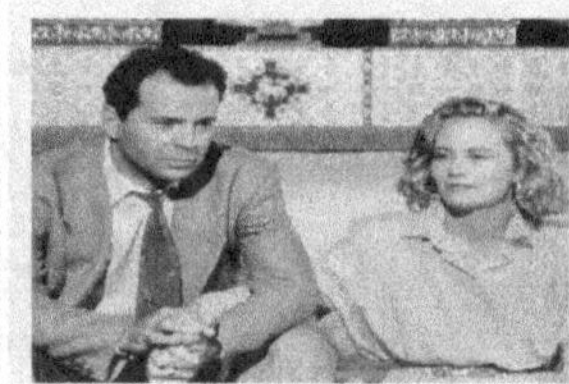 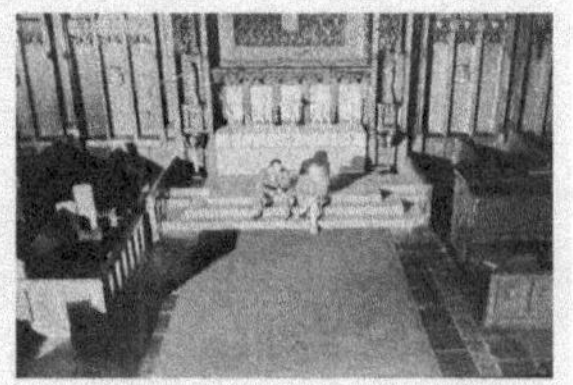

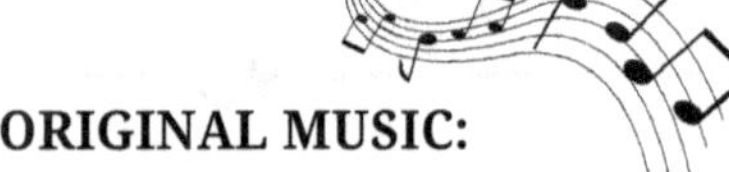

## ORIGINAL MUSIC:

**"Park Avenue Beat "**
Theme song of
*Perry Mason* (TV Series, 1957)
Written by Fred Steiner

**"We'll Be Together Again"**
Written by Laine-Fisher
Performed by Betty Carter
and Ray Charles

## LOCATION...LOCATION...

~ **First Congressional Church (final scene)** - 540 South Commonwealth, Los Angeles, California, USA

~ **Paley Residence (Bert and Agnes Wedding)** - 1060 Brooklawn Drive, Bel Air, Los Angeles, California, USA

## LOCATION...MOONLIGHTING WRAP PARTY

Curtis Armstrong mentioned in his book *Revenge of the Nerd* (Book, 2017), that *Moonlighting's* wrap party was held at the "Coconut Grove inside the Ambassador Hotel," which was located at 3400 Wilshire Boulevard, Los Angeles. The hotel was also the location shoot for s02e02, "Lady in the Iron Mask," and s05e12, "Eine Kleine Nacht Murder" — the hotel has since been demolished. The location is now the RFK Community Schools and the RFK Inspirational Park.

## ***MOONLIGHTING* MENTIONS:**

*Moonlighting* is *"lightning in a bottle"*; it has so many unique aspects to it from slapstick comedy to serious romance and everything in between. It was something special in that late eighties moment in time and absolutely became a part of the culture. When it was at its best, there was nothing more creative. The show could never be duplicated, although some have tried! *Moonlighting* has been mentioned and spoofed on so many shows over the years, it would be impossible to name them—here is a short list of mentions over the decades:

- ***Riptide*** - **Spoof (1986)**
- ***Head of the Class*** - **Spoof (1987)**
- ***Saturday Night Live*** - **Mention (1987)**
- ***Perfect Strangers*** - **Mention(s) (1987-1988)**
- ***The Tonight Show Starring Johnny Carson*** - **Mention (1987)**
- ***Muppet Babies*** - **Spoof (1988)**
- ***The Golden Girls*** - **Mention (1988)**
- ***Alvin & the Chipmunks*** - **Spoof (1988)**
- ***ALF*** - **Mention (1989)**
- ***Full House*** - **Mention (1988)**
- ***Growing Pains*** - **Mention (1988)**
- **Married . . . with Children - Mention (1989)**
- ***Teenage Mutant Ninja Turtles*** - **Mention (1990)**
- ***30 Rock*** - **Mention(s) *(2012)***
- ***Veep*** - **Mention (2012)**
- ***Hot in Cleveland*** - **Mention (2012)**
- ***Take Two*** - **Mention (2018)**
- ***The Simpsons*** - **Mention (2019)**
- ***This Is Us*** - **Mention (2019)**

# LET'S WRAP IT UP WITH A FINAL TALLY:

**DOOR SLAMS:** ...................................................... 175
**AGNES RHYMES:** .................................................. 35.5
**OUTFIT CHANGES:** .............................................. 288
(Includes Claymation Maddie Outfits) **(3)**


**FEET OUT OF ELEVATOR:** ................................... 32
**SMASHED BMW:** ...................................................... 1

## <u>KISSES:</u>

**REAL:**

- 'Twas the Episode Before Christmas ......................... 2
- Witness for the Execution .......................................... 1
- It's a Wonderful Job .................................................. 3
- Maddie's Turn To Cry ............................................... 1
- I Am Curious . . . Maddie? ......................................... 3
- To Heiress Human ...................................................... 3
- Tracks of My Tears ..................................................... 1
- Maddie Hayes Got Married ....................................... 1
- And the Flesh Was Made Word ................................. 1
- Take My Wife, for Example ........................................ 1

**FANTASY:**

- The Man Who Cried Wife ........................................... 2
- Big Man on Mulberry Street ...................................... 1
- Come Back Little Shiksa (Claymation) ...................... 1
- Tracks of My Tears ..................................................... 1

**ALTERNATE UNIVERSE:**

- The Dream Sequence Always Rings Twice ................. 5
- Atomic Shakespeare ................................................. 5
- In 'n Outlaws ............................................................. 1

**OTHER:**

- The Straight Poop ...................................................... 1

**Total Kisses:**     34

---

*Note: This is only OUR interpretation of the stats within the show. Viewers will, and should, have their own perspectives. It is with much love and respect for Moonlighting and everyone involved in making it that we present this collection of data and information. This guide is meant as entertainment only, never to criticize those who worked so hard on the production of the show. Is there more to add? Of course! But as it stands now, we hope you enjoy this companion guide and use it to add an extra layer of fun as you (re)view the series.*

# THANK YOU

***Moonlighting the Podcast*** **would like to thank:**

**Glenn Gordon Caron** for having the imagination to create *Moonlighting* and the characters of Maddie and David. To the cast and crew who worked tirelessly on *Moonlighting,* your dedication made it great. *Moonlighting* still brings so much joy to its original viewers and is finding a new audience on Hulu streaming today, which speaks to the quality of the production and entertainment value of the show. To **Glenn** and **Jay Daniel** for joining Grace and Shawna on *Moonlighting the Podcast,* being so supportive of our endeavor, and also for truly appreciating the fans of the show.

**Scott Ryan** for being a huge supporter of *Moonlighting the Podcast* from day one, being a regular guest, and for encouraging and supporting us through the journey of making this book. **David Bushman** at Tucker DS Press for editing and publishing the book.

**Scout Willis, Florence Rogers, Kara Anne Reifert,** and **Marybeth Saari** for your contributions to the research for this book. **Bob Suh** for his artwork and design on *Moonlighting the Podcast.*

**Shawna would like to thank:**

**Mom, Dad, Sis, Scott, Suzyn, Grace, Brandon, Nick,** and **Jake,** thanks for being the best family ever and indulging my passion for this show for . . . well, just about my whole life.

***Special dedication to Evan—we miss you*** ♡✈

To the bestest bestie, **Kristin**, thanks for being there and for being **you**.

To all of my friends and family who have supported my love for Bruce Willis and *Moonlighting* since the eighties. To Kelly for reciting lines from the show with me re: high school; Wednesday mornings. To Uncle Charlie and Aunt Margaret for tracking down a copy of *Moonlighting Magic* back in the day. Thank you to everyone who supports and listens to *Moonlighting the Podcast* and to my "great-great" podcast partner, Grace, for her hard work and dedication.

**Love you all to the moon and stars and back!**

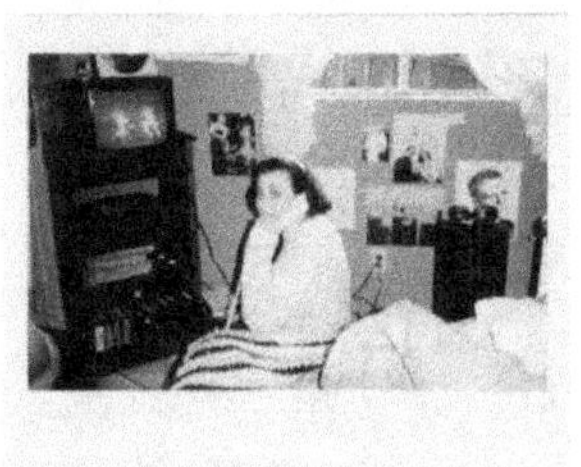

*Shawna's teen room where* Moonlighting *& Bruce adorned the walls.*

**Continued...**

**Grace would like to thank:**

To **Mum** and **Dad**, thank you for taking a massive leap back in 1954 and traveling from Italy on the *Oceania* to a strange country on the other side of the world to provide a wide array of opportunities and a better life for your girls. I miss you both so much. To **Rob** and my girls, **April** (for going to sleep at eight thirty so I could watch *Moonlighting*), **Dayna,** and **Bonnie,** thank you for your support and encouragement for me to live my passion and also for when I take on yet another project, especially this one! To the rest of my family and friends near and far, thank you for your love and support throughout the years, I am blessed to have you in my life.

To my besties, **Liz** and **Jeanette**, thank you for always being there through thick and thin; you're the best friends anyone could ever have. Thank you to all the *Moonlighting* fans out there who listen to the podcast, thank you for your continued support; we couldn't do this without you.

To the best podcast partner that anyone could ever dream of having, **Shawna**, the universe positioned itself for us to meet and begin this crazy journey together; thank you for loving *Moonlighting* as much as I do and for all your hard work on the podcast.

**Also by Grace:**
*Your Road to Success* (podcast—playpodca.st/yrts)
*Conversations with Grace* (podcast—playpodca.st/cwg)
*The Road to Success* (book
coauthored with Jack Canfield)

---•---

**Also Available:**

# Moonlighting: An Oral History

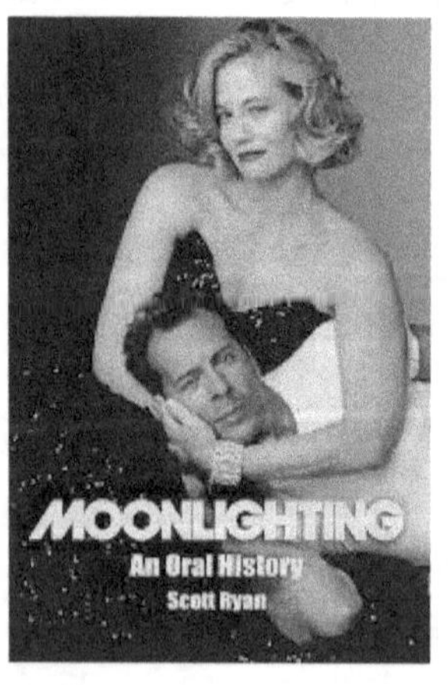


Need more *Moonlighting*? Of course you do. Check out Scott Ryan's (*The Last Days of Letterman, Twin Peaks Fire Walk With Me: Your Laura Disappeared*) *Moonlighting: An Oral History*, featuring interviews with Cybill Shepherd, Allyce Beasley, Curtis Armstrong, Glenn Gordon Caron, Jay Daniel, writers, directors, editors, and more. Order at TuckerDSPress.com

# Notes:


Armstrong, Curtis. Revenge of the Nerd: Or . . . the Singular Adventures of the Man Who Would Be Booger. New York, Thomas Dunne Books, 2017.

Chivell, Grace & Saari, Shawna. Interview with Glenn Gordon Caron, *Moonlighting the Podcast*. February 2022.

Chivell, Grace & Saari, Shawna. Interview with Jay Daniel, *Moonlighting the Podcast,* November 2022.

Finnerman, Gerald Perry, Archive of American Television. Interview conducted by Karen Herman. 2002.

Fisher, Bob. "Tender Loving Care for Moonlighting."American Cinematographer, February 22, 2021.

Rachael Ray Show, created by Harpo Productions, season 1, episode 90, CBS Media Ventures, 2007.

Ryan, Scott. Moonlighting: An Oral History. Columbus, Ohio, Fayetteville Mafia Press, 2021.

"Commentary Tracks." Special Features. *Moonlighting* DVD Collection, Lion's Gate, Seasons 3, 4, and 5, 2006; 2007.

*Moonlighting*. Picturemaker Productions ABC Circle Films, 1985-1989. Internet Movie Database. 2023.